A Manual of Library Automation and Networking

A Manual of LIBRARY AUTOMATION AND NETWORKING

Third Edition
Thoroughly Revised and Enlarged

N.R. Satyanarayana
Senior Professor of Library and Information Science
Integral University, Lucknow

With the assistance of
Abdul Mannan Khan
Deputy Librarian
Integral University, Lucknow

Ess Ess Publications
New Delhi

A Manual of
LIBRARY AUTOMATION AND NETWORKING

ISBN: 978-81-7000-721-0

₹ Ess Ess
Rs.1350/-

First Published 2014

Published by:
Ess Ess Publications
4831/24, Ansari Road,
Darya Ganj,
New Delhi-110 002.
INDIA
Phones: 23260807, 41563444
Fax: 41563334
E-mail: info@essessreference.com
www.essessreference.com

Cover Design by *Patch Creative Unit*

Printed and bound in India at Salasar Imaging Systems.

Contents

Preface to the First Edition

Computers have now become an integral part of our everyday life. They are coming to the aid of human beings in several ways. Computers are needed in industry and business, media and communications,/ defense and aeronautics, medicine and hygiene, schools, colleges, universities and R & D organizations. Libraries and information centers are no exception for the onslaught of computer.

The availability of low priced microcomputers in the 1980s has encouraged a large number of libraries and information centers to automate their activities and services. The recent advances in computer and communication technologies have made inroads into the libraries and information centers. Their activities have gradually been shifted to meeting the challenge of providing 'the right information at the right time to the user in the right format'. This process requires the right combination of the data management techniques, computer, communication and printing technologies. The attention of library and information professionals the world over is, nowadays, to how effectively and efficiently one can make use of the available technologies.

However, the thrust for computers and their use in library and information services in India is more recent. Several systems and methods were developed in respect of automation of acquisition, cataloguing; circulation and serial control. Development of retrospective information retrieval systems, CAS, SDI, and integrated information systems are also being reported. Further, several user-friendly packages such as MINISIS, CDS/ISIS, LIBSYS are available for ready information.

In this manual an effort has been made to apprise the librarians, information workers, students of library and information science and others, who have no mathematical background and computer knowledge, to become aware about computers, its basics, its programmes and its application to various activities in libraries, so that they can adopt the use of computers for their day-to-day work. This work can also serve as a textbook to the students studying Bachelor's and Master's degree courses in library and information science. The author hopes that the students will find this work useful.

The basic concepts have been explained in simple language with illustrations, examples and chapter glossaries. The text in this volume is supplemented with a detailed glossary of technical terms.

The author would feel rewarded if after going through this primer the interest of the students and practicing librarians in the subject of computerization gets cultivated. After reading this book if a librarian decides to go for computerization of his library activities the author presumes that he has succeeded in his attempt.

During the preparation of this volume the author has taken the help of M.J.M Raju (now a DRTC trainee) without whose support it would not have been possible. The author sincerely thanks him.

N. R. Satyanarayana

Preface to the Second Edition

Librarians and Information Professionals are Confronted today by the rapidly changing environment. Automation of library activitics and adoption of computers to both routine as well as non-routine activities has become almost a necessity and is being hotly discussed and debated in all professionals gatherings. There are many reasons for this change. One of the major reasons to change is the rapid developments that are taking place in information technology and potential for new services which they brings. At the same time the demands for information by the library users are also changing. The readers are now coming with new expectations and insist for high quality services. On the other hand the range and variety of information sources that librarians handle are also changing. A part from print material librarians now deal with online bibliographic database, CD-ROMs, electronic journals, digital texts supplied from a number of vendors that are downloaded from internet. Each of these format requires generic and highly specialized skills for searching, identifying, extracting and disseminating the right information to right reader at the right time and in the right format.

An attempt has been made, in this short manual, to apprise the librarians, information workers, students of library and information science and others, who have no mathematical background and no computer knowledge, to become aware about the basics of new technology and their applications to various activities in libraries and information centers, so that they can adopt the use of new technology to their day to day work. The basic concepts of library automation and computerization have been explained in simple language with a number of illustrations and examples.

In the absence of any established text book in the area of library automation and computerization that are easily available to the students in the country and also the continued and repeated representation of library and information science student to provide them a simple guide to library automation and networking to whom I had the opportunity to teach, stimulated me for the writing of this book. There is a Persian saying that 'who so desires a faultless friend, remains friendless' and 'it is' no less true that he who intends to write a faultless book, writes nothing'. I am conscious of my limitations and the magnitude of the task of presenting a guide book to the students of library and information science as well as to the working librarians.

It is my earnest desire that this guidebook will contribute to a better understanding of the objectives and processes of automating library operations and thus render it a more imaginative, fruitful and creative pursuit in this developing area of library and information science. I shall be happy to receive any suggestions for its improvements from all concerned so that I may incorporate them in subsequent edition.

During the preparation of this volume the author has taken the help of Ms. Shiva Kanaujiia, Ms. Rekha Verma, Ms. Smriti Srivastava and Mr. Samant Gupta.

The author sincerely thank them. M/S New Royal Book Company, Lucknow especially Mr. M.F. Beg and Mr. Imran Mirza deserves specials thanks for bringing this volume in the presentable form.

Budh Purnima, 2003

N.R. Satyanarayana
Department of Library and Information Science
University of Lucknow

Preface to the Third Edition

This edition reflects the changes that Information and Communication Technology (ICT) has undergone during the past ten years, there are three new chapters, viz, Library Automation Software Packages; Information Retrieval System; and Digital Library. The changes and additions in the present volume grew out of ideas, comments and suggestions from a number of my colleagues, former students and Library professionals. Even though the underlying basics of the subject remain the same, but the whats and hows are changing very fastly and quickly. Almost each and every chapter has been thoroughly revised, keeping in view of the changing environment of Information and Communication Technologies, which is compelling Libraries and Information Centers to analysis their strategies so that they can play a vital role in the emerging global knowledge society. As the technology continues to change rapidly, undermining the ability of the people to develop a reliable and interchangeable approach to their work. It also presents the library professional in developing a stable and appropriate relationship with the ICT industry. Therefore, the library professionals need to develop their level of competency and understanding the changes in the technology so that they can articulate for adopting the same for bringing improvement in the services of library and information centers.

Several library professionals especially my colleagues in the teaching profession have devoted considerable amount of time in reading he manuscript of this edition. Their critical inputs helped me greatly in giving the present shape to this volume. I sincerely think that this book will be interesting to a wide audience, especially practicing library and information professionals, students of library and information science and others who wish to understand more about computerizing library operations and services. I shall be very happy to receive any suggestions for its improvement from all concerned so that the same be incorporated in its further editions.

Lastly, as you can see from the title page, I decided that it was time to bring another person to assist me in the preparation of this and future editions. I feel happy to introduce Dr. Abdul Mannan Khan, as a junior author for this edition. He has provided me excellent comments and ideas for the present edition.

Budh Purnima, 2014

N.R. Satyanarayana
Deptt. of Library and Information Science,
Integral University, Lucknow

I have very much enjoyed assisting in the preparation of this volume. It has provided me a unique opportunity to work with someone like Prof. Satyanarayana. I am also thankful to all those people who are indirectly involved with this project. I am very much thankful to my parents for their blessings, love and support.

Abdul Mannan Khan
Central Library
Integral University, Lucknow

1

Introduction

Ever since his existence man has been inventing and devising tools and techniques to aid him. In the primitive ages, he used his fingers for counting. When the need arose, he made use of pebbles, beads, seashells, stones and the like to keep an account of large numbers. As his necessities increased further he invented newer devices. The Chinese are known to have devised abacus around 600 BC. An abacus is a clay board with a number of grooves in which pebbles are placed. These pebbles can be moved from side to side for the purpose of counting. Later on the material used changes, but the basic principle has remained the same. The abacus now has several rows of beads strung on wires in a rectangular frame. It helps in counting in the decimal system.

In the metal age with the availability of metals man derived a number of mechanical gadgets for easier calculations. Later on when electricity was discovered, these were replaced by electromechanical devices. In the twentieth century, electronic devices have helped technocrats in ushering a new era - the era of computers. Like other inventions, a computer is also a tool in the aid and service to the mankind. It is a very sophisticated and powerful tool.

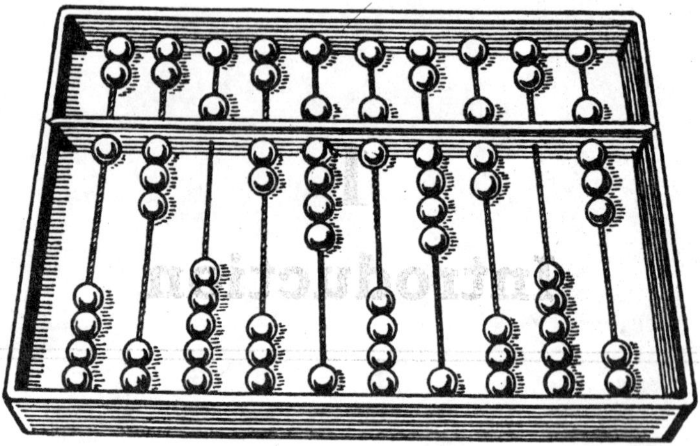

1 3 5 2 9 6 4 7 0 8

Fig. 1. Abacus

DEFINITION

The word computer according to the Oxford English Dictionary is "an automatic electronic apparatus for making calculations or controlling operations that are expressible in numerical or logical terms." The word computer has been derived from the Latin word computare which means "to calculate". This does not mean that a computer is just a calculator doing mathematical operations because nowadays 80 per cent of the work done by a computer is non-mathematical.

More accurately a computer can be defined as "a device that operates upon Information or Data". Data can be anything. It may be bio-data of various applicants when the computers are used for recruiting personnel, or the marks obtained by various students in different subjects, when computer is used to prepare results or the details (such as name, age, sex, etc.) of various passengers when computer is employed for making airline or railway reservations. Thus, data come in various forms depending upon the type of computer application. A computer can store, process and retrieve data as and when desired, so many people started calling it "data processor".

GENERAL CHARACTERISTICS

Computers are characterized by the following :

1. Speed : Computer is a very fast device. It performs operations in seconds. So whenever we talk of computer speed we say in milliseconds (10^{-3}), microseconds (10^{-6}), nanoseconds (10^{-9}) and even picoseconds (10^{-12}). A powerful computer is capable of performing about three to four million simple arithmetic operations per second.

2. Accuracy : The accuracy of a computer is consistently high. The degree of accuracy of a particular computer depends upon its design. Computers do make errors but these are mainly due to human rather than technological weakness, that is, mainly due to imprecise thinking of a programmer (a person who writes instructions for a computer to solve a particular problem) or due to inaccurate data.

3. Diligence : Unlike human beings a computer is free from monotony, tiredness, lack of concentration, etc. and hence can work for hours together without creating any error and without grambling. This diligence has made the computers do wonders. If one million operations have to be performed, a computer will perform with the same accuracy and speed, the millionth operation as that of the first one.

4. Versatility : Versatility is one of the most significant feature of the computer. One moment, it is preparing the results of a particular examination, the next moment it is busy in preparing electricity bills and in between it may be helping an office secretary in tracing an important letter in seconds. In brief, a computer can perform almost any task.

5. Power of Remembrance : As a human being

acquires new knowledge, the brain subconsciously selects what it feels to be important and worth retaining in its memory, and thus relegates unimportant details to the back of the mind or just forgets them. This is not the case with the computer. A computer can store and recall any amount of information because of its secondary storage (a type of detachable memory) capability. Every piece of information can be retained as long as desired by the user and can be recalled as and when required. The recalled information is as accurate as on the day it was fed.

6. No Intelligence : A computer cannot think like human beings. It possesses no intelligence of its own. The IQ is zero, at least till today. The computer has to be told what to do and what not to do. Hence, only the user can determine what tasks a computer will perform.

HISTORY OF COMPUTERS

The famous saying "Necessity is the mother of invention" holds good for computer. Computers were invented as a result of man's search for fast and accurate calculating devices.

The abacus, also known as "Soroban", may well be the earliest ancestor of the computer. It clearly illustrates a fundamental idea in data processing; an object, in this case a bead can be moved around according to a set of rules and the result interpreted as number.

At least two levels of translation are at work here. Suppose there is a herd of cows and you want to count them, then you move certain number of cows and move a corresponding number of beads on the abacus. In this simple mathematical device it has the capacity to memorise the simple numbers. Simple addition and subtractions can be carried out rapidly and efficiently by positioning the beads appropriately.

In theory, calculation could be speeded up by some

mechanical device that moved the beads for you. The result would be a machine that was doing your calculations for you. This is one of the elements of the computer. Although, abacus was invented around 600 BC, it is interesting to note that it is still being used in the Far East and its users can calculate at an amazing speed.

EARLY DEVELOPMENTS (EVOLUTION)

Blaise Pascal (1623-92) is credited with inventing the first calculator. A gifted mathematician, the son of a tax-collector, felt the tedious routine calculations that occupied his father could be better done by a machine. He developed the pascaline, which worked something like an odometer – every ten units counted moved the tens counter one notch and so on.

Pascal established the following principles which were important to the later development of more sophisticated calculators:

1. A carry should be accomplished automatically. The odometer of a car to measure mileage is based on this principle.
2. Substraction could be done by turning dials in the reverse direction.
3. Multiplication and division could be performed by repeated addition and substraction, just with the abacus.

However, it could only add and substract. Unfortunately, the device did not revolutionize for accounting. Perhaps the clerks saw the pascaline as a threat to their jobs.

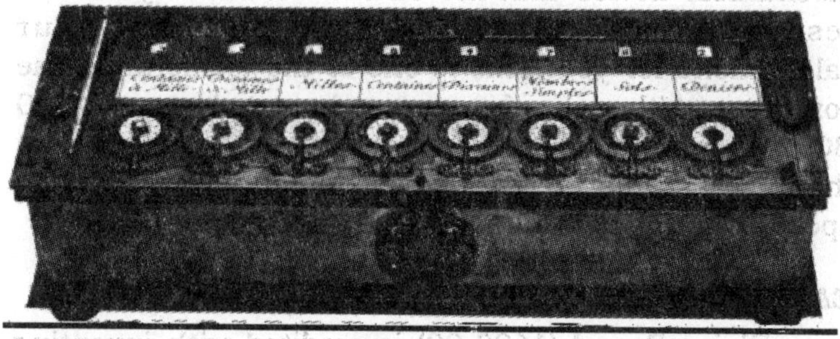

Fig. 2. Pascal's machine

The English mathematician Charles Babbage (1791-1871) formulated the concept and design, if not a working version, of the first computer. During his period, mathematical and statistical tables were prepared by a group of clerks. Even the utmost care and precautions could not eliminate human errors. Soon he became dissatisfied and exasperated with this type of monotonous job. The result was that he started thinking to build a machine which could compute tables guaranteed to be error-free. In this process he designed a "Difference Engine" in 1822 which cold produce reliable tables.

His machine was consisted of following components :

1. A STORE to hold numbers i.e. those which were to provide the data for the problems, and those which were to be generated during the course of calculations.
2. A MILL to perform operations on the numbers which had been stored. All the operations were to be carried out through the rotation of gears and wheels.
3. An INPUT device to pass into the machine.
4. An OUTPUT device to display the results.

Fig 3. Babbage's analytical engine

In 1842, Babbage came out with his new idea of Analytical Engine, which was intended to be completely automatic. It was to be capable of performing the basic arithmetic functions for any mathematical problem and it was to do so many at an average speed of 60 additions per minute. Unfortunately he was unable to produce a working model due to lack of precision engineering, but his principles paved way to designing of other digital computers.

DEVELOPMENT OF MODERN COMPUTER

The Mark I Computer (1937-44)

Also known as automatic sequence controlled calculator, this was the first fully automated calculating machine designed by Howard A. Aidkon of Harvard University in collaboration with IBM. The design is based on the punched card machinery. This machine was reliable in usage but complex in design and huge in size. It was basically an electro-mechanical device since both mechanical and electronic components were used in its design.

The Atanasoff-Berry Computer (1939-42)

Developed by Dr. John Atanasoff to solve certain mathematical equations is an electronic machine. It was Called Atanasoff-Berry computer or ABC, after its inventor's name and his assistant, Cliford Berry. It used 45 vacuum tubes for internal logic and capacitors.

The ENIAC (1943-46)

The Electronic Numerical Integrator and Calculator was the first electronic Computer. It was produced at Moore College of Engineering at the University of Pennsylvania, USA by a design team lead by Prof. J. Presper Eckert, and John Mauchly.

ENIAC was developed as a result of military need. It took up the space in a 20x40 square feet room and used 18,000 vacuum tubes. The addition of two numbers was achieved in 200 microseconds, and multiplication in 2,000 microseconds.

Fig. 4. A Vaccum Tube

The fastness is good when compared to its predecessor, but it has two shortcomings, it could store only limited amount of information and its programme wired on boards. These limitations made it difficult to detect the errors and change the programme.

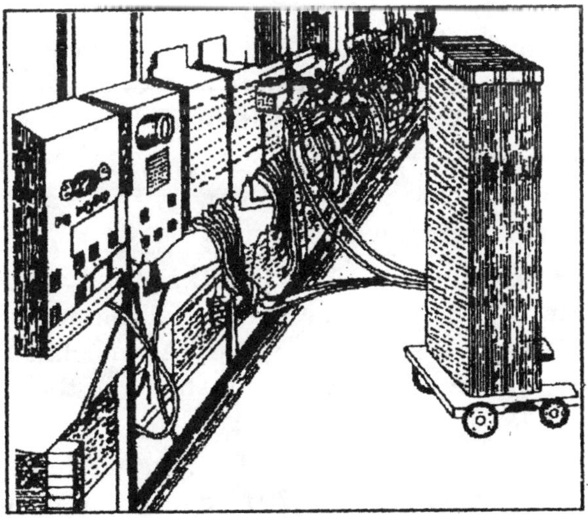

Fig. 5. ENIAC

The EDVAC (1946–52)

The Electronic Discrete Variable Automatic Computer (EDVAC) was designed by Dr. John Neumann based on the stored programme concept.

Another significant contribution by Neumann was the stored program concept in which the machine instructions are stored with data internally in the computer. The advantage of storing instructions in memory is that the computer can make logical decisions internally.

The basic idea behind the stored programme concept is that a sequence of instructions as well as data can be stored in the memory of the computer for the purpose of automatically directing the flow of operations.

The EDVAC was designed on stored programme concept. Neumann has also got a share of the credit for introducing the idea of storing both subtracts and data in the binary form (a system that uses only two digits 0 and 1 to represent all characters) instead of the decimal numbers or human readable words.

The EDSAC (1947-49) : Simultaneously with the EDVAC of the USA the British designers developed EDSAC (Electronic Delay Storage Automatic Calculator). The machine executed its first programme in 1949.

The machine was developed by a group of scientists headed by Prof. Maurice Wilkes at the Cambridge University Mathematical Laboratory.

The UNIVAC (1951) : The Universal Automatic Computer (UNIVAC) was the first digital computer which was not "One of a kind". Many UNIVAC machines were produced, the first of which was installed in the Census Bureau in 1951.

In 1952, the International Business Machines (IBM) Corporation introduced the 701 commercial computer. In a rapid succession, improved models of the UNIVAC I and other 700 series machines were introduced in 1953. IBM produced IBM-650 and sold over 1000 of these.

THE COMPUTER GENERATIONS

The word "Generation" in the area of computers is a step in technology. Originally the term used to be confined to hardware technologies but in the present context. It is extended to both hardware and software, which together stand for an entire computer system.

The custom of referring to the computer developments in terms of computer generations came into wide use only after 1964. There are five computer generations known till today. Though, there is overlapping between the generations, but the approximate datas shown against each are normally accepted.

First Generation (1942-59)

The early computers like ENIAC, EDVAC, and EDSAC are the first generation computers. They used vacuum tube which was fragile glass device that could control and amplify electronic signals.

Second Generation (1959-64)

The transistor, a smaller and more reliable successor to the vacuum tube, was invented in 1947. The second generation emerged with transistors being the brain of the computer.

It was accompanied with invention of magnetic core memory storage and high level languages like Fortran, COBOL, Algol etc. Nearly 80% of these computers were used in business and industry and almost all used the batch processing mode. Transistors replaced the valves completely as they were far more superior in performance on account of miniature size, smaller power consumption and heat production rate.

Both the first and the second generation computers had the basic component as a physical entity. The many thousands of individual components had to be assembled by hand into functioning circuits. The manual assembly of individual components and the cost of labour involved at this assembly stage made the commercial production of these computers difficult and costly.

Third Generation (164-72)

With the increasing advancements made in the electronic technology and the advent of "micro-electronics" technology, made it possible to integrate the large number of circuit elements into very small (less than $5mm^2$) surface of silicon known as "chips". This new technology was called Integrated Chips (ICS). The third generation of computers was based on these developments.

Characteristics of this generation include magnetic core and solid state main storage, smaller in size with better performance and reliability. Extensive use of higher level of programming languages and remote processing and time sharing through communications, and the speed of operation put these computers in the order of nanoscond range.

Some of the mainframe computers which belong to this generation are:

IBM – 360 series

ICL – 1900 series

IBM – 370/168

ICL – 2900

Honeywell – 6000 series

The manufacture of mini computer of third generation began after the development of large scale integration (LSI) and very large scale integration (VLSI) and microcomputer chips.

The Fourth Generation (1972 – 1984)

The development of microprocessor made it possible to place complete control processing unit of a computer on a single chip. Magnetic core memories were replaced by semiconductor memory and microcomputers became not only interrogative but also user friendly being menu driven. Memory size increased upto 16 megabytes.

ICs which have the entire computer circuitry on a single silicon chip are called MICROPROCESSORS. These are infact, the scale down versions of minicomputers.

Fig. 6. Chip and Integrated Circuit

In the initial period, the integrated circuits (IC) were confirmed to only about ten to twenty components, named as small-scale integration. With the advancements in technology it became possible to integrate hundred components on a single chip. This technology was known as medium-scale integration. Then came the era of large-scale integration (LSI) when it was possible to integrate over 30,000 components onto a single chip. Efforts are on to integrate million components on a single chip (size of a postage stamp) known as very large-scale storage integration (VLSI). Fourth generation computers have greater increase in storage capacity and speed of operation. Modular design and compatibility between equipment (hardware) provided by different manufacturers, lead to the advent of greater popularity of microprocessors and microcomputers.

Fifth Generation (1984-1990)

Scientists have worked on the fifth generation computers, which have become a reality. They aim to bring us machines with genuine IQ, the ability to reason logically, and with real knowledge of the world. Fifth generation is totally different, novel and new.

Fifth generation computers are different in various aspects to what have evolved uptill now. In structure, they will be parallel (the present ones are serial) which means they will do multiple tasks simultaneously. In function it will not be algorithmic (step by step with one step at a time).

In the nature of processing it will not be just data processing but knowledge processing. In programming it will interact with human beings in ordinary language (unlike BASIC, COBOL, FORTRAN, etc. which present computers need).

In application, it will behave like an expert. In their architecture it will have KIPS (Knowledge Information Processing System) rather than the present DIPS/LIPS (Data/Logic Information Processing System).

The odds of coming out with fifth generation computer are heaviest for Japanese. They have already started working in this direction a few years back. Japan has chosen PROLOG (Programming in Logic) language as operating software and plans to have the final machines, talk with human beings; see and deliver pictures and hear the normal and natural language.

Sixth Generation (1990 -)

Many developments that took place in computer systems since 1990 have not been fundamental changes, but they are gradual improvements over the then existing systems. The major gains of this generation are in parallel computing in the hardware and improved understanding in the development of algorithms for exploiting architecture in software.

Continued improvements are there in workstation technology, with processor designs which are now being used widely on the combination of RISC (Reduced Instruction Set Computer), pipelining and parallel processing. There is also tremendous development in wide area networks, network bandwith speed of operation and networking capabilities. Personal computers now operate with Gigabyte per second processors and multi-Gigabyte disks. They can now operate with hundreds of megabytes of RAS (Remote Access Server), color printers, stereo sound cards and graphical user interfaces. Now a days, thousands of operating systems and application softwares are existing. Microsoft Information has been a major contributor in developing operating systems and softwares.

The sixth generation has brought about micro controller technology. Micro controllers are embedded inside some other devices such as washing machines and other consumer products, as they are used to control the features and actions of the product. They work as small computers inside these products and now serve as essential parts in most machines.

TYPES OF COMPUTERS

Computers can be divided into three types :

1. Digital
2. Analog
3. Hybrid

1. Digital : A digital computer, as the name implies works on digital. In other words it is a counting device. All computers have backing storage devices which work very much similar to music tape and discs. But music is stored in wave form whereas the computer stores information in "digital" (i.e. binary) form. It works with discrete quantitites. It uses numbers to simulate real time processes. Digital computers represent data in the form of digits and then all operations are done on these digits at extremely fast rates. Digital computers basically know how to count digits.

2. Analog : Analog computers serve as models for and stimulate the rotations of an actual physical system usually operating in real time, while digital computers compound primarily arithmetic data unrelated to the system represented.

The basic difference between the earlier type and the analog computer is simple, as analog computer measures, but a digital computer counts. The barometer in your hall or speedometer in your car are some types of analog computer.

3. Hybrid : A hybrid computer is a computer which combines features of analog and digital computers. This computer system utilizes the measuring capability of an analog computer and the counting capability of a digital computer.

Hybrid computers utilise the best qualities of both the computers, and are mostly used for automatic operations of complicated physical processes and machines. But these are mostly hidden as in medical machine say ultrasound or catscan.

CLASSIFICATION OF COMPUTERS BY CAPACITY

Further Classification is based on their memory size as given below:

1. Micro Computers (upto 12 MB)
   - Home Computers
   - Personal Computers
   - Laptop Computers
2. Minicomputer (4MB -16 MB)
3. Mainframe Computers (10 MB – 128 MB)
4. Super Computers (256 MB)
5. Work Station

1. Microcomputers

Microcomputers are the smallest units. They may be tiny special purpose devices to carry out a single task such as controlling the ignition system of an automobile or may be the more visible and familiar PCs, ranging from note-book to desktop size, that we can use in countless ways. They can perform the same operations and use the same type of instructions as much as larger computers. A typical microcomputer is characterized by its size. It consists of a microprocessor chip as its CPU semiconductor ROM for storing programs and a RAM for data.

Characteristics of Microcomputers

1. These computers have C.P.U. in a single chip.
2. Low storage capacity up to a maximum of 10 kilo bytes.
3. These computers can accept and transfer data from I/O devices at the maximum speed of 5 lakh bytes/ sec.

2. Minicomputers

Minicomputers are small general purpose systems, as they serve multiple users, unlike most micro computers. Minicomputers are usually more powerful and more expansive than micros. In physical size, minicomputers vary from desktop models to units the size of small file cabinets. The difference between mainframe and that of mini is very less. It is evident in the following :

Characteristics of Minicomputers

1. **Storage :** This can store up to 2 mega bytes.
2. These computers can accept and transfer data from I/O devices at the maximum speed of 4 million bytes per second.
3. The cost is less as compared to mainframe.
4. They use winchester hard disk drives of 1200 MB each, 1 or 2 floppy drives, 7 to 8 printers, on line printers, digitizers, plotters.

3. Mainframe Computers

The advancement of technology has made it quite

difficult to draw a line of demarcation among various types of computers.

Fig. 7. Main Frame Computer

Main frame computers are systems that offer faster processing speed and greater storage capacity than a typical minicomputer. Now a days in the computer environment mainframe computers are an important part of computing. Infact, the so called supercomputers are a type of main frame. All the first to third generation computers which work with the speed of 5 to 10 million instructions per second, fall under this group.

Characteristics of Mainframe Computers

1. Mainframes can process large numbers of data at a very high speed
2. They can support many input, output and auxiliary storage devices.

3. Mainframes have multi-user facilities and can support large network of terminals and remote job entry stations.

4. Super Computers

The word "super computer" is often heard these days. They are playing a vital role in all areas from space to sports. These computers are very fast, executing more than 10,000 million instructions per second have storage capacities of millions of bits per chip. The speed is due to the use of microprocessors working in parallel and high storage densities based on magnetic memories.

Super computers are designed to process complex scientific jobs. These are the largest, fastest and most expensive computers in the world. Although, few in number, supercomputers are considered a national resource because they are designed to process important and complex scientific applications. CRAY research in U.S. and Nippon Electric in Japan are the market leaders in super computers. India is the only country outside U.S., Japan and Europe to pursue and complete with the building of PARAM 800 and PARAM 8600 range of supercomputers. The scientists at the Centre for Development of Advanced Super Computing (C-DAC) at Pune have completed the design of these super computers, belonging to the latest generation (teraflop range) in the year 1991 and will cost Rs. 200 crore. Teraflop is the unit to describe a computer which will be able to perform 20 billion calculations in the blink of an eye (i.e. one fifth of a second). Such powerful super-computers shall be used in weather forecasting (how clouds are formed, predict turbulences in air), earthquake prediction, oil exploration, analysis of satellite remote sensing data, how galaxies are formed, ocean currents and similar scientific research.

Other notable super computers in India are ANUPAM developed by BARC and PACE developed by

ANURAG (Advanced Numerical Analysis Group) of DRDO. Large classes of problems concerning ballistic missiles, reactor design, climate modeling, large linear programming, seismic data processing, etc. could not be solved by none of the third generation and most of the fourth generation computers because did not have the speed at which calculations were required to be done. The speed needed was theoretically not possible. This is the limitation of speed at which a signal can be propagated on electric conductor. Electronic signals travel at the speed of light which is approximately 30,000 km. per second. At this speed the signal travels less than 30 cm in a nonosecond. Although through miniaturization, the length of the interconnecting conductors had already been reduced substantially, lengths of more than 30 cm may be encountered, delaying the travel of signal, and thus making calculations impossible. This problem can be circumvented by parallel architecture. Super computers of use this architecture.

A super computer CRAY-1 is considered as the most powerful computer today. Nowadays super computers are being used in defence research as well.

5. Work Station

It is a type of computer used for engineering applications (CAD/CAM), desktop publishing, software development, and other types of applications that require a moderate amount of computing power and relatively high quality graphics capabilities. Workstations generally come with a large, high-resolution graphics screen, at large amount of RAM, built-in network support, and a graphical user interface. Most workstations also have a mass storage device such as a disk drive, but a special type of workstation, called a diskless workstation, comes without a disk drive. The most common operating systems for workstations are UNIX and Windows NT. Like personal computers, most workstations are single-user computers.

However, workstations are typically linked together to form a local-area network, although they can also be used as stand-alone systems.

ORIGIN OF PERSONAL COMPUTER (PC)

Microcomputers are often called personal computers or PCs. Since They were originally intended to single user devices either at office or at home. The home computer is a PC which allows the home appliances on input/output devices, viz., TV and the cassette tape recorder as the output and input/output devices, respectively.

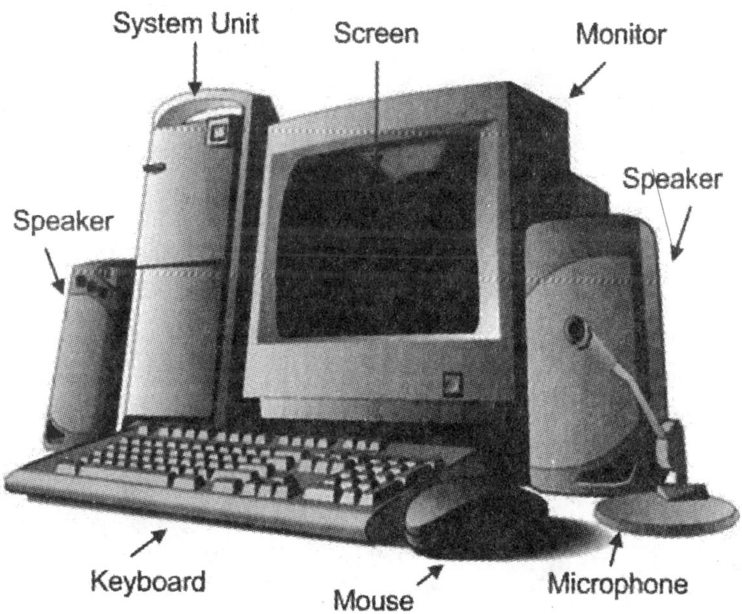

Fig. 8. A personal computer

The origin of personal computers took place due to the increasing influence of computers in every area and due to the price reduction of computer parts. The personal computer is significant because of its cheapness that turned the rationale for data processing development on its head. The equipment became so inexpensive that, for some applications it was possible virtually to ignore its cost. The desktop computer became a background tool to be used when the user chose, and as the user chose. On the other hand, creating software became increasingly expensive, and at times prohibitively so as the number and complexity of potential applications began to mushroom. The origin of personal computer revolutionized the entire concept of computing and by spread to all areas of human knowledge.

Today, the world of personal computers is basically divided between Apple Macintoshes and PCs. The principal characteristics of personal computers are that they are single-user systems and are based on microprocessors. However, although personal computers are designed as single-user systems, it is common to link them together to form a network. In terms of power, there is great variety. At the high end, the distinction between personal computers and workstations has faded. High-end models of the PC offer the same computing power and graphics capability as low-end workstations.

Personal Computer Types

Actual personal computers can be generally classified by size and chassis/case. The chassis or case is the metal frame that serves as the structural support for electronic components. Every computer system requires at least one chassis to house the circuit boards and wiring. The chassis also contains slots for expansion boards. If you want to insert more boards than there are slots, you will need an expansion chassis, which provides additional slots. There are two basic flavors of chassis designs – desktop models and tower models – but there are many variations on these two basic types. Then come the portable computers that are computers small enough to carry. Portable computers include notebook and subnotebook computers, hand-held computers, palmtops, and PDAs (Personal Digital Assistants).

Tower model

The term refers to a computer in which the power supply, motherboard, and mass storage devices are stacked on top of each other in a cabinet. This is in contrast to desktop models, in which these components are housed in a more compact box. The main advantage of tower models is that there are fewer space constraints, which makes installation of additional storage devices easier.

Desktop model

A computer designed to fit comfortably on top of a desk, typically with the monitor sitting on top of the computer. Desktop model computers are broad and low, whereas tower model computers are narrow and tall. Because of their shape, desktop model computers are generally limited to three internal mass storage devices. Desktop models designed to be very small are sometimes referred to as **slimline models**.

Fig. 9. Desktop computer

Notebook Computer

An extremely lightweight personal computer. Notebook computers typically weigh less and are small enough to fit easily in a briefcase. Aside from size, the principal difference between a notebook computer and a personal computer is the display screen. Notebook computers use a variety of techniques, known as flat-panel technologies, to produce a lightweight and non-bulky display screen. The quality of notebook display screens varies considerably. In terms computing power, modern notebook computers are nearly equivalent to personal computers. They have the same CPUs, memory capacity, and disk drives. However, all this power in a small package is expensive. Notebook computers cost about twice as much as equivalent regular-sized computers. Notebook computers come with battery packs that enable you to run them without plugging them in. However, the batteries need to be recharged every few hours.

Laptop Computer

A small, portable computer – small enough that it can sit on your lap. Nowadays, laptop computers are more frequently called notebook computers.

Fig. 10. Laptop Computer

Subnotebook Computer

A portable computer that is slightly lighter and smaller than a full-sized notebook computer. Typically, subnotebook computers have a smaller keyboard and screen, but are otherwise equivalent to notebook computers.

Hand-held Computer

A portable computer that is small enough to be held in one's hand. Although extremely convenient to carry, handheld computers have not replaced notebook computers because of their small keyboards and screens. The most popular hand-held computers are those that are specifically designed to provide PIM (personal information manager) functions, such as a calendar and address book. Some manufacturers are trying to solve the small keyboard problem by replacing the keyboard with an electronic pen. However, these pen-based devices rely on handwriting recognition technologies, which are still in their infancy. Hand-held computers are also called PDAs, palmtops and pocket computers.

Palmtop

A small computer that literally fits in your palm. Compared to full-size computers, palmtops are severely limited, but they are practical for certain functions such as phone books and calendars. Palmtops that use a pen rather than a keyboard for input are often called hand-held computers or PDAs. Because of their small size, most palmtop computers do not include disk drives. However, many contain PCMCIA slots in which you can insert disk drives, modems, memory, and other devices. Palmtops are also called PDas, hand held computers and pocket computers.

PDA (Personal Digital Assistant)

Short for personal digital assistant, a handheld device that combines computing, telephone/fax, and networking features. A typical PDA can function as a cellular phone, fax sender, and personal organizer. Unlike portable computers, most PDAs are pen-based, using a stylus rather than a keyboard for input. This means that they also incorporate handwriting recognition features. Some PDAs can also react to voice input by using voice recognition technologies. The field of PDA was pioneered by Apple Computer, which introduced the Newton Message Pad in 1993. Shortly thereafter, several other manufacturers offered similar products. To date, PDAs have had only modest success in the marketplace, due to their high price tags and limited applications. However, many experts believe that PDAs will eventually become common gadgets. PDAs are also called palmtops, hand-held computers and pocket computers. A most recent version of PDAs is I-Pads, I-Pods.

Present Scene

The growth of computers is multifold and multidimensional. Focus has diverted from hardware and software to performance: on making life easier, not for the computer, but for the end users.

Desktop and Laptop computers are going ahead and are being produced on large scale. Nowadays, there is information explosion which can be controlled by no other machine other than a computer. The present-day Research and Development activities are concentrated on developing parallel processing systems, knowledge-based information processing and user friendly computer systems. The emphasis is on tools that ease the programmer's task, often by increasing the computer's processing burden.

Forecast

It is only a matter of time before the computer will be able to interpret a wide range of vocal commands. When this technology becomes reality and is combined with existing synthesized-speech technology, we should be able to have a meaningful verbal dialogue with a computer. Instead of keying in a computer program on a keyboard you would simply enter each line verbally.

We are still a few steps away, but life saving computer implants are only around the corner. These tiny computers will control mechanical devices that can replace living organs that have ceased to function. Other medical research has given paralegics renewed hope that they may someday walk again with the assistance of a computerised nervous system. Within a few years, pocket computers will be able to read 50 different newspapers, turn on the heat at home, call a cub, order groceries, buy share of stock, make hotel reservations. Our pocket computers will also serve as credit cards.

Albert Einstein once said that "concern for man himself and his fate must always form the chief interest of all technical endeavors". There are those who believe that a rapidly advancing computer technology exhibits little regard for "man himself and his fate". Whether it is good or bad society now has reached the point of no return with regard to its dependence on computers.

REFERENCES

- Ahmad, S. Computer in Library Management. New Delhi: A.P.H. Publishing, 1996.
- Bagga, R.K. Computer and Defence Application. 2nd ed. Delhi DESIDOC, 1971.
- Bishop, P. Computing Science, 2nd ed. Walton-on-Thomas : Nelson 1987.
- Burstein, Jerome S. Computer and Information System. New York: Holt, Rinehart and Wilson, 1986.
- French, C.S. Computer Science. 4th ed. London: D.P. Publications, 1992.
- Jaggi, V.P. and Jain, Sushma. Computer for Beginners. 10th ed. New Delhi: Academic (India), 1990.
- Maynord, J. Computer Programing Made Simple. London : ELBS, 1983.
- Miller, M. Easy Computer Basics. New Delhi : Pearson, 2014.

- Rajaraman, D. and Rajaraman, V. Computer Primer. New Delhi: Prentice Hall, 1986.
- Rajaraman, V. Fundamentals of Computers. 4th ed. New Delhi : Prentice Hall of India, 2010.
- Sehgal, R.L. Computer Based Information Processing Techniques for Libraries. New Delhi : Ess Ess, Publication, 1998.
- Shelly, G. and Vermaat M. Introduction to Computers. Bosteon : Course Technologies, 2011.
- Singh, P. Basics of Computer. New Delhi : V.K., 2010.
- Wells, D. Computer Concepts : Basics. New York : Cangage, 2010.
- Wilkinson, G.G. Fundamentals of Information Technology. London : John Wiley, 1987.
- Zuboff, S. In the Age of the Smart Machine. New York: Oxford University Press, 1988.

2

The Machine

Computer is a machine that is all concerned with the "data". Data are a collection of facts in raw form which become information after proper organization or processing. For processing the data, we need to have an input device through which we put in the data and a processing unit which processes the data. Later on the processed data need to be retrieved, for which an output device is necessary.

The modern computer uses electronic circuits instead of gears that were used in the early computers and used the binary numbers system for all its operations. The binary numbers system has only the digits 0 and 1. For example, in the decimal system, the number 2107 can be thought of as 2 x 1000, plus 1 x 100, plus 0 x 10, plus 7 x 1. The "place" on the left has a value 10 times its neighbour on the right. That is, there is a ones place, a tens place, a hundreds place and so on. In the binary system the number 1101 can be thought of as 1 x 8, plus 1 x 4, plus 0 x 2, plus 1 x 1. In this system the "place" on the left has a value 2 times its neighbour on the right. There is a ones place, a twos place, a fours place, and son on. One digit in a binary system is called a bit.

The computer stores all its information in the form of bits. In terms of electricity, think of a computer as a very large collection of switches, each of which can be on or off. The "ON" state can be defined as 1. The "OFF" state can be defined as 0. This is the level of the data the computer actually deals with. It can change 1 to 0 or 0 to 1. The power of modern computer is that it can throw these switches very, very fast.

In most of the microcomputers bits are grouped as eight-digit number called bytes. So each byte can have 256 different values (0 through 255 in the decimal system). Data in bytes are moved around the computer system through eight parallel wires known as a data bus.

The bytes used by the system are stored in a memory location which can be thought of as a pigeon-hole with an address label. The pieon-holes are organized in a long sequence starting with address 0 and in the case of the other computers over to a million and above. Each location can hold one byte of data. Accessing or getting to a specific data in a specific location (address) is what happens when we address information.

Basic Computer Organization

All computer systems perform the following five basic options:

1. Inputting : The process of entering data and instructions into the computer system.

2. Storing : Saving the data and instructions so that they are available for initial or for additional processing as and when required.

3. Processing : Performing arithmetic operations or logical operations (comparisons like equal to, less than, greater than etc.) on data in order to convert them into useful information.

Component of processing

a) Arithmetic & logic unit

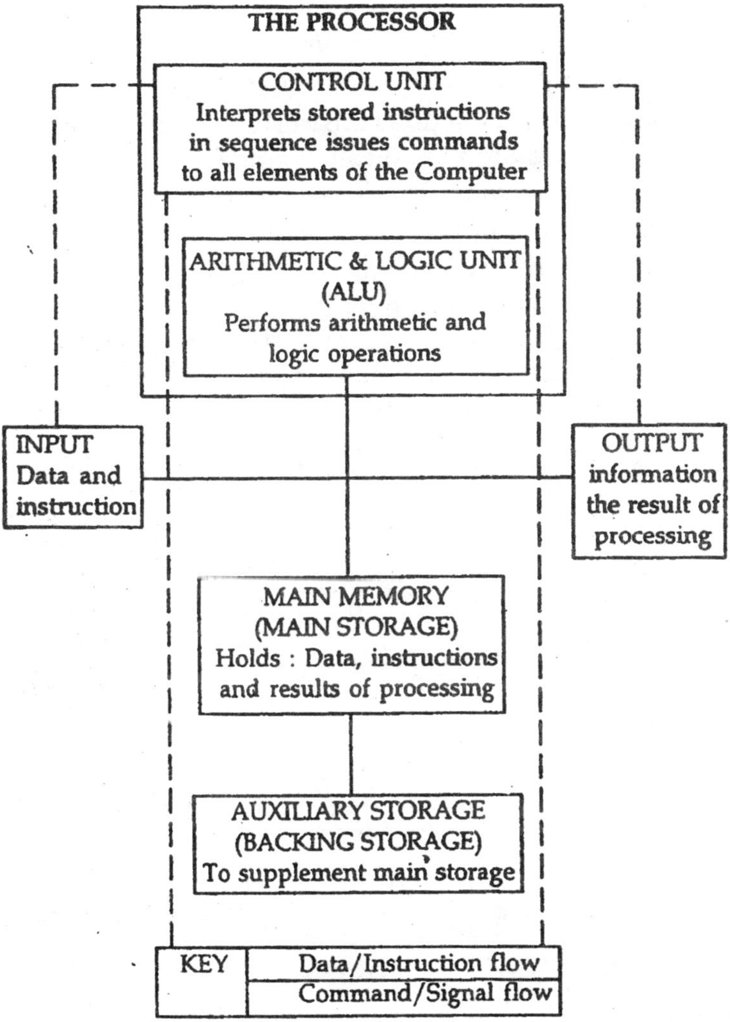

Fig. 11. The elements of a Computer System showing its "Logical Structure"

b) Control unit

c) Internal memory (immediate access storage, IAS)

4. Outputting : The process of producing useful information or results for the users, such as a printed report or visual display.

5. Controlling : Directing the number and sequence in which all of the above operations are performed.

How do the system units work together?

When the system units are working together, results of computations are periodically being saved in memory for read-out at a later time or new data is being written into the memory and saved for use at a later time.

The central processing unit (CPU) controls the functions of the system units. It tells the input when to bring information into the system, or tells the output when to write information. It sends signals to the output to turn on a motor or form a letter or number on a display. It controls when and at what time each operation is to be accomplished. The CPU does this by following instructions stored in memory in a step-by-step sequence called program.

Inside the computer, the information is not recognizable as written letters or numbers because it is all converted into electrical signals of digital codes so that it may be handled easily inside the computer system. Let's see how these signals are handled.

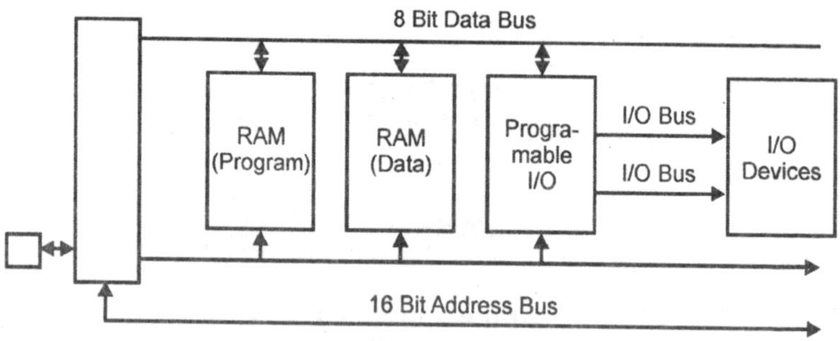

Fig. 12. Three Principle Busses of a Computer

The digital codes carrying the information inside the computer system must be coupled from one unit to another. The multiple wires which do this are called buses. There are three principle buses in a computer system.

Input Unit

Data and instructions must enter the computer system before any computation can be performed on the supplied data. There are various types of input devices that are being used depending upon the condition where the computer system is put to use. The input devices range from well-known punched card to magnetic character readers.

Punched Card

A punched card is divided into eighty columns, are numbered from 1 through 80 (predictably). The rows run down the card 12, 11, and 0 through 9. Originally the card was intended to be used for numerical data only (Hollerithis census application). Thus early cards had only ten punch positions per column 0 through 9. These were only numeric positions which were extended to 12 and 11 when the need arose.

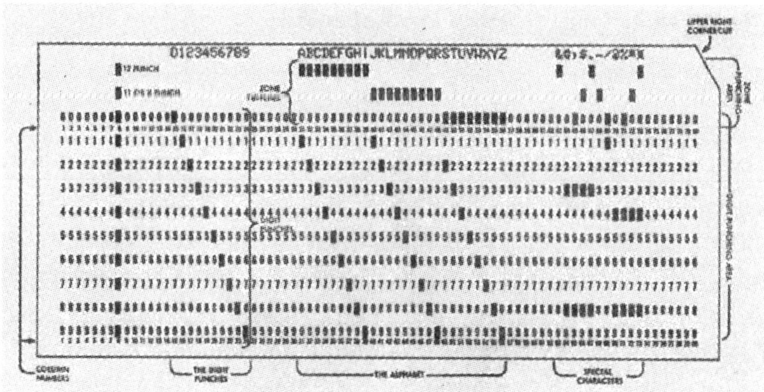

Fig. 13. Punched Card

Each column of the card holds one character, a letter, a digit, or a special symbol such as a punctuation mark. The position of holes punched in the column determines the character.

Key Board

The commonest way to input data is by pressing keys. Since each key is marked with one (or more) character of some control function. It is easy for the operator to use these keys. Since each key pressed sends a unique signal through the CPU to the main memory, it is simple for the computer to understand.

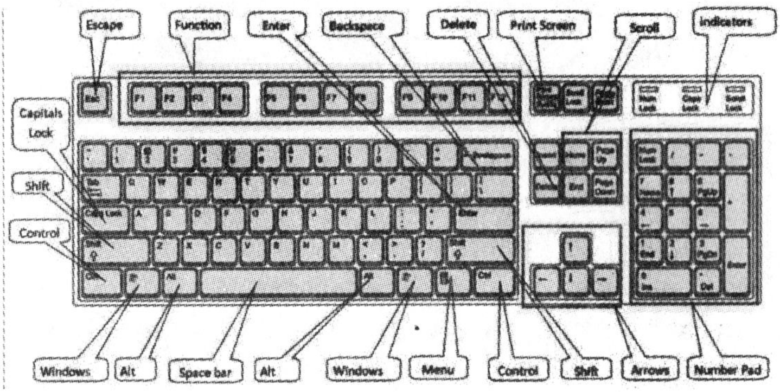

Fig. 14. Keyboard

Computer input key-boards are similar in appearance to typewriter keyboards with the standard QWERTY layout. Inside the keyboard unit, there is electronic circuitry to generate the correct electronic signals for each key pressed and usually a temporary store, called a buffer to hold data until the computer is ready to receive it. Keyboard is usually operated with some form of visual output, so allowing immediate inspection of each typed character and deletion and correction as necessary.

1. In the past few years, considerable interest has been accorded to the DVORK keyboard which arranges keys differently. The DVORK keyboard is designed for rapid data entry, or typing, and we should expect to see many more such keyboards in the near future. It gets is name from its invention, August Dvork.

2. Mouse : Mouse is a pointing device with whose help the user can nagivate any where on the screen (i.e. VDU) connected with the computer. The mouse is connected through one of the ports to the computer. Pointing a cursor with a mouse is easier for non-typists than pressing various key combinations.

3. Light Pen : Light pen is a device seldom used with desktop applications except in the cases where the PC is used as graphic terminal in CAD or similar applications. The light pen, is a stylus connected by a cable to a terminal. It can be touched to the CRT (Cathode Ray Tube) screen where it can detect the flying spot or roster on the screen as it passes, the computer can detect accurately the position of the light pen.

Character Readers

MICR (Magnetic Ink Character Recognition): Direct input is achieved by the use of special readers which can read characters printed in a special format on the source documents themselves.

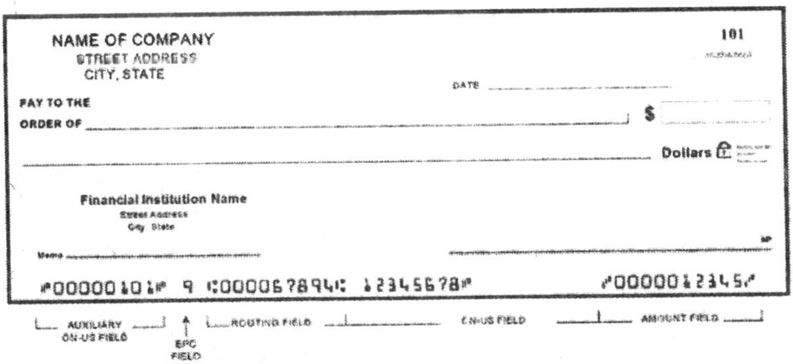

Fig. 15. MICR

The best known "special format" is the one used on the bottom of cheques. The shape of these characters is a bit odd, but you can read them. They can also be read by a special purpose magnetic reader, direct into the computer memory. This reading method is called MICR.

OCR (Optical Character Recognition)

OCR is like MICR, it uses a special odd-shaped character set which can be sensed and interpreted to binary by optical methods. Optical readers can also be used to interpret marks made on documents in significant places. This is called OMR (Optical Mark Recognition) or simply "Mark-sensing".

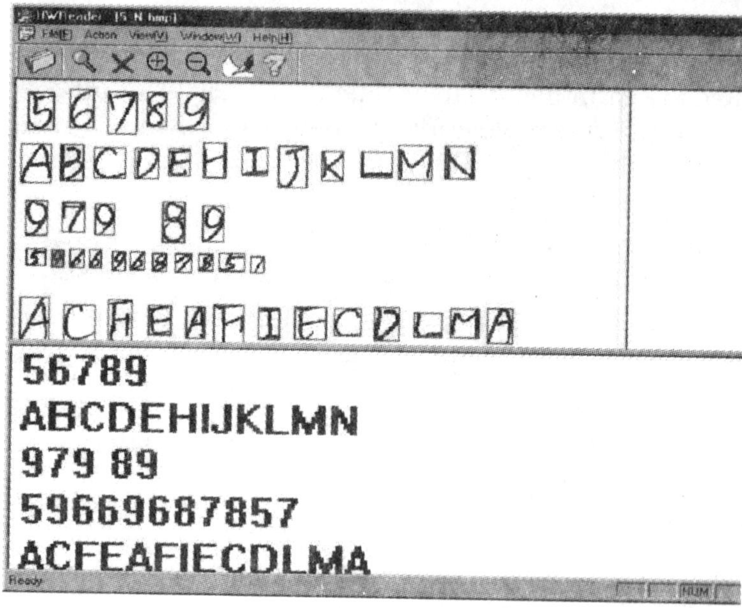

Fig. 16. OCR

Voice Input

Computers are being developed to input data voice. There are problems which arise because of different dialects and the way different people speak. But, this is technically feasible to convert the spoken word consisting as it does or pressure variations in the air to varying electrical voltage by means of a microphone. The voltage patterns so produced may then be identified by electronic circuitry within the computer.

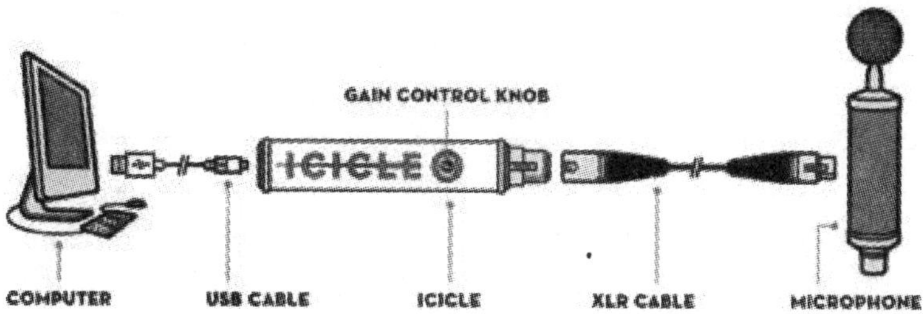

Fig. 17. Voice Input

Bar-code Readers

Data coded in the term of light and dark lines or bars known as bar-codes. Bar-codes are used particularly by the retail trade for labelling goods. They are used for numbering books in libraries so that when a book is borrowed or returned it can be

Fig. 18. Bar-Codes

Storage or Memory Unit

Storage and memory are two words used for the same meaning. The word memory is an unfortunate choice as it implies a human capability; the word storage is a better choice to use.

Storage unit of a computer can be compared with a chalk-board when we write something on the board it can be read or copies. As the board space is only limited, eventually it has to be erased and reused. Once this happens, the data are lost forever. It can of course be rewritten, but the original piece of data is gone.

Computer memory is similar to an electronic chalkboard. Once information enters in a computer's memory, it stays there exactly as entered and the computer has the ability to recall the data. The capacity is only limited, eventually all memory gets filled, then it has to be erased and re-erased.

A computer is an electronic device. Is it mechanical? Whether it is mechanical or not, at least not in the commonsense. We easily manipulate ten different digits, twenty-six letters and any number of punctuation marks and other symbols. Such diversity is not convenience for an electronic device. Thus, before we try to understand how a computer stores data it is better to know about the binary system.

Binary System

It is number system using only two digits 1 and 0 to represent a number, as compared with ten digits of the more familiar decimal number system. This is exclusively used in computers because it corresponds to the on and off status of the electrical switches.

The decimal number system is very familiar to all. Consider two numbers 5 and 50. Both have five as common digit, but both are different numbers, the difference is in the position of numbers. The first five is in units position and the second five is in the tens position. Closer analysis reveals that the number 50 is really another way of saying "five tens and no one's". So any decimal number consists of a series of digits 0, 1, 2, 3, 4, 5, 6, 7, 8, 9- written in precise, relative positions. The number fifty-seven is written as 57, and by mere interchange results in seventy-five which is written as 75.

Take for example a number 8670. The combination of digits really represented are:

8 6 7 0

Unit	- 0 times	1 -	0
Tens	- + 7 times	10 -0	7
Hundred	- + 6 times	100 -	600
Thousand	- +8 times	1000 -	8000
			8670

In other words, to find the value of any number, multiply each digit by its positional value, add these products. This is known as the digit – times – place – value rule.

In the example above, we started with 1, then went to 10, then 100, then 1000. The next value is 10,000. To move up to the tens position, we multiplied this starting value by 10 which is the base value, so the base value of decimal system is number 10.

In the figure below we have written a series of places or positional values along a horizontal line, showing these same values in scientific notation below the line. Starting at the right, we find that the number 1 can be written as 10^0. Taking this as starting point, the place values for the decimal number system can be written as 10, the base raised to a series of sequential integer power – 0, 1, 2, 3, 4, 5, 6, 7, ...

100,000	**10,000**	**1,000**	**100**	**10**	**1**
10x10x10x10x10	10x10x10x10	10x10x10	10x10	10	1
10^5	10^4	10^3	10^2	10^1	10^0

As in decimal numbering system, the digit-time-place -value rule still works; it is just that the place values are different representing powers of two rather than power of ten. Consider for example, the binary number 1101.

1 1 0 1

2^0 or Unit	- 0 times	1	-	1
2^1 or twos	- + 7 times	2	-	0
2^2 or fours	- + 6 times	4	-	4
2^3 or eights	- +8 times	8	-	8
				13

There is nothing to restrict the application of these rules to a base ten numbering system. The positional values are represented as powers of two instead of ten. As in the decimal numbering system, the digit zero (0) is needed to represent "no value" in a given position. In addition to zero, the binary numbering system needs only one other digit, a one (1) in order to form numbers. Only the values less than the base can be represented in single position since the base of the binary system is two (2), only number less than 2 can be presented 0 and 1.

Any whole number can be written in binary. The difference is, normally the binary number is enclosed within a set of parentheses, and or subscript is used to indicate the base like $(1101)_2$. The base ten system is predominantly used because we are used to it since childhood, and as we have 10 fingers in our hand we used base – ten which is convenient to us.

As far as the computer is concerned it is an electronic device, binary numbers are much more convenient to use than base – ten numbers. Since data representation requires only two digits, 0 and 1. The computer, using binary numbers can work with the simple on/off logic of electrical circuits. Binary number system is truly an electronic numbering system.

There are other number systems, notably octal or base-eight and hexadecimal (base 16) are also used with computers. The octal system used powers of eight to represent positional values, using the digits 0, 1, 2, 3, 4,

5, 6 and 7 with this framework. The hexadecimal system uses powers of 16 representing 0, 2, 3, 4, 5, 6, 7, 8, 9, A, B, C, D, E and F. The most important point is that there is no computer using either octal or hexadecimal number (table below). They all work in binary.

Conversation tables : (Before codes)

Octal	Binary	Hexadecimal
0	0000	0
1	0001	1
2	0010	2
	0011	3
3	0100	4
4	0101	5
	0110	6
5	0111	7
6	1000	8
	1001	9
7	1010	A
	1011	B
	1100	C
	1101	D
	1110	E
	1111	F

The value of base-8 and base-16 number systems lies in the case of conversion to or from binary. Circumstance that allows numbers written in these systems to be used as a shorthand for displaying the actual binary contents of a computer's memory. Each octal digit is equivalent exactly to three binary digits; each hexadecimal digit is equivalent to exactly four binary digits.

When a programme goes wrong the programmer often finds it necessary to look at a dump of the contents of the computer's memory in order to figure out the defect.

Codes

Numeric data are not the only form of data that are handled by a computer. There is often a need to process alphanumeric data which include the alphabets from A – Z. In Morse code, for example, letters are represented by a pattern of dots and dashes for instance (.__.__..__.__ __.__ __.__) in the international distress signal SOs. If we were to substitute a 1 for each dot and a 0 for each dash, we would have a binary code capable of communicating letters as well as digits.

B C D

The Binary Code Decimal (BCD) code is one of the early memory codes. It is based on the idea of converting each digit of a decimal number into its binary equivalent rather than converting the entire decimal value into a pure binary form. This facilitates the conversion process to a great extent.

The BCD equivalent of each decimal digit is shown in (X). 42_{10} is equal to 10100010_2 in a pure binary form.

Converting 42_{10} into BCD, however, produces the following result:

42_{10} – 0100 0010 as a 01000010 in BCD
4 2

In the above discussion, we have used a group of 4 bits to represent a digit (character) in BCD. 4 bit-BCD coding system can be used to represent only decimal numbers because 4 bits are insufficient to represent the various characters used by a computer. Instead of using 4-bits with only 16 possible characters (2^4), computer designers commonly use 6 bits to represent characters in BCD code which has possible character (2^6).

EBCDIC

Extended Binary Coded Decimal Interchange Code (EBCDIC) was developed to remove some of the drawbacks of BCD coding system. The major problem with BCD code is that only 64 different characters can be represented in it. This is not sufficient for providing decimal numbers (10), lower case letters (26), and a large number of other special characters. So, BCD code was extended from a 6 – bit to an 8 – bit code. The added two bits are used for additional Zone bits, expanding the Zone to 4 bits. This coding system is known as EBCDIC. In this code, it is possible to represent 256(2^5) different characters instead of 64 (2^6). In addition to the various character requirements mentioned above, this also allows a large variety of printable characters and several non –printable control character. All of the 256 combinations have not yet been assigned characters, so the code can still grow as new requirements develop.

ASCII

One more computer code, that is, widely used is ASCII (American Standard Code for Information Interchange). This code is popular in data communication and is used almost exclusively to represent data internally in microcomputers.

Storage Devices

Any storage unit of a computer system is ranked according to the following criteria :

1. Access time : This is the time required to locate and retrieve stored data from the storage unit in response to a programme instruction.

2. Storage capacity : The amount of data that can be stored in a storage unit.

Based on the above-mentioned criteria, storage units are basically of two types: Primary and Secondary.

Storage locations and address : A primary or internal storage section is basic to all computers. It is made up of several small storage areas called locations or cells. Each of these locations can store a fixed number of bits, called word length of that particular primary storage.

Storage capacity : The storage capacity of large computer systems is more than that of small systems. This capacity is defined in terms of bytes or words. A symbol commonly used to denote the storage capacity is letter K (kilo) which is equal to 1024. Thus a 32 kilobyte memory is capable of storing 32x 1024 = 32768 bits. Memory size ranges from a few K bytes of words in small machines to several thousand K bytes or words in large machines.

Bits and computers : Computers are normally known by 8-bit computers, 16 – bit computers and 32 – bit computers etc. This refers to the word size of particular computer in terms of total number of bits. Word size is an important architectural factor. Small machines have 8 bits or 16 bits, large machines have 32 bits or more. The question is what is the advantage of having more number of bits per word instead of having more words of smaller size.

To answer the above questions, imagine a highway with 8 lanes, and heavy traffic. Then, when it is expanded to 16 lanes the flow of traffic eases. Similar is the case with the 8 bit and 16 bits. Greater bits means a more rapid flow of electronic signals. Thus, a 32 – bit computer is much faster than an 8-bit or 16-bit computer. Data and instructions are moved to and from memory in word-size bunches. So, even if the electronic circuits used are comparable in speed. Small machines are slower than the bigger machines. This difference is analogous for providing a user of a small machine with a small data shovel and user of a large data machine with a large data shovel. Even though they both may be shovelling at comparable speeds, the user with the smaller shovel will be slower because more and more shovelfuls are needed to move the same amount of data.

PIMRARY MEMORY DEVICES

RAM : Primary storage is usually referred to as random access memory (RAM) because it is possible to randomly select and use any location of this memory to directly store and retrieve data and instructions. RAM is said to be volatile. That is its contents are lost when power is turned off, which is also called user memory.

ROM : Read only memory (ROM) is the one in which information is stored permanently. It can only be read and it is not possible to write fresh information on it. ROM is non-volatile, that is, its contents are not lost, when power is turned off unlike RAM.

PROM : Programmable Read Only Memory (PROM) is stored on chips that you can programme yourself (though special hardware is necessary). After they are programmed they function like ROM chips.

Other Chips : EPROM (Erasable Programme Read Only Memory) and EEPROM(Electrically Erasable Programme Read Only Memory).

Cache Memory : A special very high speed memory is sometimes used to increase the speed of processing by making current programmes and data available to the CPU (Central Processing Unit) which processes the data. As the CPU speeds are quite high compared to the access time of main memory, there is the need for memory which has to be small and fast to compensate for the mismatch in operating speed between CPU and the main memory. This type of memory is called a high speed buffer or cache memory.

Cache memory is a memory in hiding, and is not addressable by the user of the computer system. It is very expensive as compared to the main memory.

Registers : The instructions are interpreted and executed by CPU and there is a movement of information between the various units of the computers system. In order to handle this process satisfactorily and to speed up the rate of information transfer, the computer uses a number of special memory units called registers.

The number of registers varied among computers as does the data-flow pattern. Computers use several types of registers, each one designed to perform a particular function. The length of the register depends upon the number of bits it can store. Thus a register which can store 16 – bits is referred as 16-bit register. Registers do very from one computer to another but some are common to all.

SECONDARY MEMORY DEVICES

The processing of data is done with the fast primary storage devices. But with the increase of data sometimes which goes to million and even billions of bytes of data, it cannot be stored in primary storage devices alone because of the cost per bit increase. So to help to solve this problem, cheaper secondary storage devices are used which are otherwise called auxiliary memory. Eventually the storage capacity is large, but these secondary storage devices generally have an operating speed far slower than that of primary storage.

Several different devices can be used as a secondary storage, but the one selected for a particular application mainly depends upon how the information needs to be accessed. Basically there are two ways of accessing information, i.e., 1) Sequential or serial access and 2) Direct or random access.

Sequential access device is the one where the information to be retrieved need to the traced in a serial way for e.g., applications like monthly pay-slips, electricity bills, etc.

Random access or direct access is the one where the information can be retrieved directly and instantaneously, for example, in a computerised bank, computerised train ticket booking system, where the information needs to be retrieved at the same instant.

Punched Paper Tape : This a sequential-access storage device. Data are coded on a tape in the form of punched hole combination. The tape is normally 1 inch wide, comes in rolls, and may be used in any length up to several hundred feet. There is a line of sprocket holes in the middle of the tape for the purpose of feeding the tape through punching and reading device.

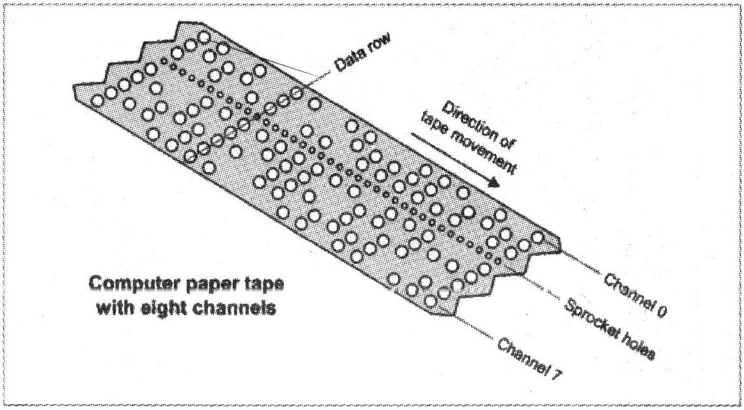

Fig. 19. Punched Paper Tape

Magnetic Tape : Magnetic tape is one of the most popular storage medium for large data and that are sequentially accessed and processed. The tape is a plastic ribbon, usually half a inch wide that is coated on one side with an iron-oxide material which can be magnetized. The tape ribbon itself is stored in reel of 50 to 2400 feet or a small cartridge or cassette. It is similar to the tape used on a tape-recorder except that it is of higher quality and is more durable. Computer tapes can also be erased by recording on the old data.

Tapes, Cassettes and Cartridges : Magnetic tapes reels are suitable for use only with large and medium size computers. The same magnetic tape is used in smaller systems in the form of cassettes and cartridges.

Fig. 20. Cartridge

Fig. 21. Cassette

Magnetic Disk : A magnetic disk is a thin, circular metal plate/plates coated on both sides with a magnetic material. It is very similar in appearance to a LP gramophone record. A disk pack consists of a number of these disks, three or more, mounted about half an inch apart from each other on a central shaft which rotates at a speed of 2,400 or more revolutions per minute (rpm). All the disks of a disk pack move simultaneously in the same direction, and at equal speed.

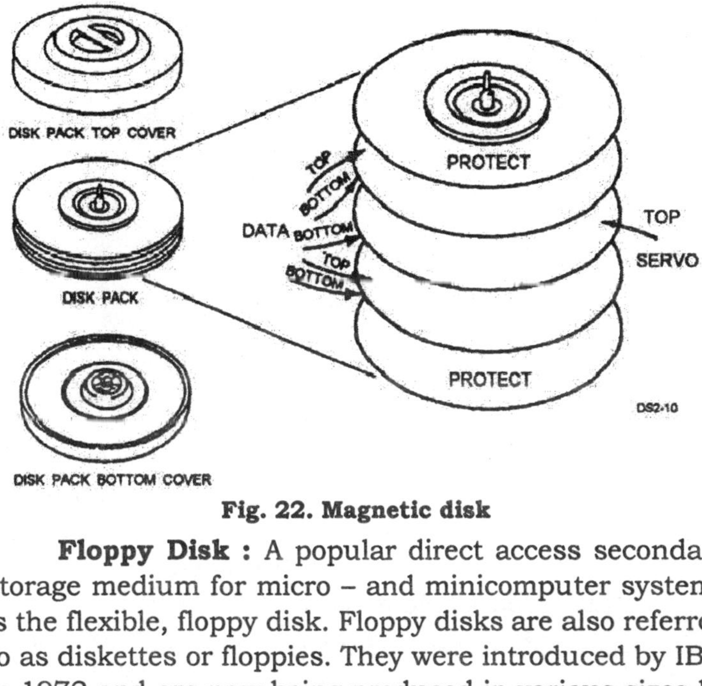

Fig. 22. Magnetic disk

Floppy Disk : A popular direct access secondary storage medium for micro – and minicomputer systems is the flexible, floppy disk. Floppy disks are also referred to as diskettes or floppies. They were introduced by IBM in 1972 and are now being produced in various sizes by many manufacturers.

A floppy disk is made of flexible plastic which is coated with magnetic oxide. The flexible disk is enclosed within a square plastic which is called jacket. The jacket gives handling protection to the disk surface and the read/write head.

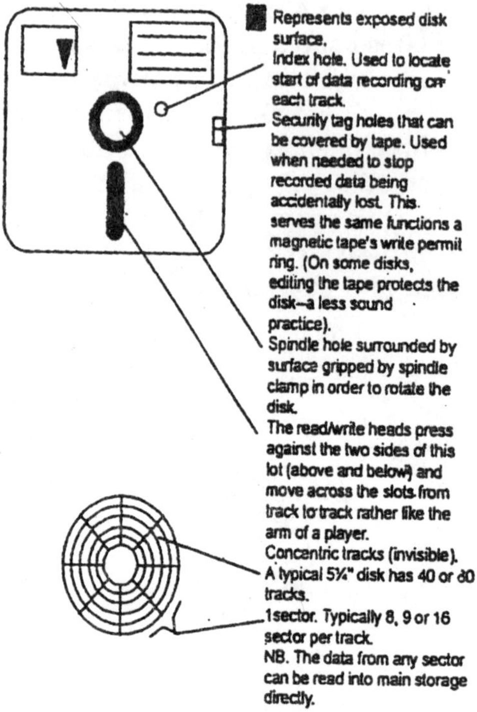

Fig. 23. Floppy disks

Floppy disks are typical 3.5, 5.25 or 8 inches in diameter. They come either in single or double-density versions and record on one or both surfaces of a diskette. There are basically four types of diskettes:

a) Single-sided-single-density

b) Single-sided-double-density

c) Double-sided-single-density

d) Double-sided-double-density

Winchester disk : There is one more type of relatively new disk storage unit known as Winchester disk. In this, disks are permanently housed in sealed and contamination-free containers. Winchester disks are fast and highly reliable, yet low-priced compared with conventional hard-disk device. They are normally 5.25; 8 or 14 inches in diameter and storage capacities of 10,

20 and 40 megabytes are typical. Some Winchester units employ dual disk drives in which case the storage capacity is doubled.

Magnetic Drum : Magnetic drum is a direct access storage device that can be used for both sequential and random processing. It consists basically of a cylinder whose outer surface is coated with a thin layer of magnetizable material. A motor rotates the cylinder on its axis at a constant and rapid rate.

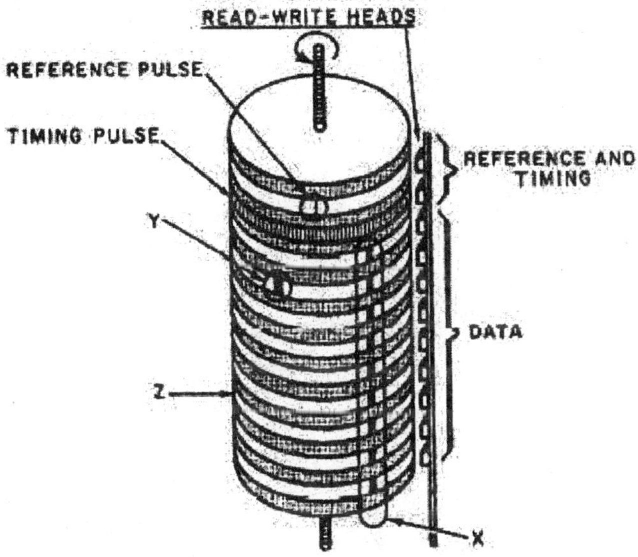

Fig. 24. Magnetic Drum

OPTICAL STORAGE DEVICES

The most popular alternative to magenetic storage systmes are optical storage media. The most widely used type of optical storage medium is the compact disk (CD), which is used in CD-ROM, DVD-ROM, CDR, CDRW and Photo CD systems.

Since the mid 1990s nearly all PCs have been sold with a built in CD-ROM drive. Consumers are now buying more systems with DVD-ROM drives rather than standard CD-ROM units. These devices fall into the optical storage category because they store data on a reflective surface so that it can be read by a beam of laser light. A laser uses concentrated, narrow beam of light, focused and directed with lenses, prisms and mirrors. The tight focus of the laser beam is possible because all the light is of the same wavelength.

CD-ROM

The familiar audio compact disk is a popular medium for storing music. In the computer world, the medium is called compact disk read only memory (CD-ROM). This uses the same technology used to produce music CDs.

The CD-ROM drive for music or data reads 0s and 1s from a spinning disk by focusing a laser on the disks surface. Some areas of the disk reflect the laser light into a sensor, other areas scatter the light. A spot that reflects the laser beam is interpreted as a 1 and the absence of a reflection is interpreted as a 0.

Data is laid out on a CD-ROM disk in a long, continuous spiral that starts at the outer edge and winds inwards towards the centre. Data is stored in the form of lands, which are flat areas on the metals surface, and pits, which are depressions or hollows. A land reflects the laser light into the sensor (a data bit of 1) and a pit scatters the light (a data bit of 0).

On a full CD-ROM the spiral of data stretches almost 3 miles long. A standard CD can store 650 MB of data or about 70 mins of audio.

CD-ROM Speeds

Compared to hard disk drives CD-ROM drives are quite slow, because the laser reads pits and lands one bit at a time. Another reason is the rotational speed of the disk. Like a track on a magnetic disk the track of an optical disk is split into sectors. However the sectors are laid out quite differently than they are on magnetic disks.

The sectors near the middle of the CD wrap farther around the disk than those near the edge. For the drive to read each sector in the same amount of time it must spin the disk faster when reading the sectors near the middle and slower when reading the sectors near the edge. Changing the speed of rotation takes time – enough to seriously impair the overall performance of the CD-ROM drive. The first CD-ROM drives read data at 150 KBps and were known as single speed drives. This rate is much slower than that of a typical hard drive which transfers data at rates of 5 – 15 MBps.

Presently CD-ROM drives read data 2 '!52 times faster than first models (300'!7800KBs). Even with the changing speed of the disk reading data from an optical medium is a relatively simple undertaking. Writing data however is another matter. The medium is a foil disk that is physically pitted to reflect or scatter the laser beam. The disk is then covered in a plastic coating and it is difficult to alter the surface of the disk after it has been stamped.

CD-ROM Uses

The fact that you must use special technologies to write data to an optical disk does not mean that this storage medium is not useful. In fact many applications rely on huge volumes of data that rarely change. Because of the high precision and data density possible with CD-ROM, a single CD typically can hold about 650 MB of data.

Software companies can distribute their products on CD-ROM, because of the high capacity and the fact that 1 CD is much cheaper to produce than a set of diskettes. Many software publishers regard CDs as the distribution medium of choice.

DVD-ROM

Digital video (or versatile) disk read only memory,

is a high-density medium capable of storing a full-length movie on a single disk the size of a CD. It achieves such high storage capacities by using both sides of the disk and special data compression technologies. The latest generation of DVD-ROM use layers of data tracks; the laser beam reads data from the first layer and then looks through it to read data from the second layer. Each side of a standard DVD-ROM can hold up to 4.7 GB. Dual layer DVD-ROM can hold 17 GB of data.

MEASURING DRIVE PERFORMANCE

Average Access Time

For a storage device the average access time (or seek time) is the amount of time the device takes to position its read/write heads over any spot in the medium. This measurement is an average because access times can vary greatly depending on the distance between the heads original local and their destination.

For storage devices access times are measured in milliseconds (ms). For memory devices access times are measured in nanoseconds (ns). In a disk drive the access time depends on a combination of 2 factors.

1. Revolutions per minute (rpm).
2. Time taken to more the heads from one track to another.

Device	Typical Access Time
Static RAM (SRAM)	5 – 15
Dynamic RAM (DRAM)	50 – 70 ns
ROM	55 – 250 ns
Hard disk drives	6 – 12 ms
CD-ROM drives	80 – 800 ms
Tape Drives	10 – 500 s

File Compression

One solution to the storage problem is to compress

data. File compression or data compression is the technology for shrinking the size of a file, thereby freeing up space for more data and programs to reside on the disk.

Entire hard disks, floppy disks, or individual files can be compressed as much as a 3:1 ratio. File compression is performed by software that uses mathematical algorithms to squeeze the data into smaller chunks by removing information that is not vital to the file or data. When the file is returned to its original size this data is reinserted so that the original data is reproduced exactly as it was before compression.

A utility used to compress one or more files shrinks the selected files and stores them inside a new file with its own name. The resulting file is called an archive file because it stores the compressed data inside.

Data transfer rate

The speed at which a device can transfer data – how long it takes for one device to transfer data to another device. Speeds are expressed as a rate, or as some amount of data per unit time. When measuring a devices data transfer rate (throughput) the time is measured in seconds, but units of data may be measured in bytes, KB, MB or GB.

Speeds for hard disks are generally high, from around 15 MBps to 80 MBps and higher. CD-ROMs and diskettes are the slowest storage devices.

Drive Interface Standards

An important factor in determining how quickly a drive can read or write data is the type of controller that the drive uses. A disk controller connects the disk drive to the computers bus enabling the drive to exchange data with other devices.

EIDE

Enhanced integrated drive electronics (EIDE) is

an enhanced version of IDE. It is a catch all term for drive interfaces based on this standard. Supports transfer rates of 33 MBps. The standard variants go by many different names including Fast IDE, ATA, Fast ATA and more.

SCSI

Small computer system interface (SCSI) was originally developed as a way to connect third party peripheral devices to mainframe computers. One way to think of SCSI is as an extension to the computers bus. As such all interface circuitry needed by the device has to be on the device itself. One benefit is to improve efficiency, allows higher transfer rates than EIDE.

Storage Hierarchy

The storage hierarchy will let us know about cost effectiveness, assess time and capacity. The pyramid explains the concept. Thus each memory which is plugged in between the CPU and the main memory is the fastest one, next comes the secondary storage devices and then the off-line secondary storage devices.

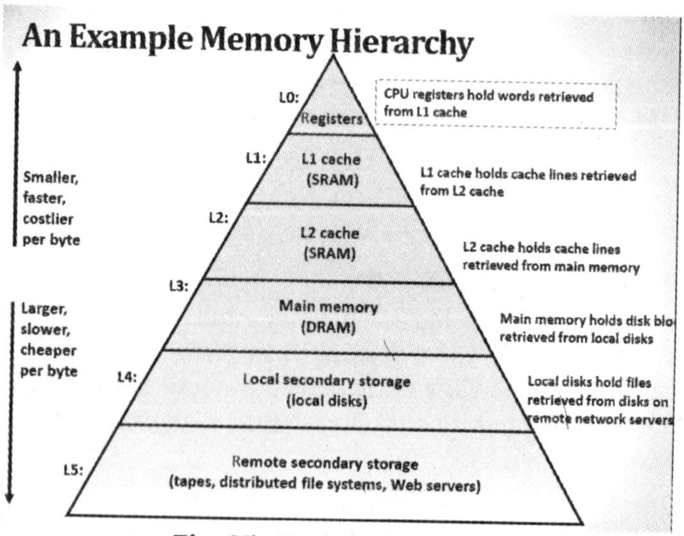

Fig. 25. Storage Hierarchy

Processing Unit

Processing of the data, that is input, is done by the Central Processing Unit (CPU), which has control unit and logic unit. CPU is like human brain. It decides what to do and what not to do. It uses logic to take decisions. Logical decisions like IF, THEN, ELSE, etc. are done by the CPU.

The difference between a CPU and a processing unit is quite simple. A CPU consists of main memory unit, a logic unit and control unit. A processor is CPU without memory unit.

Arithmetic and Logic Unit (ALU)

A computer has to do a large number of calculations and computations. It has to add, substract, multiply and divide. It has to apply logic. By logic we mean:

i) Comparing two quantities to see which one is bigger.

ii) Courting any element and testing whether the desired value has been reached.

iii) Deciding the next route.

All such calculations and comparisons are done in this unit. This unit takes instructions from the control unit. It takes data from the memory unit and returns information to it.

Output Unit

Processed data, need to be output in the relevant way to be used by the user. The output devices are the link to the outside world.

Printers

Printers are the most commonly used output devices that can be found in almost all computer centres. There are several types designed for different types of application. Depending on their speed and printing, printers are classified as character printers, line printers and page printers. In addition, there is another classification according to which printers are of two types

– impact and non-impact. Impact printers use the familiar typewriter approach of hammering a typeface against page and inked ribbon. Non-impact printers do not hit or impact a ribbon to print.

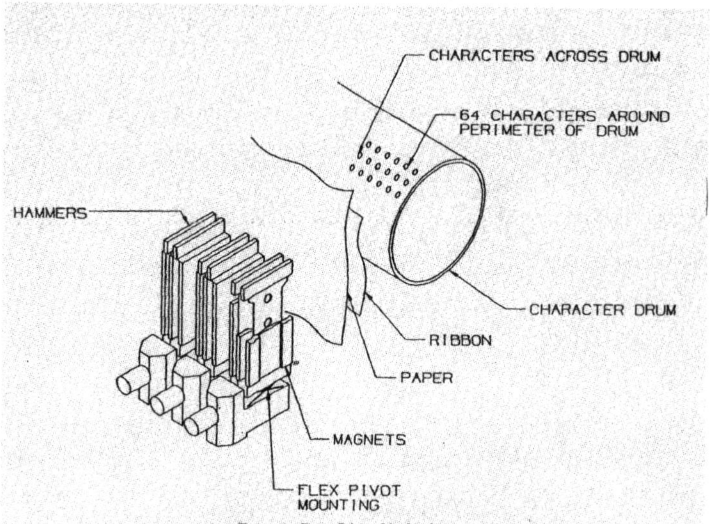

Figure 1. Drum Printer Mechanism

Fig. 26. Printers

1. Impact printers can be further grouped as Serial or Character impact printers
   a) Dot Matrix Printer
   b) Daisy Wheel Printer
   c) Golf Ball Printer
   d) Cylinder Printer

Line Printers

   a) Chain
   b) Band
   c) Drum

2. **Non-Impact Printers :** Non-impact printers are categorized under five types:
   a) Thermal

b) Laser
c) Inkjet
d) Electrostatic
e) Electro-graphic

Character Printers

Character printers print only one character at a time. A typewriter is an example of character printer. Commonly used character printers are letter quality, printers which use print wheel are known as daisy wheel. Each petal of the daisy wheel has a character, embossed on it. When the desired character spins to the correct position, a print hammer strikes it to produce the output. Another type is DOT-MATRIX printer which prints each character as a pattern of dots.

MATRIX PRINTING

DAISYWHEEL PRINTING

LINEPRINTER PRINTING

LASER PRINTING

Fig. 27. Character Printers

Line Printers : Line printers are impact printers used with most medium and large computer systems, for producing high volume paper output. They are fast printers having speed in the range of 300 to 2500 lines per minute.

Visual Display Units or VDU : These are the most widely used output devices connected on-line. VDUs are of different kinds depending upon their application. The TV screen like VDUs provide most of the feedback you need to run your programmes depending upon the application.

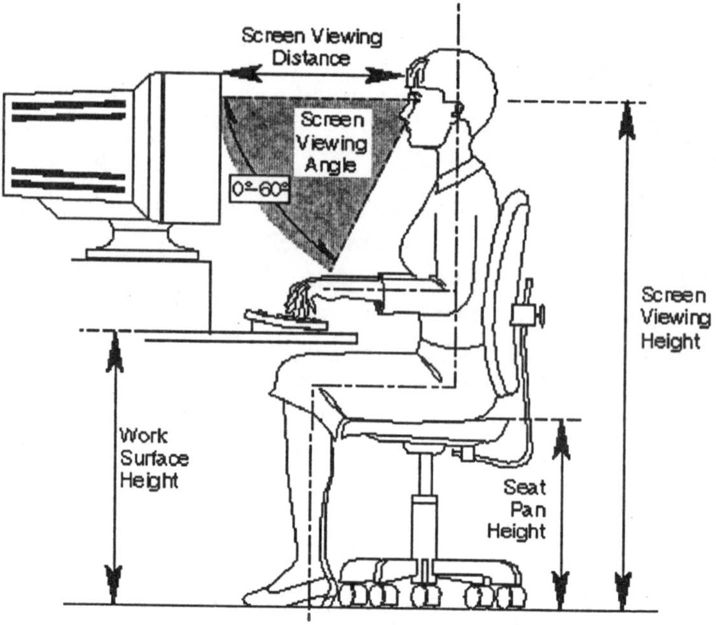

Fig. 28. VDU

The screens of visual display unit and PC systems are used to receive output in alphanumeric form – as letters, numbers, and special characters. A Cathode Ray Tube (CRT) screen is generally found in desktop work-stations, and in the larger transportable PC models. Visual display unit have separate storage of about 1K capacity in the form of core or IC memory. The memory relieves the computer during display by storing the data.

They use colour monitors, i.e. Multichrome, Monochrome, etc. High resolution VDUs are also used which means that the resolution is high as compared to less resolution VDUs. High resolution implies that the number of points across the screen and the number of rows up and down are larger than in medium or low resolution. These points or dots are often referred to as lines. The higher the resolution the more detailed is the image on the screen.

Control Unit

Control Unit helps all the devices to work in co-relation to each other. These operations include functions like, how does input device know that it is time to feed data into the storage unit and how is it that only the final results are sent to the output device and not the intermediate results. All this is possible due to control unit. The control unit selects, interprets and sees to the execution of the programme instructions. The control unit is able to maintain order and direct the operations of the entire system.

This unit has an electronic clock that sends millions of pulses in a second and this frequency of the clock decides the speed at which the computer works. Control unit is truly the nerve centre of the computer, because it controls and co-ordinates all hardware operations i.e., those of the CPU and I/O devices.

The Future

Advances in material science, manufacturing, and concepts of computing, promise to maintain the historic growth pattern in hardware power. Over the last 50 years, the cost dropped by a factor of 10 each decade and the capability increased by a factor of atleast 100 each decade. There are four areas in which this momentum will most likely be maintained, i.e. increasing switch speed, shrinking distances, developing superchips (which are called as Very High Speed Integrated Chips, VHSIC), and lastly development of hardware depending on parallel and vector processing.

REFERENCES

- Blundell, B. Computer Hardware. Middlesex : University Press, 2008.
- Burstein, Jorome S. Computer and Information System. New York: Holt, Rinehart and Winston, 1986.
- French, C.S. Computer Studies. 4th ed., London : DP Publications, 1992.

- Hunt, Roger. Computers and Commonsense. 4th ed., London: Prentice Hall, 1988.
- Introduction to Computer Science. Delhi : Pearson, 2011
- Krishnamurthy, E.V. Introductory Theory of Computer Science, 1991
- Norton, Peter, Introduction to Computers. 7th Ed. New Delhi : Tata McGraw Hill Education, 2013.
- Preeze, A.D. and Dyk, V.V. Computer Hardware and Software. Cape Town : Imani & Rose, 2008.
- Rajaraman, V., Fundamentals of Computers. 5th Ed. New Delhi : PHI Learning, 2010.
- Rowley, J.E. The basics of Information Technology. London : Bingley, 1988.
- Rowley, J.E. Computers for Libraries, 2nd ed. London : Bingley, 1985.
- Shelly, G., and Vermaat, M. Introduction to Computers. Boston : Course Technologie, 2011.
- Sinha, Pradeep K. and Sinha, Priti. Computer Fundamentals. 6th Ed. New Delhi: BPB, 2011

3
Software

The terms hardware and software are being used widely in connection with computers. Hardware is the term used for the machinery itself and to the various physical devices of a computer system. Thus the input, storage, processing, control and output devices are hardware. This has already been dealt in chapter 2.

Software

A computer with the hardware is just an useless machine. It needs to be instructed to do a desired job. Hence, it is necessary to specify a sequence of instructions that a computer must perform to solve a problem. Such a sequence of instructions written in a language that can be understood by a computer is called Computer Programme. The programme controls the computer to process data and to do what it wants to be done.

The term software refers to a set of computer programmes, procedures, and associated documents (flow charts, manuals, etc.) that describe the programme and how they are to be used. To be precise, software is a collection of programmes to enhance the working capabilities of the hardware.

Major Types of Software

1. System software
2. Application software
3. Dialogue/query software

Each of these kinds of software specializes in a set of capabilities. The different kinds, as illustrated above, interact with each other in maximum utilization of hardware. As shown, the system software surrounds the hardware and controls access to the hardware. Application software must work through system software to operate. Lastly, dialogue and query languages frequently have to work through application software and translators, and finally through system software, in order to operate.

System software includes the management software of computer resources such as processing time, storage and memory, printers, terminals, communication links and all of the peripheral equipment that surrounds a central processing unit. The special set of programmes that manages and controls CPU is the operating system. The interaction of users with the PC or microcomputer is controlled by and takes place through operating systems.

Application software refers to programmes that are written for or by a user in order to accomplish a specific task. There are various special software programmes written to apply for a specific application.

The third kind of software, which appeared in the 1980s, called by a variety of names, such as user friendly, fourth generation, dialogue/query, and very high-level languages.

Relationship between Hardware and Software

For the maximum utilization of computer output, hardware and software need to work together. They are complimentary to each other. One cannot work independently without the help of the other.

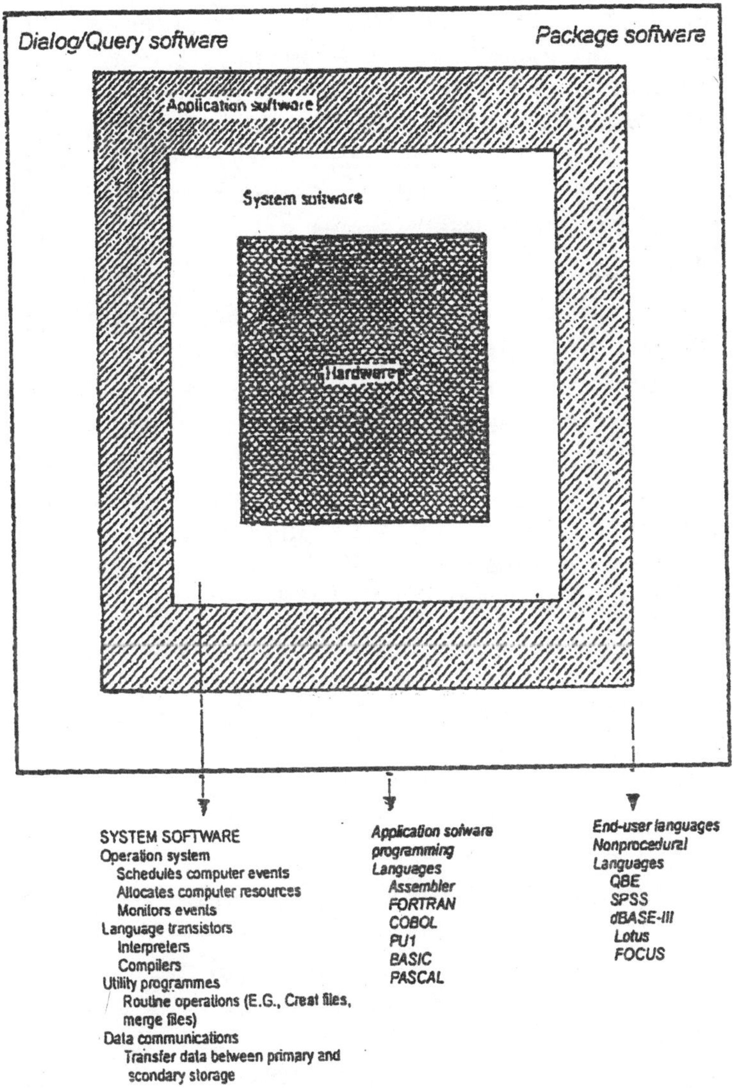

Fig. 29. Software

To tell an analogy, a video cassette player or an ordinary audio-cassette player and cassettes are hardware. However, the songs recorded on the cassette are its software. To listen to a particular song one has to record it and put the cassette in the player and listen to it. Similarly to get a job done by a computer relevant software should be developed. Software production is difficult and expensive. Hardware is one time expense and software is a continuous one. Different softwares can be loaded and run on the same hardware to perform different types of jobs, just as different cassettes can be used on the same cassette player.

System Software

System software includes Operating System (OS), languages, translators and utility programmes.

Operating system is an integrated set of programmes that is used to manage the various resources and overall operations of a computer system. It is designed to support the activities of a computer installation. It works like a manager of a company. An operating system is responsible for the smooth and efficient operation of the entire computer system.

An operating system mainly performs three functions. First, it allocates resources to the application jobs in the execution queue. It provides locations in primary memory for data and programme and controls the input and output devices such as printers, display terminals, and telecommunication links.

Secondly, the operating system schedules the jobs that have been submitted. There are several ways in which jobs come to the attention of the CPU operating system, viz., (a) telecommunication links present many jobs to the CPU and there is always one job waiting for the CPU to handle; (b) a job can be submitted directly by the system operator, (c) batch jobs are executed out of which operating system should be in a position to differentiate between high priority and low priority jobs according to the requirements of the organization.

Thirdly, the operating system translates the high level language programmes and dialogue/query programmes such as BASIC, COBOL, FORTRAN and

FOCUS, into machine language that the computer can understand and execute. These translators are called compilers and interpreters.

Operating system is the component for the hardware to be utilized to its full potential. Unless the operating system is activated, hardware cannot be used. Operating system comes in floppies like MS-DOS for microcomputers and disks/takes for mainframes. Mostly it is stored in the hard disk, so that once the power is switched on, operating system immediately takes over the control of hardware and ensures that the instructions are obeyed.

Capabilities of Operating System

Multi-programming permits several programmes to share a computer system's resources at any one time through concurrent use of a CPU. The word concurrent would mean that only one programme is actually using the CPU at any given moment but that the input/output needs of the other programmes can be served at the same time. Small processors, terminal channels, which are limited in their circuiting to input/output processing functions, actually provide all the input and output. When two or more programmes are active at the same time, but they do not use the same computer resources simultaneously.

As illustrated in the diagram if there are three programmes, A, B and C, programme A output data is being stored in the secondary device and the programme B is being processed by the control processing unit and the third programme C is waiting for the CPU to get processed.

In multiprogramming there are three states. They are (a) running, i.e., the CPU is being used; (b) blocked, i.e., input/output operation in being done; and (c) ready, waiting for the CPU. As an example, we can take programmes, A, B and C are in blocked, running and

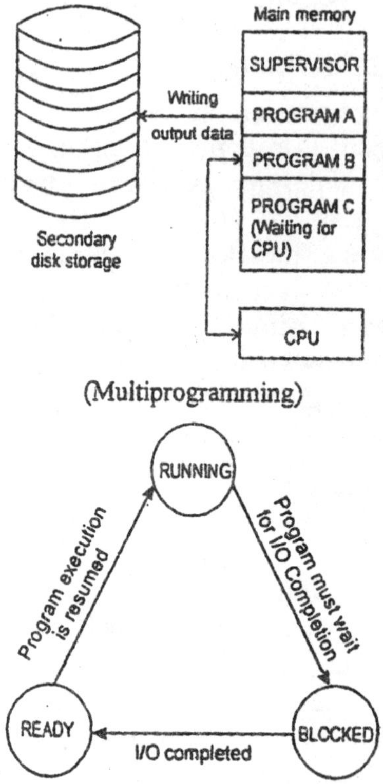

Fig. 30. Illustrating the Operation of Multi-programming

ready states, respectively. If programme A is in blocked state it means that it is doing input/output operation, programme B is running which means that it is using CPU and programme C is in ready state which means it is waiting for CPU. So if one programme, say A, completes its output operation it will be in ready state for the CPU and CPU is taken over by programme C and similarly CPU is used by all the programme without keeping it idle. So, in multiprogramming CPU is always busy. Thus, multiprogramming has two main advantages : (a) Through put is increased which means that rate of data transfer from input to output, (b) Lowered response time which means that the user should not feel that someone is on-line in a multi-user system.

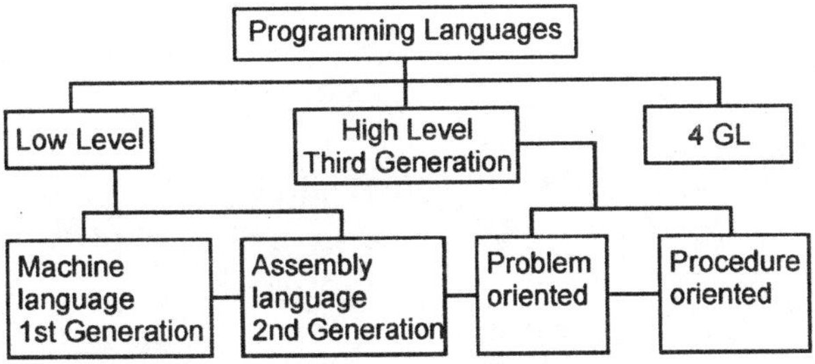

Programming Languages

Fig. 31. The three different states of a programme residing in main memory in case of multiprogramming

Multiprocessing is the use of several independent computing units in the same system environment. This may involve the simultaneous use of many CPUs to accomplish the work by dividing it among themselves.

Difference between Multiprocessing and Multiprogramming

Multiprocessing is the use of two or more CPUs and multiprogramming is the use of two or more programmes to be processed by a single CPU.

Time-sharing

Time sharing is a form of processor management. It is like multiprogramming but in time-sharing it is time driven and whereas in multiprogramming it is event driven. In a time sharing environment, thousands of users are allotted a tiny slice of computer time, say 2 milliseconds. In this time slot, each user is free to perform whatever operations are required, at the end of which another user is given this time slot. So, this way it is also called multi-user environment. Examples of operating system are CP/M, MS-DOS, UNIX, etc.

CP/M : Control programme/microcomputer is an operating system for 8-bit machine/computer and is produced by digital research. This is based on the Zilog Z50 and the Intel 8080 microprocessor chips. This was improved for 16-bit microcomputers known as CP/M-86 operating system. This is based on Intel 8086 and 8088 microprocessor chips. (The 8088 is the microprocessor used on the IBM PC).

MS-DOS : Microsoft Disk Operating System is an operating system which was adopted by IBM for its Personal Computer. IBM was in need of an operating system for its PCs as only CP/M was available at that time. But this was only for an 8-bit microprocessor, whereas IBM is 16-bit machine which required a different disk operating system which led to the use of MS-DOS.

MS-DOS programme allows one to communicate with the machine. It helps to control over all aspects of computer system working. It acts as an interface between man and machine.

UNIX : Unix is an operating system developed by Bell Telephone Labs for mini and microcomputers. This is a real-time multi-tasking operating system, written in the language 'C'. It was written originally on a DEC PDP-11 machine for Bell Laboratories. Unix supports multi-user, multi-taks environment. As far as signle user is concerned it is only the MS-DOS. Unix is the most widely used operating system. It has facilities like multiprogramming and multiprocessing.

Application Software

Operating system software seeks to optimize the utilization of the hardware and to meet the demands of the users, whereas application software is just in contrast to the operating system software. It is primarily concerned with accomplishing the tasks of end users.

Evolution of Software

At the beginning there was only the machine language programming. In the early 1950s machine language was replaced by symbolic language, using symbols as records than 0s and 1s. This first symbolic language was called assemble language. In the middle and later 1950s, there appeared the first high level languages (FORTRAN and COBOL), which relied on

English-like or mathematics-like phrases.

Types of Programming Languages

There are two major types of computer or programming languages: low-level and high level. As shown in, the low-level language can be further divided into machine and assembly languages.

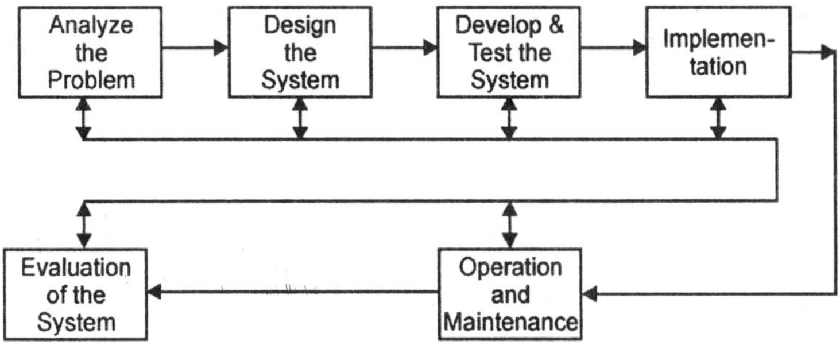

Fig. 32. Programming Languages

Low-level languages are divided as following :

1. Machine language
2. Assembly language

Machine language

This is a low-level computer language, i.e. directly understandable by the computer system. Each model of a computer has a unique machine language. This is generally written as a string of binary 1s and 0s.

Assembly language

One of the first steps in improving the programme preparation process was to substitute letter symbols-mnemonics for the numeric operation codes of machine language. A mnemonic (or memory aid) is like any kind of mental trick we use to help us remember. Mnemonics come in various shapes and sizes, all of them are useful in their own way. For example, a computer may be designed to interpret the machine code of 1111 (binary) or 15 (decimal) as the operation 'subtract', but it is easier for a human being to remember it as SUB.

While assembly language gives programmers great control, it is costly in terms of programme time, difficult to read and debug, and difficult to learn. An assembly is used for converting assembly language programme (source programme)into machine language programme (object programme).

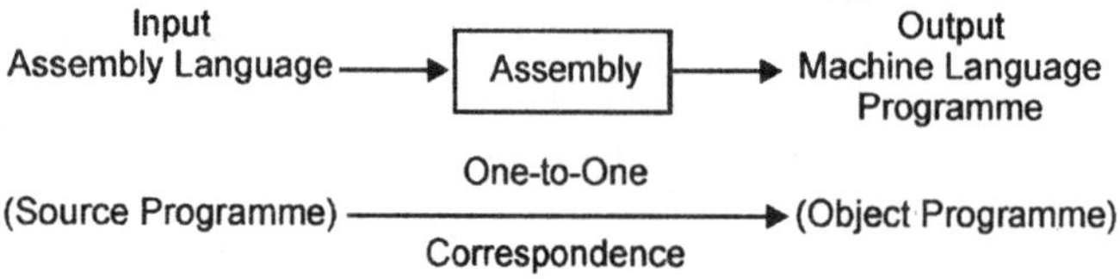

Advantages of Assembly language

1. Mnemonic code allows programmer to save time and reduce detail in writing a programme.
2. Since words or symbols are used instead of numbers, that too binary numbers, fewer errors result, and those that are made are easier to find.
3. It is easier to modify programmes written in assembly language rather than machine language programmes.

High-level languages

Developing an assembly language or a machine language one needs to know about the internal structure of the computer. So, in order to develop a programme independently without any knowledge of internal structure of the computer, high-level languages were developed. The languages instead of being machine oriented are problem oriented. These were developed by using English language and some mathematical symbols.

Compilers

Since the computer is capable of understanding only machine-level instructions it is necessary for the high-level language to be translated into the machine language. So computer acts as a translator.

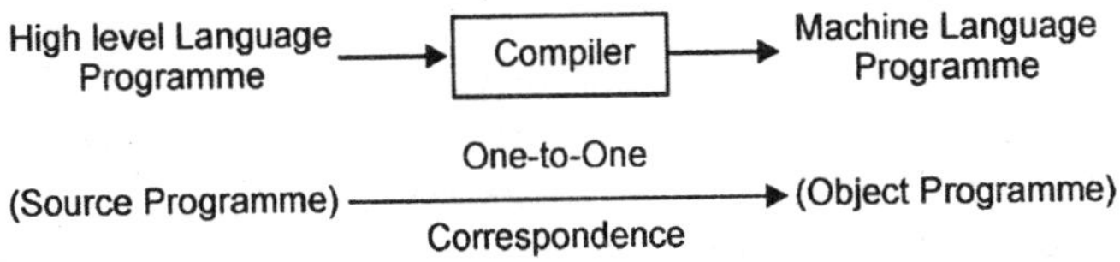

A compiler can translate only those source programmes which have been written in the language for which the computer is meant. For example, a FORTRAN compiler is only capable of translating source programmes which have been written in FORTRAN and, therefore, each machine requires a separate compiler for which high-level language that it supports. Compilers are large programmes that reside permanently on secondary storage.

Interpreters

An interpreter is another type of translator used for translating high-level language into machine code. It takes one statement of a high-level language and translates it into a machine instruction which is immediately executed. It differs from compiler as it translates as well as executes, whereas a compiler translates the whole source programme. Interpreters are often used in small computers. Compiler is a large and complex programme compared to an interpreter.

SOME HIGH-LEVEL LANGUAGES

FORTRAN : (FORmula TRANslation) was developed in 1956 to provide an earlier way of writing scientific and engineering applications. FORTRAN is especially useful in processing numerical data. FORTRAN had undergone several revisions so that the language has been evolving into a wider and more useful language with time.

FORTRAN is not very good at providing input/output efficiency or in printing and working with lists. The syntax is very strict and keying errors are common, making the programme to debug.

COBOL : (Common Business Oriented Language) came into use in the early 1960s. It was originally developed because the defense department wished to create a common administrative language for internal and external software.

COBOL was designed with business administration in mind, for processing large data files, with alphanumeric characters (mixed alphabetic and numerical data) and repetitive tasks like pay-roll.

The weakness of COBOL is a result of its virtue. It is poor at complex mathematical operations. There are many versions of COBOL and not all are compatible with each other. Lengthy COBOL programmes, some hundreds of thousands of lines for e.g., major pay-roll programme can become so complex as to be virtually incomprehensible.

BASIC : (Beginners All-purpose Symbolic Instruction) was developed by John Kemeny and Thomas Kurtz in 1964 at Darmouth College, U.S.A. Their purpose was to develop a language which can be used by all and easy to learn particularly by the undergraduate students in all fields of study. This language has few syntax rules and can be learnt with a bit of concentrated study. A person with little or no knowledge of computers or programming techniques can learn to write BASIC programmes, because of its simplicity and its bias towards users.

Unlike FORTRAN or COBOL, BASIC is an interpreter based language. Instead of compilers interpreters are used. As soon as a BASIC statement is entered they are checked for syntax errors which can be immediately corrected. This feature makes it a popular computer language used in microcomputer systems.

The weakness of BASIC is that it has not yet been standardized. The language varies significantly from one computer system to another. Thus, a BASIC programme written on one computer may not work on another unless modified.

PASCAL : Named after the French mathematician Blaise Pascal. This language was first inducted in 1971 by Professor Niklaus A. Wirth of Federal Institute of Technology in Zurich, Switzerland. PASCAL was the first language to fully embody in an organized way, the concepts of structural programming. The language is relatively easy to learn and it allows the programmer to structure the programming problem. This means that the programme must be written in logical modules which in turn are controlled by main module.

PASCAL is weak at file handling and input/output and is not easy for beginners to use.

PL/1 : PL/1 stands for Programming Language One. It was developed by IBM in 1964. It is the most powerful general purpose programming language, as it can handle mathematical and business applications with ease. It is highly efficient in input/output activities, and can handle large volumes of data. PL/1 was developed to create a universal language which can be programmed in any application.

Structured languages

In 1965, a Dutch academic named Edsgar Dijkstra presented a paper in which he described how programming could be reduced to a few basic rules. One of these rules called for the elimination of GOTOs from programming languages. The other rules detailed how programmes could be built from the three basic constructs :

- Sequence
- Selection, and
- Iteration

This, in essence, stimulated structured programming movement.

Other language

There are many more languages that do not have wide application in the world. Depending upon the application various other languages are being used.

GENERATIONS OF LANGUAGES

First Generation Languages

Instructing the machine through direct binary codes. Closely associated with the architecture of the host processor complex to write, read and debug.

Second Generation Languages

Uses symbolic codes, machine instructions given by mnemonic alphabetic codes. Easier to understand although still closed allies' to machine architecture.

Third Generation Languages

Higher level languages such as FORTRAN, COBOL, PL/1 and BASIC, written in procedure code, largely independent of the hardware architecture permitting portability. Much easier to use.

Fourth Generation Languages

There is no agreed definition as to what constitutes a Fourth Generation Language. It might be safer to suggest that it consists of everything which is not in the first three categories: In general such products are marked by :

- non-procedural programming code
- a simple query language
- centered around a database

Characteristics of a Good Language

A language has got to have some characters which makes it a good one. This is the reason one user uses a particular language while another uses another language. Depending upon the nature of application one language is preferred over the other. Some characters that makes a language a good language.

Simplicity : Programming languages that are simple and easy to learn and use are liked by programmers. This is the reason why BASIC is being used by many programmers.

Naturalness : A language should be natural for the application area as it has been designed. In other words, it should be problem-oriented. Often if a major amount of programming in a particular area is required, it is extremely useful to develop programming language just for that class of applications. FORTRAN and COBOL are examples of scientific and business applications.

Efficiency : Efficiency is certainly a major element. A programming language should be such that it's programmes are efficiently translated into machine use, efficiently executed, and acquire little space in the memory as far as possible.

Structured : The language should follow the necessary features to allow the users to write their programmes based on concepts of structured programming. This helps the programmers to write, test and maintain the programmes.

Extensibility : A good programming language should also allow extension through simple, natural and elegant mechanisms.

Suitability of Environment : Depending upon the type of application for which programming has been designed, the language must also be made suitable to its environment. For example, a language designed or real-time application must be interactive in nature. On the other hand, languages used for data processing jobs like pay-rolls, stores, accounting etc., may be designed to be operative in batch mode. So a programme for real time may not be useful for batch mode and vice-versa.

DIALOGUE/QUERY SOFTWARE

These softwares are also known as end-user language which are non-procedural. In general, these tools permit the development of some applications by end-users without professional intervention. There are different languages. Query languages (such as IBM's Query for example) allow a user to query a file or database for an inquiry, such a query might be "List of employees in the Library less than 50 years of age". Repeat generators are used to extract data from files and create customised reports. Graphic languages (such as SAS graph) retrieve data from files and display it in user-defined graphic formats.

Application generators contain preprogrammed modules that can generate applications based on the user's specification of what needs to be done (such as relational database product like dBase III or Paradox).

d-Base : d-Base is a package which is used for data-base management. d-Base has many revised versions out of which d-Base IV is the latest one. d-Base can be used to create a vocabulary and thesaurus of some 200 terms for a specific subject area. d-Base is used for Data Base Management Systems, which is a common area in the library services. d-Base packages are hence widely used for in all areas of library management. The management of a data base includes adding new information, sorting, searching for records, printing the reports, editing of the existing records and deleting the data. d-Base IV is a popular example of the relational approach where it relates the data or records. It also has a retrieval language which can employ indexes for faster retrieval of data. d-Base has facilities of interacting with other packages like Word Processor, Visicale, and Lotus 1-2-3 and others which helps in the organisation of data in the form of tables.

Spread sheets are powerful and flexible number

manipulators, the mathematical equivalence of word processors. They emulate a large sheet of paper with rows and columns marked out. Numbers in both rows and columns can be manipulated in many ways. Totals can be calculated and automatically entered into specific locations. This helps in automatic recalculation wherever a number is altered, saving hours of work. Spread sheet helps in annual examination of salaries, repairs, etc., of the library.

Spread sheet will print data exactly as they are recorded and most allow the presentation of graphs, bars, charts, etc., which may be more effective.

Word processing packages like Word Perfect, Word Star are used to create and edit the text as easy and powerful as possible. In the past, word processing did not allow to incorporate graphics into the documents but the recent packages had helped in this field to develop Desktop Publishing (DTP).

Word Processing software is used to turn the computer into an extremely sophisticated electronic typewriter, with the ability to store and manipulate documents on floppy disks. Features offered in word processing programmes include text manipulation, such as insertion, deletion, duplication, replacement of words and phrases with alternative words. Printing and formatting functions allows one to select bold, italics or underlined type, with justified or centered type. The number of characters per line and lines per page can be re-set and varied for each printing and the software also provides automatic page number and headings. Modern word processing software includes automatic spelling checking and mailing list generation.

Word Star : Word Star, by Micro Pro International, is probably the most widely used word processing programmes in the world. Word Star is page-oriented word processor which does not keep the entire document in the computer memory all at the same time. As one works on the package it keeps on stored that part as you are working. This system of loading and saving considerably reduces the speed of working.

Word Perfect : Word Perfect is very much similar to the Word Star. Both of them are being used extensively for storage and production of standard documents to which minor changes are made and to draft documents which can quickly and easily be amended to produce perfect copy, to listing of catalogues etc.

Dialogue/query softwares usually are not to be used to develop an entire system. Instead it is used to permit untrained users either to use a system or to build a simple application (e.g. to create a report).

CDS/ISIS : Computerised Documentation Service/ Integrated Set of Information System, is a generalized information storage and retrieval system designed to manage non-numerical databases. CDS/ISIS is a microcomputer based software package, written in Pascal language, designed specifically for managing information storage and retrieval system. It has all the facilities to support the library and information usage.

The minimum hardware requirements for running CDS/ISIS are: (a) a PC/XT with 412 KB of RAM (MS-DOS operating system environment); (b) a floppy drive: (c) a hard disk; (d) a monitor and (e) a printer. Larger the capacity more records can be accommodated.

CDS/ISIS is a database with files of related data. Even though it deals with only text it does more than just text processing. The system is menu driven, so needs no special training for users of this package.

Software development is increasing at a faster pace as compared to the hardware. Software is something that needs to be changed time and again, depending upon the need of the hour. Without systems and applications software, the computer revolution would have been still unborn. It is through software that computer hardware becomes useful.

REFERENCES

- Baluja, G.S. Computer Concepts and Programming. New Delhi : Dhanpat Rai, 2011.
- Beiser, Karl. Essential guide to dBase IV for Libraries. London : Meckler, 1991.
- Bissmer, R.H. Introduction to computer concepts. New Yok : John Wiley, 1993.
- Depace, M. dBase IV : A Practical Guide. London : BSP Professional 1989.
- Crashing, Joanna. The Word Star 2000 Companion. London : Paradigm, 1987.
- Jain, V.K. "O" Level – Information Technology. New Delhi: BPB, 2000.
- MS-DOS version 5.0. London: Microsoft, 1991.
- Maynord, J. Computer Programming Made Simple. London : ELBS, 1983.
- Rajaraman, V. Fundamentals of Computers. 5th Ed. New Delhi : PHI Learning, 2010.
- Schneidewind, N.F. Computer, Network, Software, and Hardware Engineering with Applications. New York : John Wiley, 2012.
- Simpson, Alan. Understanding dBase III Plus. New Delhi : BPB Publications, 1986.

4

Programming Languages

Languages are generally used by people to communicate with other people. They learn the language by using it. Computer programming languages are languages used by people to communicate with the computer. In fact people specify the actions to be taken by computers in solving their problems. As the needs of different types of users to solve problems with computers vary, so do the computer programming languages. We, the library and information professionals, need to know the aspects of computer programming languages, both for storing of information and retrieving the same when warranted. Therefore, a brief attention to languages and approaches to languages and their application to activities, is required.

Computers have their own internal languages, private jargons of strings of numbers. These are difficult for most people to learn. They are rarely used as programming languages. A single computer may have more than one language, and different computers may have different languages, even though made by the same manufacturer. Usually a list of numbers direct the machine to perform certain simple action. For example, the number 103344 might be an "instruction" or an "Order" or a "Command" to add two numbers stored in location 33 and 44. Where as the same number 103344 may be an instruction to print the character in location 3310 to another. Thus the choice of numbers may vary from machine to machine. Such lists of numbers are almost as cryptic as the codes used by spies. Thus each machine require a programmer to specify in full detail what is to be done. These continued set of instructions are called "machine" languages. Even a slight conceptual change can require large portions of a programme to be rewritten.

In order to save the effort of writing a new programme for each machine every time to solve the same problem, many programming languages for computer have been created. These languages make computers accessible to more people. This also increases the chance of writing instructions for computers correctly. Programming languages express the actions to be performed in terms of more comprehensible to people and in ways that allow the same programmes to be used on many different types of computers.

Some languages are close in style to the operation of computers, consisting of sequences of actions to be taken. such a style simplifies efficient translation of a problem specification into the internal language of the computer. But a strained interpretation may lead to increase in the chances of programming effors. In order to reflect the demands of the problem to be solved more naturally rather than the demands of the computers, languages using other styles of programming have been developed, such as object – oriented, functional and logic programming. These offer promise of increased productivity for appropriate problems.

Early Developments

The history of computer programming languages is intimately related to the history of computers themselves. In fact, many of the drawbacks of the early languages were reflections of the limitations of the computers of the time. Thus, the changes in hardware had a significant and direct impact on the development of programming languages.

First Programming

Perhaps, the first programming of computers was for Babbage's Analytical Engine, by Augusta Ada in 1842. The programming was in direct machine language with a manual translation from normal mathematics notation. The fundamental concepts of operations (actions to be performed), variables (information that may change during the calculations) and consonants (numbers that would not change) were established. In Babbage's time, cardboard cards with holes pushed into them were used for the control of looms. He choose such punch cards as a mechanism for specification of both operations and variables. In 1890 Hermann Hollerith invented a series of electromechanically punch card devices under the control of wired in programme of simple actions. "Programming" such machines consisted of throwing switches and inserting jumper wires into plug boards (something like a telephone switch board). In the mid 40s' Mark – 1, in addition to its internal plug board wiring, started accepting a general programme of instructions on paper tape. Programming the machine was a complex process of preparing tapes, cards and switch settings.

Stored Programme

A great simplification of programming came with the creation of digital electronic-stored programme computers, because a programme was stored in memory as numbers. The concept was pioneered during Woycon ENIAC by Eckert and Mauchly. ENIAC was programmed by wiring, but Wilkes' EDSAC in 1949 fully implemented stored programme computer design. As the early internal memories were small they have limited programme size. However, the ability to store data made the possibility to reuse the same sequence of instructions rapidly without having reload them per each execution. Thus commonly used modules of code were programmed in the native language of the machine, "machine language" and saved for use with many programmes.

Assembly Language Programming

If computer used decimal numbers internally, programming could be a simple translation of operations into appropriate decimal digits, and laying out of locations of instructions and operands in memory. Thus, in the 1950s, machine language programming was replaced by assembly language programming. An assembler translates names for operations such as ADD and SUB into appropriate numbers and keep track of memory locations using already stated instructions, variables and consonants. A programmer refers to them by name rather than by number.

A program which translates an assembly language program into machine language program is called an assembler. A program of instructions written in assembly language is called as a source program. After this source has been converted into machine code by an assembler it is referred to as an object program.

This was a significant improvement in making it easier to write programmes.

Low level and High level languages

A language in which each statement is directly translated into a single machine code is known as low level language. Examples of low level language are the assembly languages. The basic problem of an assembly language is that it is more closely related to the structure of a computer than to the performance of the tasks which is to be performed.

To overcome the difficulties associated with assembly languages, High Level Language (HLL) or Procedure Oriented Language (POL) were developed. High level languages permit programmers to describe tasks in a form which is problem oriented rather than computer oriented.

The instructions written in high level languages are called statements. The statements more closely resemble English and mathematics as compared to mnemonics in assembly languages. Examples of high level languages are BASIC, PASCAL, FORTRAN, PL/1 etc.

Birth of FORTRAN

In 1959 for business applications, compilers for a "Common Business Oriented Language" (COBOL) based on earlier work by Grace Hopper were developed. For such applications language this is still in heavy use. The style is closer to English than the mathematical formula FORTRAN.

The great success of FORTRAN and COBOL and the increasing power of computers led to the attempts to create better languages. Starting from 1950s Peter Naur and others worked on "Algorithmic Language" (ALGOL) intended to provide code more structured and easier to read and maintain than FORTRAN. ALGOL did not achieve great popularity in the U.S., but did attract a wide following in Europe in 1960s.

Birth of PL/1

By creating PL/1 in 1964, IBM attempted to correct some of the limitations of FORTRAN and combine it with all the business-oriented features of COBOL. PL/1 is still in use, but has not attracted a large following.

Birth of Pascal

In 1971 Niklaus Wirth, proposed alternative language, called PASCAL, that proved effective for that purpose, and was simple and clear. In the mid 1970s attempts were made for the development of a language specially suited to programming computers operating in real time and embedded in military hardware. Jules Schwartz's JOVIAL (Jule's Own Version of the International Algebric Language) was a real time programming to control computers with a mixture of assembler and FORTRAN.

Birth of C

A compiler language called C was designed in 1972 by D. Ritchie. C provides the user oriented economy of expression of FORTRAN and PASCAL with the access to hardware features of assemblers, and has replaced a major portion of the use of assemblers for time critical, real – time programme in operating systems and device control code.

C++

Just as one person is associated with the development of Pascal (Niklaus Wirth), a single individual is generally credited with development of C++. Starting with C, Bjarne Stroustrup developed an effective language that kept the efficiency of C, yet added the power of object inheritance. In order to understand C++, it is assumed that C is already known.

Brief Overview of the Language

C++ is a language derived from C. The major change is the addition of classes and a mechanism for inheriting class objects into other classes. The design of C++ was guided by three principles.

1. The use of classes would not result in programs executing any more slowly than programs not using classes.
2. In order to make sure that the addition of classes did not cause other needed features to be omitted. C programs should run as a subset of C++ programs.

3. No run-time inefficiency should be added to the language.

For the most part, the three goals were met. Most C programs can be compiled by a C++ compiler, although there are a few inconsistencies between the languages. Strong typing is stronger than the "weak" strong typing of C. Certain new reserved words have been added to C++.

New languages

The 1980's have seen an explosion of new languages and extensions of existing languages to handle various types of systems – super computing, parallel computing etc. Of particular interest is the language LINDA with data structures based on the concept of Tuple Space. Tuples are ordered sets of values. In a sequential language we would expect to have a fixed address telling us where the tuple is to be found. In the Tuple Space approach we find the tuple partly by the contents of its fields and partly by its structure, so that the necessary addressing information is carried out by the tuple.

In the early days of computing, there was a feeling of moving from one generation of computers to another, and from one family of language to its descendants. With the faster pace of developments today, it is hard to distinguish any clear boundaries making the end of one generation and the start of another. "Fourth Generation Language" 4 GL, has come to mean packages and systems of powerful tools for programming that allow someone who is not particularly familiar with the intricacies of programming to solve problems with computers. This includes powerful data base query languages, spread sheet systems, graphic tool boxes, and systems integrated with the text processing for the production of complex and compound documents. In many cases the need to programme is avoided by the use of menus or graphic user interfaces allowing the nonprogrammer to piece together the solution to his problem out of simple known steps and objects. It is to be hoped that the fourth generation packages will be followed by a "Fifth Generation" of even more powerful systems functioning as expert systems able to assist the user actively in finding the solutions to his problems.

Characteristics of Programming Languages

Now a days computers are put to a variety of uses. The complexities in the use of computers has led to the creation of more languages than any one person could learn or use in a life time. Infact, it is common to extend languages affectively to invent whole new vocabularies, when faced new problems. Efficient programmers are writing extensive set of "functions" and "subroutines" that they try to use and extend for additional applications.

In any particular application on any particular machine, the specific instructions for use of the dialects of languages used must be consulted.

Digital stored program computers provide the means to manipulate numbers and other data by sequences of operations. The data and the memory locations within which they are stored are "objects" on which a computer performs a sequence of "actions". Computer programming languages are tools to perform actions, explicitly or implicitly, on objects. They are designed either to work directly with representations of concepts that derive from the structure and functions of digital stored programme computers or to work with representations of concepts that derive from representations of other concepts. That means, the language translator must translate these representations into terms appropriate to computers. The objects that must be manipulated are the equivalent of nouns and pronouns in human languages. These objects are called "variables", "constants", "parameters", "arrays", "strings", "pointers", "arguments", etc. in programming languages.

There are actions that may be taken either simply as actions themselves or on some of these objects, the equivalent of intransitive and transitive verbs in human languages. These actions are called "operations", "functions", "subroutines", "procedures", "handlers", "drivers" etc., in programming languages. The basic elements of a language are enriched by additional descriptive elements that describe various properties of objects and actions, and provide a context that may change the meaning of objects and actions. These are some thing like as descriptive sentences involving adjectives and adverbs.

Varieties of Programming Languages

In programming languages we usually use the name "statement" for sentences of the language. Similar to that human languages, the actions (verbs) and objects (nouns and pronouns) may be in a variety of relative positions. When the emphasis is on the sequence of actions, (doing one thing after another) it is called a "statement-oriented" or "imperative" or "procedural" programming. When the emphasis is more on objects and the consideration is towards the actions as an internal mechanism of the objects that communicate messages among themselves, it is called "object-oriented" or "non-procedural" programming.

Procedural and Non-Procedural Programming

A programme that is written in an imperative programming language will consist of a number of related modules containing some declarations that establish the environment in which the work is to be done, i.e., specifying the data-structures of the objects to be manipulated. And then the sequence of steps to perform on these objects is well defined. The most powerful action to be taken is the execution of an assigned statement. In other words, it is a statement that puts new information into an object, usually based on the evaluation of arithmetic expressions, possibly containing references to functions of previously computed data. This statement is a generalization of the simple computer order to "store". For improving the readability and maintainability of imperative programming language programmes, it is necessary to keep small the context of objects that any actions may effect. This is done by breaking up the programme into procedures, modules, packages, etc. FORTRAN, BASIC, PASCAL, C are the examples of languages in this category

Imperative and Object-Oriented Programming

In object-oriented programming, attempt is made to solve problems by working with objects that can send message to one another. These messages may cause the objects to take appropriate actions. These actions are basically hidden, i.e., due to internal mechanism within the objects. This is a realistic model of the behaviour of the system. An early example of a computer system operating in a similar manner was the CDC 6600 of 1963. It is a complex of 11 processors communicating via messages left in mail-boxes. This approach was used to provide a highly efficient operating system, but was not made available for user programs. MODULA-2, SMALL TALK, C++ come in this group.

The major distinction of imperative programming and object-oriented programming is in the difference of entire mechanism of how the data would be manipulated. In imperative programme the data-manipulation is normally visible, allowing programmer to build assumptions about the internals of manipulation. Thus allows to add new features to the data structure. In an object oriented language, by associating the manipulation of the data with the data structures themselves, the internal mechanism is hidden and the effects of changes in routines can be kept purely internal.

Functional and Logic Programming

There are also two more styles of programming languages : (1) Functional Programming and (2) Logic Programming. In functional programming (or application programming) problems are solved by pure function evaluations. Here the procedures that express functions themselves are valid data, which will be evaluated in some manner consistent with their definition, but not in a strictly determined order. APL, LISP, ML are few functional programming languages.

Logic programming is one step further in trying to focus on the application rather than on the operation of computer hardware. It considers only the relationships among objectives of interest rather than the implicit actions of functions. It deals with the specification of problems on a high level, as statements about objects and the relationship among them, and then allows the user to ask questions about those relationships, making the logical inferences from what is known to what has been asked. Hence the term 'Logic Programming' PROLOG is an appropriate example for work in artificial intelligence.

Some Important Programming Languages

When a problem pushes a computer resources to its limits, there is need for languages that will make optional use of those resources. This can easily be achieved by using languages whose structures corresponding to the structures of computers, in terms of sequences of actions to be taken on appropriate data. Efforts are being made to create more flexible and more enduring languages from 1959 (since the creation of FORTRAN) till date that allow a machine to achieve maximum performance. In earlier days, assemblers were used to allow instructions to be written which would extract the last bit of efficiency. Today, this is more commonly being done by programming languages (such as C).

BASIC

(Beginners All Symbolic Instruction Code) is the most widely used general purpose programming languages for personal computers. Though it was developed in 1990s, it is still being regarded as a friendly system easy to pick-up and easy to expand. There are many dialects of BASIC now. Programs in BASIC consists of sequences of numbered lines. The variables used may be sometimes restricted to single letter names. Sometimes it is common to allow at least a letter and a digit. The most recent versions allow full strings of letters and digits starting with a letter.

BASIC follows the operation which can be grouped and stated as :

1. Arithmetic operations. Addition ("+"), Subtraction ("-"), multiplication ("*"), division ("/"), exponentiation ("^")
2. Relational operations, Less than ("<") less than a equal to ("≤"), greater than (">") greater than or equal to (>=") equal to ("=") not equal to ("< >").
3. Logical operations "AND" "OR" "NOT"

The flow of programme control is keyed to the numbers put on each line.

The "GOTO" and "GOSUB" statements transfer control to the designated line number. That line and following lines are executed as a subroutine to be executed until a "RETURN" statement. The "RETURN" statement transfers control back to the place immediately after the "GOSUB". The "FOR" statement causes repeated execution of the following statements in the statement number order until a matching "NEXT" statement. The "IF" statement, "THEN statement" and "IF" "ELSE Statement", evaluates the logical expression and executes the statement after the "THEN" if the expression is true.

The assignment statement is as in FORTRAN, except

some versions require the word "LET" before the statement.

Files are manipulated by INPUT and PRINT statements.

FOR device control, many versions of BASIC add an "INP" statement to read device registers and an "OUT" statement to store new values into device registers.

In BASIC the example of adding 10 numbers might READ

```
100 sum = 0
110 FOR COUNT% = 1 to 10
120 INPUT MYINP
130 SUM=SUM +MYINP
140 NEXT COUNT%
150 PRINT SUM
160 END
```

C Language

"C" is general purpose programming language. It was developed by Bell Laboratories in the early 1970s. Today there are many versions of C that run on personal computers's and larger machines.

Although C is a general purpose high-level language, it also allows programmers to write low-level machine instructions that approach in density and efficiency those that are loaded in a machine or assembly language. It is thus a favourite language of professional programmers who write operating system and other software packages for machines of all be used to solve each task. Thus C programme may be come a grouping of functions that are linked together to produce the problem solution.

Sl. No.	Language	Development and Use
1.	FORTRAN	Developed by IBM in 1957. Earlier version was named as FORTRAN II, which was later modified to FORTRAN IV. Now other version such as FORTRAN 77 are becoming very popular. It is primarily used for scientific work.
2.	ALGOL	Developed in Europe in the earlier part of 1960. Mostly used in East European Countries. ALGOL is a block structured or modular language that is well suited for use in structured programming.
3.	COBOL	Designed by CODASYL (Conference of Data System Languages) in the year 1960. The earliest COBOL – 60. Later versions were COBOL-61, COBOL-65. The ANS/COBOL was standardized in the year 1974. This is the most commonly used version.
4.	BASIC	Designed by John Kemeny and Thomas Kurtz at Darmouth College in the mid 1960. It is one of the most popular language used on micro-computers. It was standardized by ANSI in the year 1978. Initially developed for beginners, for elementary applications it is now being used for advanced applications in wide variety of fields such as business, science, engineering and mathematics. To translate BASIC instructions into machine language codes, BASIC language compilers are used.
5.	PASCAL	Developed by Niklaus Wirth at University of Zurich as a programmers' trainer language because it is very easy to learn. Now it is considered as a general purpose language and it uses nested blocks of instructions. Highly suited for small computers. It is used for general purpose

		problems and also meets the needs of the computer scientists. The programme compiled from PASCAL runs several times faster as compared to the same programme compiled from FORTRAN or BASIC.
6.	PL/1	Designed by IBM in the year 1960. More powerful than other languages because it combines the best features of various languages. Used for scientific and business applications. PL/1 is a multipurpose language. Later improved versions are PL/2, and PL/M. It is designed to include the features of FORTRAN as a scientific language as well as COBOL as a business language.
7.	ADA	Developed by the Defence Department of USA. It is being used for real time problems faced by the defence department.
8.	C	Designed by Richie in 1972. C allows users to write low level machine instructions that approach in density and efficiency that are coded in machine language. C programme may represent a grouping of functions that are linked together to produce the solution of the problem. This language is used by system programmes to develop complex programmes such as an operating system and application programme.
9.	PROLOG	Developed in 1972 by Alain Colmerauer P. Rouse. It is an object oriented language and uses only data about objects and their relationships with emphasis on symbolic processing. With PROLOG, the user defines a goal and the computer must both the programme procedure and solution. A Prolog programme is a collection of data

	(or facts) and the relationship among these facts. It is mainly used to develop software for expert systems. Japanese have chosen it as the main language for their fifth generation computers.
10. 4 GL	4 GL has come to mean packages and systems of powerful tools for programming that allow some one who is not familiar with the intricacies of programming. This includes data base query languages, spread sheet systems, graphic tool boxes and systems integrated with text processing.
11. SQL	It is a popular language for data retrieval. It assumes the discipline use of top-down concepts to decompose main functions into lower-level components for modular coding purpose.
12. LISP	It stands for list processing. LISP is suitable for non-numeric operations involving logical operations. It is used extensively in artificial intelligence.
13. LOGO	It is an abbreviation of Logic Oriented Graphic Oriented. It is used in scientific work in universities. It has also been popularized as a first educational language that children use to achieve intellectual growth and problem solving skills sizes and it is used to create graphics and special effects in films. Programs written in C can be shifted from one machine architecture to another without much difficulty, but the language is not designed to be used by beginning programmers. A small concise language C makes use of a library of functions that are equivalent of subroutines. These functions are self-contained pieces of code that carry out some task. A C programme can use modular and structural concepts, i.e., a problem may be broken into smaller tasks, a function

	may be used to solve each task. Thus C programme may become a grouping of functions that are linked together to produce the problem solution.

Data Base Programming Languages

Computers manage information. They provide the tools to scan large amounts of information and extract what is needed. Data retrieval works with objects that are identified by their contents, rather than by their physical location. The contents may include explicit keys to help in the search or may stand by themselves.

The paradigm now used for database languages is one in which data is considered as a set of tables, the columns of which identify attributes of data, and the rows of which are the data items of interest. Some columns, or set of columns, serves as the key to identify uniquely the data items to be retrieved.

The operators used are union (combining the rows of two tables with matching columns to form one with the combined information from both), intersection (combining to retain only the common information from both), difference (combining to obtain information in the first table that is not in the second), cartesian product (combining tables with different columns to make all possible combinations), select (extracting selected rows from a table), project (extracting selected columns from a table), inner join (combining tables by matching entries in a common column), outer join (like inner join, but including rows with no match), and divide (extracting particular rows and columns on the basis of a match in other columns).

SQL

A popular language for data retrieval is SQL (Structured Query Language). The typical command in this language has the form

SELECT the names of columns

FROM the name of a table

WHERE the criteria to be satisfied in selecting

ORDER BY the order of presentation of the columns.

The criteria may include relational, arithmetic, and pattern-matching operators.

There are some difficulties in applying this paradigm to data that have search criteria based on considerations other than positions of values within tables. For example, a search on the shape of particular images, or on the symmetries of lattice involving experimental error, may strain this paradigm, and may require the explicit creation of inverted indices organized on the basis of the anticipated search.

Programming Languages

JAVA

Java is an extension of C and C++. Originally known as Oak. It was designed to be a platform independent language. Java gained popularity when it provided support for "Applets", programs that could be embedded in web pages.

Three factors worked toward the sudden popularity of Java:

1. Web Applications. 2. Use of C syntax. 3. Growing frustration with C++. The reason that should have contributed to the rise of Java: 1) Clean and simple language design. 2) Use of garbage collection. 3. Built-in support for event-driven programming and concurrency.

Java is not, by means, a perfect language. The main problems include: 1. Lack of support for parametric polymorphism. 2. Weak support for modules. 3. Overly complex. 4. Use of C syntax.

ML

ML is developed in Edinburgh in late 1970's as meta-language for automated theorem proving system. Designed by Robin Milnor, Mike Gordon and Chris

Wadsworth.

The important attributes of ML are:

- Primarily applicative
- Functions are first class values
- Statically scoped
- Static typing via type inference
- Polymorphic types
- Rich type system including support for ADT"s.
- Support for exception handling.
- Automatic storage management via garbage collection.
- Incremental compiler supporting interactive program development.

LISP

LISP was developed by John McCarthy in 1960. LISP is functional programming language which works on the basis of symbolic computation (math, logic). LISP provides a chance to think differently then C language. LISP use the simple machine models and given attention to theoretical considerations like recursive function theory, and Lambda calculus. LISP supports various good ideas like program as data and garbage collection.

Ada

Ada programs represent different types of real-world objects using different *data types*. The built-in data type are defined in a package called standard which is always available automatically in every Ada program.

PROLOG

Prolog is logical programming language and it all about programming in logic. Complete prolog is works on facts, rules and queries. For example:

Fact : Socrates is a man

man (socrates)

Rule: All men are mortal.

moral (x):- man (x)

Query: Is Socrates mortal?

mortal (socrates).

To work on the prolog, we should create our own "database" (Program) in any editor and save it as text only, with a 'pl' extension. Here's the complete program:

man (socrates)

mortal (x) :- man (x)

Prolog is completely interactive and its interpreter is invoked by typing siestas. Then we load our programme/consult ('mortal.pl'). Then finally we ask our question at the prompt:

-mortal (socrates).

Progol responds: - Yes

REFERENCES

- Bajpai, S., and Yadav, D., Introduction to Computers and C. Programming. New Delhi : New Age, 2002
- Bagga, R.K. Computer and Defence Applications. 2nd ed. Delhi : DESIDOC, 1991.
- Burstein, J.S. Computer and Information System. New York: Holt, Rinehart and Wilson, 1986.
- French, C.S. Computer science. 4th ed. London: D.P. Publications, 1992.
- Horowitz, Ellis. Fundamentals of Programming Languages. 2nd ed., Rockville, Maryland: Computer Science Press, 1984.
- Jaggi, V.P. and Jain, S. Computer for Beginners. 10th ed. New Delhi: Academic (India), 1990.
- Jevapoovan, T. Computer Programming : Theory and Practice. New Delhi : Vikas, 2006.
- Knuth, D.E. The Art of Computer Programming : Fundamental Algoriths, 2008.

- Mayanord, J. Computer Programming Made Simple. London : ELBS, 1983.
- Pratt, T.W. and Zelkowitz, M.V. Programming Languages : Design and Implementation. 4th Ed. New Delhi : Pearson Education, 2003.
- Puri Y.P. and Puri, V. Computers and Information Technology. New Delhi: Global Business Pr., 1992.
- Rajaraman, V. Computer Basics and C Programming. New Delhi : PHI, 2008.
- Reynolds, J.C. Theories of Programming Languages. Cambridge : University Press, 1998.
- Taxali, R.K. PC Software Made Simple, New Delhi: Tata McGraw-Hill, 1995.

5

Data Base Management Systems (DBMS)

Now a days a large number of application packages are available for the users of personal computers. Among them three types of programmes have become very popular among the users. They are spread sheets, word processors and databases. Although the use of all the three application packages grew during the last fifteen years, the increase in the use of database management systems have been most significant. There are several reasons for the gain of popularity of databases. Computer technicians would attribute the phenomenal growth in data base use to improved hardware such as larger RAM capacity and the availability of hard disks which permit the use of more powerful programmes. However, software developers would attribute the growth of data base use to more sophisticated programmes that provide easier, more flexible information storage and retrieval.

Larger storage capacity permits users to handle

more files. RAM and hard disks also improve processing speeds. This increase in storage capacity and speed enable users to create larger databases than that was possible with the older programmes. With the increasing enhancement of communication, increasing availability of sophisticated software packages, programmes with menu-driven query facilities, dialogue prompts using natural languages interface and simplification in report formatting capabilities, information retrieval has been simplified. Now programmes permit simultaneous sorts using multiple categories, cross-referenced data and easily recognized files. The most significant software advances, such as applications generators, helps users to design their own data base management systems. Thus enabling the executives to structure their own menus, data entry and retrieval, and reports. All these features are possible without any programming.

The simplicity of the new data base management systems and the ability to create a work environment that closely meets the needs of individual managers, have enabled data base management systems to become leading business applications packages.

HISTORY AND DEVELOPMENT

Although the terms "database" and "database management system" did not become part of computer jargon until about 1966, the basic underlying techniques were developed in the early sixties. The initial emphasis was very much on the effective use of direct access storage. Towards the end of the sixties it was realised that the systems thus built were costing even more resources to maintain and expand than installations. The realization led to the emphasis on "data independence" and the data base management systems were then the emerging trends. The relational approach found in 1970 helped to improve the independence of programmes from the way in which the data was structured.

The early 1970s saw the emergence of data base management as a respectable research topic in U.S. It was realised that in order to retrieve information quickly and easily from a database, it has to be stored and before it is stored, it has to be validated. In the early 1980s several papers appeared on "emantic integrity". Another significant development during this period was the realization that there must be a way of first analyzing and then structuring data which must be independent of any DBMS which can subsequently be used to define and manage the database, thus leading to the concept of data modelling. The 1980s has further seen the emergence of easy to use tools available as part of the DBMS packages for actively constructing an information system once it has been designed.

One of the most significant development is that class of DBMS labelled "network", the most popular being the network database language (NDL). In the late 1980s, ISO agreed to a formal standard for Relational Database Language, SQL. An improved version of SQL with integrity enhancement is also available, called SQL-2.

Now, database technology must be viewed in terms of functionality provided by the complete package. It is predicable that products which are better integrated and organised internally and which offer improved functionality to all levels of users are almost ready for use. Database technology now can be seen as potentially having a major influence on the way the computer systems are designed.

Components of DBMS

Originally the DBMS was used to very specific functions. The core of such a system is a data definition language or describing data structures and the programmes that are used to build, update and retrieve data from the database. The trend is for vendors of database management systems to create integrated tools for building and operating databases. An overview of the DBMS is given below:

The starting point for the DBMS is the study of the way data travels and is transformed within database. The basic tool to describe this is the Data Flow Diagram (DFD) which describes in a pictorial way how data flows.

To be able to 'read' DFDs, all one needs to know is the following set of definitions of the elements and conventions for the symbols used to depict them.

- Data flow is a pipeline through which packets of information of known 'composition flow', and it is represented with a vector;
- Process is a transformation of incoming dataflow(s) into outgoing data flow(s), and is represented with a circle ('bubble');
- File is 'a temporary repository of data', and is represented with two parallel lines;
- Data source or sink is 'a person or organisation, lying outside the context of a system that is a net originator or receiver of system data', and is represented by a box.

'While the data flow diagram seeks to capture how information passes through a system, and what is done in the various processing stages, it does not concentrate on the actual detail of the data itself or on the overall coherence of the data. It is therefore appropriate that a deeper analysis of the data to be used. Description of logical data modelling, data analysis are useful in its own right and can also become the starting point for design of an actual database. Taken together, a data model and a set of leveled DFDs provide a co-ordinated set of tools for the DBMS. The linking of the two techniques is made easier by the use of a data dictionary.

In true sense data dictionary is 'a repository of data about data'. The data dictionary is used to store and define definitions of data including identifiers, location, format for storage and other characteristics. The data dictionary can be used to retrieve the definition of data that has already been used in an application so that standards for naming can be enforced across applications. Depending on the specific system, the database administrator might also store some of the description of the data structures in the dictionary, for example, entities, attributes, and relationship. The data dictionary must have software to update itself, produce reports on its contents, and answer queries. A complete system will also tie into the data definition components of the DBMS.

The language must identify various subdivisions of data, for example, items, segments, records and files. There should be unique names for each data-item type, record type, record type, file type, database, etc. The language should specify how data items are grouped in aggregates, records or other subdivisions and show repeating groups of items. The language must make it possible to designate data items as keys. It is also necessary to specify how various subdivision or record types are related to make different logical structures, and it should be possible to give names to relationships among data groupings. Additional capabilities that the language may possess, includes the specification of privacy locks to prevent unauthorized reading or modifications. The language should be concerned only with logical data description and specific addressing, indexing, or searching techniques, or the placement of data on physical storage. These topics belong to the physical definition of the files, not the logical definition.

An integrated data dictionary (DD) generates a file for the data definition language (DDL) which it uses to generate the scheme for the DBMS. Such an interface between the DD and DDL can be batch mode, that is, the DD generates a file, which is passed to the DDL. A dynamic interface involves the DBMS software actually consulting the DDL and DD during its execution. Such a dynamic link means that changes are automatically reflected in all components of the database environment as soon as they are made.

Given the data definition and the database, the database management system constructs all pointers, linkages, and directories automatically. The application programme issues calls for the data it desires. The database management system examines the data request and determines where the records of interest are located; it returns the entire record or the field requested to the calling program.

Typically, the programmer inserts some type of all to the DBMS to access the database. The actual statements used in the programme differ among DBMS vendors; the specific commands are also very dependent on the underlying structure of the DBMS: hierarchical, network or relational.

While the DBMS does provide a great deal of assistance to the programmer, individuals still must write programs to load the data, maintain it and answer inquiry requests.

Important Data Base Management Packages

The objective of a database management system is to facilitate the creation of data structures and relieve the programmer of the problems of setting up computerized files. DBMS have developed from a concept of a database as something different from the programmes accessing to it. This approach highlights the importance of data as resource in the organization and as something that has to be carefully managed.

The choice of a particular database management system is a complicated one. We should ask if the system is easy to use, understand, manipulate, and implement. Just as with any other package, the computer department will be interested in the quality of the computer code in the system and with its documentation.

There are advocates of all three major data models : hierarchical, network and relational. Academically, the choice is relational because of the many features it offers. Relational data models can be analyzed formally which gives them a strong foundation and some degree of standardization across implementations.

Relational models are also favoured because the retrieval and data manipulation languages tend to be easy to understand and use. Also, relational systems tend to appear simple to the user, making retrieval and manipulation easier. Thinking of data in the form of tables is conceptually more simple than complex hierarchical or flex relations.

Hierarchical Data Base Management Packages

In a hierarchical structure, the data is organized in records into a hierarchy of fields and subfields. For example, the imprint field in the MARC format which has three subfields place, publisher, date of publication. Fields for name loadings have sub-fields for different parts of the name depending on the form of the name. Hierarchical structures have the advantage that the programme can refer to and process different levels in the hierarchy. But, the major disadvantage in the hierarchical structure is they do not enable the programmes (the users) to go quickly from one customers field to another (customer) field in the next record. To do that it is necessary to go to the top of the hierarchy (i.e. to the level of the records). That means the record with the desired customer has to be read from the file, there by showing the process. The database management packages based on hierarchical structure are not used for PCs. They are designed for minicomputers and mainframe systems.

Network Data Base Management Packages

This database management system features two kinds of files, a master and a variable file. The master file is accessed on some key and is linked to the variable file.

Associations among entries are linked by pointers. Thus, a network database management package permits connection of the nodes in a multi – directional manner, unlike that of a hierarchical package which does not permit the connection of branches. In a network programme each node may have several owners and may inturn any number of other data units. Data management software permits the extraction of the needed information from such a structure by beginning with any record in a file.

Relational Data Base Management Packages

These database management packages are regarded as the ultimate form among all the varieties of DBMS. They are the ones considered best.

Relational DBM systems have the same aims as any other kind, the means by which they are achieved are generally described in what sometimes appears to be an unnecessary complicated way, with terminology which reflects the mathematical origin of the ideas rather than the needs of those who have to understand how they work. The basic idea is that the collection of data which is to constitute a database should be organized into groupings of different kinds, so that a particular kind of information will be given only once in one grouping, and nowhere else. When it is needed the system will find it within the grouping. If it has to be altered only once, at that place in the grouping. The altered form will be available for whatever purpose it is needed. To ensure that the system works the framework of groupings is created by a process of normalization.

The groupings in a relational database are called relations. A relation consists of a two-dimensional table, in which there are columns and rows. Although a relation is not the same as a file, elementary understanding is helped by overlooking the differences (as do many of the manuals which describe relational DBM software packages). At the top of the first relation (as headings for the columns) are shown what in a formatted file would be field names: these are referred to as attribute names. Each row contains the data which in a file would be considered to constitute a record. In relational terms, the rows (more exactly their contents) are referred to as tuples. At the intersection of a particular row with a particular column is to be found the value of the attribute for the tuples. Domains are sets of possible values of attributes. A particular item of data may appear in more than one domain : Lucknow University, for example, may belong in the domain of the customer as well as of the employer attribute. Each relation has its own name.

Each column in a table has a predetermined width, i.e., there is a maximum number of characters or bytes available to describe or contain the value of an attribute in a tube. Relations and the tuples within them are therefore essentially in fixed format with the consequent disadvantages.

An important feature of a relational DBM system is that, in using the data, it is possible to move up and down the columns, i.e., to jump from value to value of the same attribute in different tuples. It is also possible to select certain attributes in a relation for display and processing and to avoid the others. The columns can appear in whatever order is needed.

Relational database packages employ relatively new data storage and retrieval concepts. They are more flexible and more powerful programmes and rank among the most popular of PC software products.

Most of the DBMS packages have built-in-data manipulation languages that are able to accept dozens of special commands. These commands are being used to develop custom programmes that will instruct the package to carry out countless logical procedures.

Programming Languages Oriented to Specific DBMS Packages

In the computer field, the machine language, assembly language and high level languages are given "generation" designation by some people. They note that the move from first generation machine languages to second generation assembly languages brought approximately seven to one improvement in programmer productivity. A similar improvement has taken place when high-level languages (third generation languages) were introduced. Now a number of software vendors are producing a variety of application development tools that may offer further improvements in productivity. These are often referred collectively as fourth generation languages (4GLs).

Fourth Generation Languages (4GLs)

A 4GL DBMS software interacts as a tool to store, manipulate and retrieve the data needed to satisfy user requirements. A high level language is usually a procedural language, the one which requires the programmer to spell out the steps in the processing procedures needed to achieve the desired result. But a 4GL is a non-procedural language that allows users to simply specify what the out put should be without describing all the details of how the data should be manipulated to produce that result. Thus it is difficult to arrive at a satisfactory definition for 4GL, as each tool (or language) is the product of a specific vendor and these suppliers do not agree on definitions. However, in general they can be grouped into two categories based on the application development tools, viz., End-user oriented 4GLs and DBMS oriented 4GLs.

Now a days, the use of 4GLs is increasing. These tools are often easier to use than high-level languages.

Structured Query Language (SQL)

SQL consists of English like statements, designed

to select records from tables of the database. SQL statements can be used at run time. To find a record one can use the simple method with a SQL statements, as find first to find the first record. SQL is very effective for modifying a table data.

The Structured Query Language (SQL) is a database querying language codified as a standard for inter connection of database products and applications by American National Standards Institution. As many of the library operations such as circulation control are of transaction – processing nature that can be supported by SQL and SQL-based database management systems. These application development features include tools for user-programming of reports and data entry forms. These tools use SQL internally to communicate with the database processing.

SQL is based on relational modelling of data, where data is arranged in two or more dimensional tables with rows and columns. SQL is a language for querying, that is for retrieving subsets of the database according to search criteria. Selection is the basic operation supported by SQL.

Some of the products of SQL based database products can be used in mainframe, minicomputers or personal computer environment. ORACLE, INGRES and UNIFY are some of the SQL based database product run on large range of computing equipment.

ORACLE

ORACLE is a SQL based database system in the relational database management category. It is one of the most exciting DBMS for microcomputer systems in the market-to-day. In the Late 1970s IBM developed SQL, as relational database interface. Prior to SQL there was no standard data access language. The 1990s viewed SQL as widely accepted standard language for data manipulation, definition and control. Applications written with SQL can easily be moved from one computer platform to another. ORACLE has followed this standardization painstakingly. ORACLE can be adopted for a wide variety of tasks, such as to create primary database storage structures, modify the structure, add, edit and delete data, secure data from public access, transfer data between database and external file, communication within networks, monitor user access to the database ORACLE attempts to meet all these needs and perform all these tasks in order to handle today's multi-user database applications. It provides an outstanding set of tools for data management and applications development, as well as a versatile working environment for end users ORACLE is now available in many versions, 10-I is the latest.

dBase III

dBase III is one of the 4GL. dBase was developed by Ashton-Tate during mid 1980s. dBase III is now available for many personal computers and operating systems as a fully implemented version. Besides being used as a programming language it also has the essential features of a good DBMS. It supports relational model. One of the significant feature of the model is its activity to manage unforeseen changes in requirements. It is good at handling complex dynamic data that has many inter-relationships. Though the relational DBMS in the larger computer system are supporting relational algebra and relational calculus, dBase III supports only the aspects of relational algebra.

The fundamental issue regarding design and programming is how to systematize the transformation of the DBMS specifications into a machine executable system and to achieve the following qualities.

- Reliability
- Efficiency
- Maintainability
- Utility

RDBMS

The Relational Database Management System (RDBMS) is the modern day database technology. It is a commonly used database software for data processing. There are many RDBMS software packages which are based on the relational technology. Some of the commonly adopted commercial RDBMS software's are Oracle, DB2, MS SQL Server , MS Access, Sybase, etc. The relational database management systems are based on the rules of relational model suggested by Dr. E.F. Codd in the year 1970. In this model, the data is modeled as relations or tables.

Characteristics of RDBMS

The great strength of RDBMS is that data are represented in simple logical constructs: relations or tables. It is based on the set theory. From the set theoretical stand point, each relation is a set and therefore we can manipulate each relation using set theory rules like union and intersection of sets.

From user point of view, the RDBMS database is perceived as collection of well-organized tables. Each table corresponds to independent entity, and there is no relationship between tables. It eliminates parent chain relationship (as it was in network and hierarchical models) and represents data in database as simple row, column (two-dimensional) tables of data values. The objects about which we wish to store the data are stored in tables as rows that represent individual record and columns that represent characteristics (attributes) of the object. There are no limits to the number of rows or columns except that such limitations may be imposed by a typical RDBMS implementation. The records in the table have no specific order, and the columns can appear in any order. Each row which represents a record is an instance of the object.

A column, which represent attribute, holds a value for each record in a specific format. The values confirm to the domain from which they are assigned. Two or more attributes can get their values from the same domain. For example, a customer name and employee name can come from the same domain. A domain is a set of permitted values for an attribute. The values may be defined by type such as integer, character, string, etc.

Data in a table may be retrieved by a query (data language). Data language also allows data manipulation. The query language is known as data language, and it is non-procedural language since it is not necessary to write the procedure for the work to be done but can only specify what needs to be done. The language used for manipulating data is called Data Manipulation Language (DMN) and consist of set of commands. In the chapter we will discuss keys, relational operators, data integrity, data dictionary and types of relationship.

DBMS and RDBMS – A Comparison

A DBMS is a collection of software programs that enables the storage and management of data within database. Within database architecture there are different theories and implementations for storing the physical data. An RDBMS is a special case of DBMS that stores data in a simple, logical structure called tables with relationships to other tables. Both DBMS and RDBMS are models for storing information in a physical database. One can manage large sets of data by RDBMS.

The flat file is allowed in DBMS design, but not accepted in RDBMS design. A flat file is data that is 'flat' in logical nature. The data in flat file has no relationship to other data. It is necessary to describe the data in the program that uses data from flat file and requires programming logic to retrieve records from a storage device.

Data Mining

Data mining is the computational process of discovering patterns is large data sets involving methods at the intersection of artificial intelligence, machine learning, statistics, and database systems. The overall goal of the data mining process is to extract information from a data set and transform it into an understandable structure for further use. Aside from the raw analysis step, it involves database and data management aspects, data pre-processing, model and inference considerations, interestingness metrics, complexity considerations, post-processing of discovered structures, visualization, and online updating.

The term is often misused to mean any form of large-scale data or information processing (collection, extraction, warehousing, analysis, and statistics) but is also generalized to any kind of computer decision support system, including artificial intelligence, machine learning, and business intelligence.

The actual data mining task is the automatic or semi-automatic analysis of large quantities of data to extract previously unknown interesting patterns such as groups of data records (cluster analysis), unusual records (anomaly detection) and dependencies (association rule mining). This usually involves using database techniques such as spatial indices. These patterns can then be seen as a king of summary of the input data, and may be used in further analysis or, for example, in machine learning and predictive analytics. For example, the data mining step might identify multiple groups in the data, which can then be used to obtain more accurate prediction results by a decision support system.

Data Warehouses

Dramatic advances in data capture, processing power, data transmission; and storage capabilities are enabling organizations to integrate their various databases into data warehouses. Data warehousing is defined as a process of centralized data management and retrieval. Data warehousing, like data mining, is a relatively new term although the concept itself has been around for years. Data warehousing represents an ideal vision of maintaining a central repository of all organizational data. Centralization of data is needed to maximize user access and analysis. Dramatic technological advances are making this vision a reality for many companies. And, equally dramatic advances in data analysis software are allowing users to access this data freely. The data analysis software is what supports data mining.

REFERENCES

- Brown, A.M., Computer Databases. New York : Create Space, 2009.
- Charafer, D.N. Fourth and Fifth Generation Programming Languages New York : McGraw-Hill, 1986
- Database Management Systems. New Delhi : ITL Educational Solutions, 2012.
- Goel, S. Computer and Database Management. New Delhi : Anmol, 2000.
- HofferJeffrey A., V. Ramesh and Topi Heikki. Modern Database Management. 10th Ed. New Delhi : Pearson, 2011.
- Leigh, William and Paz. Noemi The use of SQL and Second Generation DBMS for Data Processing in Libraries: In Information Technology and Libraries, December 1989
- Lucas, Henry C. Information Concepts for Management. 3rd ed. New York: McGraw-Hill, 1982
- McFadden, F.kR. and Hoffer, J.A. Database Management, New York, Benjamin Cummuns, 1985
- Majumdar, Aru and Bhattacharya. Database Management Systems. New Delhi : Tata McGraus-Hill, 1996.
- Patel, Ashok and Shah, Arvind. Database Management System: Concept Design, Architecture and SQL. New Delhi :Macmillan, 2011.
- Pratt, P., and Adamski, J. Concepts of Database Management. New York : Course Technology, 2012.
- Ramakrishnan, Raghu and Gehrka, Johannes. Database Management Systems. 3rd Ed. New York : McGraw-Hill, 2003.

- Ratnaswamy, M. and Satyanarayana, N.R. Database Programming Impact on Bibliographical Previews. In Modernization in Libraries, Seminar Papers of the Thirty-Third All India Library Conference, December 1987, Delhi: ILA, 1988.
- Sanders, Donald H. Computers Today. 3rd ed. New York : McGraw-Hill, 1988.
- Silberschatz. Database System Concepts. New Delhi : Tata McGraw – Hill Education (I) Limited, 2013.
- Singh, S.K. Database Systems : Concepts, Design and Applications. Noida: Dorling Kindeersley, 2011.
- Smith, David A. A dBase Program for Bibliographic Databases. In Programme, Vol. 23, No. 2, April 1998.

6

Library Automation

Library automation implies a high degree of mechanization of various routine and repetitive tasks to be performed by human beings. With the advent of automation the human intervention is reduced to a great extent. The appearance of computer has greatly increased the library automation. In addition to computers advancement, telecommunication and audio-visual technologies gave way to new possibilities in information handling. In India, the use of computers is limited to only some specialized libraries unlike the case of developed countries. Library automation includes use of computers and other semi-automatic devices like punched cards to reprography. These are semi-automatic because human intervention is greater in extent. So, when we talk of library automation, these days, it is principally the use of computers; associated peripheral media (magnetic tapes, disks, optical media, etc.); computer based products and services in library work.

Need for Automation

The need for automation has several reasons. Need of computers is present in all areas depending upon its usage. They range from acquisition control, serial's control, cataloguing and circulation control. They are also used for library manager's evaluation of reports, statistics etc. For the good administration of the library computers are used in all levels of workfolk. Above all, the unique characteristics of computer made it the right choice for the library world.

The factors responsible for the use of computers consists of all the reasons including economical and technological. The factors are:

Information explosion : Multifold increase in the information output and its usage has made it a problem for the librarians and other information scientists to organize. For organizing this enormous information, manual and conventional methods of information organizing were not sufficient.

Economic feasibility : Increase in information has made the cost of publishing and distributing very high, so the whole affair had become costly. To make it economical, use of computers was made compulsory for sharing the resources and also sharing the same with other libraries. This rendered the libraries to automate.

Routine Jobs : Relieving the professionals with the routine jobs of filing, sorting, typing and other repetitive works, to concentrate themselves upon the technical service. This switchover helps professionals to help them to serve the user better and at a cheaper cost.

Increase in users : As information exploded, so does the users also. There was an increase in number of students and faculties of the universities and researchers in the R & D organizations particularly after the Second World War. Information users and the specialization of the information rendered special methods to be developed. Old methods had to be abandoned and new methods like SDI (Selective Dissemination of Information), etc., are being used.

Speed : With the advent of computers there is faster

dissemination of information to all areas through telecommunication networking.

Accuracy : Even though it is not 100% accurate, it is accurate to a great extent.

Storage capacity : Increase in technology of storage devices made it possible to store huge amounts of information in a very small and compact media for the proper utilization of the space available.

Special features of Library/Bibliographic data handling

1. Nature of data

- Information is largely textual in nature
- Bibliographic record is of variable length
- A field may repeat many times or may not exist at all
- Fields may need to be grouped together and these groups themselves may repeat
- Bibliographic fields are often large and sometimes may include several thousands of items.

2. Manner of handling Bibliographic data

- Items of information in a file may need to be accessed simultaneously by several users/subsystems, for reading and updating.
- Many files may need to be updated extensively on a day-to-day basis.
- Outputs of varying formats may need to be generated
- Special data capture devices may be needed (e.g., for circulation data collection).
- Records may need to be sorted in special sequences.

History of Library Automation

In the early 1960s several libraries of North America and UK began to experiment with computers. In the USA this work of experimenting was mostly confined to special libraries and university libraries.

In the year 1961 H.P. Luhn of IBM developed programmes for producing keyword indexes to titles of articles appearing in Chemical Abstracts. In the UK public libraries have always been as much involved as that of academic and special libraries in developing computer-based systems. In 1965, the metropolitan boroughs of London were reorganized and the chief libraries were forced with the problems of producing a unified catalogue of their stock and four of these boroughs decided to use a computer system to achieve this.

Computer specialists not familiar with library problems underestimated the complexity of these and promised too much. The result was the systems were costly and inadequate. By the end of the decade, reality began to approach expectation, but only a small fraction of library operations were computer based.

1970s saw the emergence of computer-communication networks. Earlier, computer usage was confined only to the four walls of the library, but telecommunication networks have changed the library automation. Libraries started using the networking to a particular geographical area for the purpose of sharing resources. One such project is On-line Computer Library Centre (formerly Ohio College Library Centre). This decade saw the growth of resource-sharing amongst libraries. OCLC, after its birth for the support of library services to Ohio, rapidly expanded to the whole of North America and in the early 1980s to Europe. The other major North American co-operatives are RLIN (Research Libraries Information Network). Subsequently several co-operative networks were developed.

The trend for libraries to acquire their own computing facilities accelerated in the 1980s with the availability of microcomputer systems. The usage of microcomputers as "intelligent" terminals to remote areas by the small libraries to maintain databases, serial controls and acquisition etc., has revolutionized the library automation. Another trend that put great impetus on library automation is the provision of "packaged" hardware. Mid – 1980s saw new developments which are microcomputer related, which are cheaper to library automation. CD-ROM is a product of this range.

CD-ROM (Compact Disk Read Only Memory), is an optical disk with a storage capacity of 550 million bytes (characters). The equivalent of 2,75,000 pages of printed matter. CD-ROM has become a tool for providing cost effective access to large quantities of information using a desktop microcomputer and a relatively inexpensive CD-ROM player/scanner.

Digital optical disks fall into two categories. One is WORM (Write Once Read Many times) and erasable (rewritable disks). WORMs are blank disks that are recorded on by the user. To write later, a powerful beam of laser light burns tiny spots or pits into the coating that covers the surface of these disks. Once burned in, the spots are not erasable.

Erasable optical disks use lasers to record and write information to and from the disk. To write on such a disk, a laser beam heats a tiny spot on it, then a magnetic field is applied to reverse the magnetic polarity of the spot. Because of this property, they are often called magneto-optical disks.

Areas of Automation

Computer has brought in a new impact to the library and information usage. It is used in various fields of library activities. Some of the areas of automation are:

Acquisition

The library has to maintain and use various records of the acquisition section. An acquisition librarian purchases material for a library which accounts for a large part of the budget.

Manual acquisition system faces the problem of

maintaining huge data and files, records, book orders etc., which involve routine jobs. Use of computerized acquisition system reduces the routine, clerical and repetitive tasks. This will help in the professional staff for qualitative improvement in their work.

The functions of an ideal acquisition system which are similar to most libraries are:

1. To search a bibliographic file to determine the status;
2. To order for a duplicate copy;
3. To search the book-seller file so that it helps in deciding to order books of interest immediately through on-line with the book-seller;
4. The capacity to provide detailed financial information in a variety of ways;
5. The capacity to select books from an external database (e.g. Whitaker's Book Bank on CD-ROM); and
6. The system needs to be capable of accommodating wide variety of materials, including monographs, serials, government documents, bulk orders, gifts and exchange materials, etc.

As a matter of fact, large number of book-sellers started using computers for a variety of uses. They use computers for building large bibliographic databases and update them so that librarians can use these databases for ordering. Most of these services are accessible using teletype compatible terminals. This type of services are mostly confined to developed countries like the UK and USA. They are less prevalent in India.

Increasing automation in the book trade and library acquisition systems is leading to a new type of interface and relationship between book-sellers and libraries. Databases are becoming very prominent. Bowker's Books in Print database, for instance contains more than

7,45,000 records of titles produced by 13,500 US publishers and distributors, i.e., available on BRS and Dialog on-line research services. Similarly, Whitaker's Book Bank of the UK is also available on on-line.

More recently, an interesting development has taken place in UK between publishers and book selling trade which is called teleordering. Intelligent terminals in bookshops are used to record details of book orders, using their ISBNs. These ISBNs are sent to the publisher via telephone to the teleordering computer system, where ISBNs are checked against Whitaker's British Books in Print database and the full author/title details are retrieved. The advantages of Teleordering system include cost savings, fewer errors, improved reporting and speedier distribution, all of which will result in an efficient computerized acquisition system.

Cataloguing

Catalogue is a very good information retrieval tool which helps to locate the holdings of a library. Different library professionals gave different definitions of which Charles Ammi Cutter in 1876, wrote that catalogue is used for achieving the following objectives:

1. To enable a person to find a book of which either the author or the title or the subject is known.
2. To show what the library has by a given author, or a given subject or in a given kind of literature.
3. To assist in the choice of a book or to its edition (bibliographically) or as to its character.

Catalogue is an organized record of the holdings of a library. It gives access to a library collection. Conventional cataloguing involves the use of many man-hours of professional staff, production of variety of cards i.e., author, title, subject, serial etc. With the use of computers and high-speed printers, production of these cards has become faster. Catalogues, on microfilms are also being used popularly due to the inexpensive nature and their durability.

MARC (Machine Readable Cataloguing)

The MARC (Machine Readable Cataloguing) project of the Library Congress is the application of computers in a controlled cataloguing. MARC project started in 1966 was completed in 1967. The greatest contribution of MARC project to library services was designing of bibliographic record format. The MARC record format designed by Library of Congress was adopted by British Library also. Taking Library of Congress and British Library as an example many libraries in the USA, UK and other European countries developed computer readable catalogues.

Advantages of MARC

1. A centrally prepared catalogue can be distributed to the receiving libraries in a machine readable form.
2. Up-to-date maintenance is possible without employing additional staff.
3. MARC system is cheaper than the LC catalogue cards.
4. The MARC tape can be utilized for acquisition functions i.e. selecting and ordering and claiming unsupplied books without any additional cost.

COM (Computer Output Microfilm)

The COM was developed in the USA by Stremberg Carlson Co. COM is capable of recording photographically a full page at a time as compared to a line only printed by a line printer.

The former are wound in cartridges while the later are cut into microfiche. The end product of a COM is a magnetic tape while it contains the requisite bibliographical information besides the concerned printing and format control codes provided for the final images.

Advantages of COM

1. Easy to handle
2. Compact storage
3. Less expensive for storage & duplication
4. Less expensive accumulations
5. Requires no binding
6. Take lesser time
7. Less in production & distribution cost
8. Easy availability

OCLC (Ohio College Library Centre)

OCLC started in August 1970 is a non-profit corporation which was originally planned to be a network of academic libraries but now it has more than 700 user libraries with 1200 terminals in various types of libraries including one national library i.e. the National Agriculture Library.

Advantages of OCLC

1. The system is very effective as the response time for title searches was 25-30 seconds.
2. OCLC enables its users at remote places to search the central catalogue by author, title and subject approaches.
3. Its common products include computer line-printed catalogue cards besides spine and book labels' accession list and OCLC catalogue tapes for the purpose of producing COM catalogue.

The Ohio College Library Centre (OCLC) in the USA has one such catalogue which caters to the needs of the users in North America which is on-line. In 1974 four large North American research libraries (Columbia University, Harvard University, New York Public Library and Yale University) formed a group with the aims of co-operative sharing the resources and the creation and operation of sophisticated bibliographic tools. To fulfil the above aim the Research Libraries Information Network (RLIN) was set up.

Advances in telecommunications have paved the way for the cooperative cataloguing.

Functions of OCLC

1. On-line access to a database with bibliographic record.
2. Capable of inputing complete details of new documents.
3. Cataloguing should be flexible in doing functions like add, delete, and modify, etc.
4. Computerized catalogue system should be in a position to generate output in various physical forms for appropriate use.
5. Access to the master file.
6. On-line authority control.
7. Cataloguing should be able to work in correlation with circulation system.

While developing cooperative computer based cataloguing various constrains need to be solved. Other factors include economics, telecommunications, likely use by the staff and users and how the catalogue is to be consulted.

In the developed countries the developments are breathtaking. In the British Library in London, users are able to access a new electronic catalogue called the on-line public access catalogue or OPAC.

India is still in its infancy in this area due to lack of telecommunication facilities at economic rates. India needs to develop local controls so that they can be linked first and then regions, and then the whole country.

Serials control

"Serials' are defined by AACR2 as a publication in any medium issued in successive parts bearing numerical or chronological designations and intended to be continued "indefinitely". Serials include periodicals, newspapers, annuals (reports, yearbooks, etc.), the journals, memoirs, proceedings, transactions etc., of societies and numbered monographic series.

Serials are very different from books which pose several problems like :

1. The serials change their names quite often, either they are divided into two or merged into one, the publication seizes or lies inactive for quite long.
2. The number of serials is generally large.
3. To keep track of the large number of serials which are not received and the claim to be sent to the supplier or publisher or distributor.
4. They may release many supplements, indexes and special issues.
5. The serials sometimes are not brought but are gifted or exchanged.
6. The problem of storing and circulating individual issues.
7. To overcome the problem of when and where to send for binding.
8. To keep a track of the amount being spent for the serials i.e., for acquisition, dissemination, and binding etc.

Special libraries and the academic libraries are mostly using computers for serials control due to economic facility.

Evolution

In 1960s computers for the first time were used for serial control which are mostly batch processed. In 1970s some libraries in the US developed on-line real time systems which were cost effective. Slowly systems were developed all over the developed world with services for serial control being offered by library cooperatives and some software for serials control for microcomputer systems.

To identify a serial is a big problem. There are two currently used numbering systems for this purpose. One is the old, CODEN. It is controlled by Chemical Abstracts service and covers mainly scientific and technical literature. CODEN consisted of a code of six digits. The first four of which are assigned mnemonically from the title of the journal, the fifth one is made unique and the sixth character is check digit. The second numbering system is the International Standard Serial Number (ISSN). The ISSN is an 8-digit number with the last digit being a check digit.

At North Western University Library the serials control system, which covers the major functions described earlier, is part of the integrated system – NOTIS. About 50,000 current and retrospective serial titles are included in the control database and, being part of an integrated system, searching of these titles is carried out by the general on-line public access module. Blackwell's and Dawson group both supply serials control software with optional links to their respective databases of serial titles. In this software the user can borrow, order titles and download record data for the control routines, then eliminating a considerable amount of relying of data. Dawson's programme also provides analyzing of circulation lists by borrower and department.

Circulation

Circulation is an important area which needs to be automated, because of the nature of job that prevails in the circulation. Circulation involves the charging and discharging of library materials, reservations, statistics, sending of reminders for the over-due material, etc.

Circulation is an area which needs no professional talent but it is highly labour-intensive and time-consuming. Circulation counter transactions are not evenly distributed throughout the working day. There are some prime periods when the counter is busy. It varies from one library to another. It is different in public library as compared with an academic or a special library.

Early circulation systems are error-prone particularly in the US in the early 1960s and in the UK in the late 1960s. The first systems in the UK were those at the University of Southampton and at the Atomic Weapons Research Establishment at Aldermaston. In the early systems this was achieved by taking the data of the book details on an 80-column punched-card and the borrowers' details on the special badge, similar to a credit card. In the late 1960s and early 1970s libraries in the UK and other developed countries started using more sophisticated devices like light pens for reading bar-coded labels, reading of non-magnetic metallic lables and cards for recording OCR (optical character reader) labels. 1970s saw the batch processed circulation systems which provided fast and reliable collection of data. In the early 1980s several organizations have started producing turn-key, on-line, real-time circulation control systems. They are constantly changing with the need of the hour and the place of application. The trend nowadays is towards integration of other functions such as on-line public access systems and to the other important areas of the library functionary.

Information Retrieval

Information retrieval is a new concept as compared with others like cataloguing, classification etc., even though catalogues are examples of an information retrieval system. It deals with the techniques and processes of representation, storage and retrieving information pertaining to a set of items, which may be documents, serials, microfiche, microfilm etc.

Project MAC at Massechusets Institute of Technology, one of the most acclaimed, is a general purpose information retrieval system in which a number of users can simultaneously make inquiries, via, remote terminals. Its importance lay in the demonstration of the potentialities of the computer as an information storage and retrieval device.

Evolution

The use of computers in the retrieval of the scientific literature in the early 1960s has started with the production of printed indexes. By the early 1970s, several indexing and abstracting journals like Biological Abstracts, Chemical Abstracts, Engineering Index etc., were produced by computer.

The MEDLARS project of the National Library of Medicine in the United States was directed towards the mechanization of publishing of Index Medicus, but outside interest in its has focussed more on its potential for mechanized retrieval of medical information.

Interest in mechanized information retrieval has led to research in new indexing techniques. There evolved new classification systems, thesaurus construction and statistical analysis of language to create abstracts automatically. The most widely used technique for indexing by computer is KWIC (Key-Word-in-Context) Index.

Computerization of Indexing

Indexes are main retrieval tools for any documentation work. Computers were used, both for preparation of in house indexes to reports, local abstracting & indexing bulletins, patent lists etc. Computer generated indexes mostly rely on automatically assigned index terms.

For quick production of these indexes, computers have been used increasingly since 1950, which began with Luhn's work on KWIC indexes in 1957. There are different types of computer produced indexes.

Keyword Based Indexes

KWIC, KWOC, KWIT and KWAC these indexes can be easily generated entirely with the help of a computer. The elimination of personal interpretation enhances consistency and automatically lead to the use of current terminology.

Indexes Based on String Manipulation

Computers definitely have a role in the production of indexes based on intellectually assigned index terms. For example a series of terms from a controlled vocabulary of single concept terms is to present a document then these terms are composed into an index string. PRECIS and the Index generation algorithm used in Abstracts in New Technologies and Engineering (ANTE) are subject indexes based on a rigid framework of conceptual analysis.

The specially of CI is that given one document in a field, the searcher should be able to trace other related documents. Citation Index provide a valuable additional approach to the identification of related documents.

Computer usage to produce indexes comes in a variety of physical forms, such as by computer typesetting, on-line printer paper or on COM film or fiche. Indexes started coming in on-line. KWIC (Key-Word-In-Context) index is a widely used indexing system developed by H.P. LUHN of IBM in 1961.

KWIC indexes can be used in academic libraries for getting information about materials present in the libraries by putting in the keyword in the title.

The disadvantage lies with the reliability of the words made in the title which may be uninformative or misleading. This problem can be overcome by enriching the title with extra key-words at the input stage.

Information services

Providing the latest information to the users may

be through personal contacts, telephone, etc. With computer impact information service is by producing information bulletins, Selective Dissemination of Information (SDI) and evaluative reports.

The older Information Retrieval Systems (IRS) were batch-oriented which mean queries to be submitted in batches and the results used to be available only after some time. Development of real-time and time-sharing systems and faster storage access devices made the queries answerable in the moment unlike the batch-processor system.

Content Analysis

Content analysis includes indexing and abstracting. Automation of these areas is attempted by using statistical methods. That means if a term is repeated more number of times than other words then it is imperative that the document is concerned with that word. This keyword is taken as an index word. In automatic abstracting one can extract those sentences of a document which contain frequently used terms or phrases. Thesaurus construction is also being developed by computers using linguistic analysis rather than statistical methods.

Managerial Application

Automation of library will help the manager of the library in the formulation of policies. Automation can generate the statistics at a faster pace and hence the faster approach to manage the things in the library. Statistical analysis of the performance of the library will help in formulating policies for the coming year. Automation helps to retrieve data at a very speedy pace.

REFERENCES

- Brown-Syed, C. Parents of Invention: The Development of Library Automation Systems in the late 20th Century. New York: Libraries Unlimited, 2010.
- Boss, R.W. Library Manager's Guide to Automation. 2nd ed. New York: Knowledge Industry, 1984.

- Gilliman, P. and Peniston, Silvinia, Library Automation . A Current Review. London: ASLIB, 1984
- Head, J.W., & McCabe, G.B. Introducing and Managing Academic Library Automation Projects. N.Y.: Greenwod Press, 1996.
- IgLesias. Problems and Failures in Library Automation. N.Y.: Idea Group, 2013.
- Information Today Inc. Directory of Library Automation Software, Systems, and Services. Pennsylvania: State University: Information Today, 2004.
- Kochar, R.S. Library Automation: Issues and Principles. New Delhi: APH Publishing, 2007.
- Lancaster, F.W. Problems and Failures in Failures in Library Automation. New York: Read Books, 2008.
- Ravichandra Rao, I. K. Library Automation. 2nd ed. New Delhi: Wiley Eastern, 1992.
- Rowley, J.E. Computers for Libraries, 3rd ed. London: Bingley, 1992.
- Tedd, Lucy A. An Introduction to Computer Based Library System. 2nd ed. London : John Wiley, 1985.

7

Library Automation Software Packages

Library automation is the process to mechanise or computerize all the activities of the library such as acquisition, circulation, serial control, cataloguing etc. The word automation generally refers to something which has the power of spontaneous motion or self movement. It is the performance of either one operation or a series of operations. In other words it is a process by self activating, self controlling by automatic means. In Library management context, automation implies the use of automatic data processing such as computer or by using any other labour saving devices. It is the technology concerned with the design and development of process and system that minimize the necessity of human intervention in operation. Library automation is a phenomenon where a computer system manages many library key functions.

In Indian scenario of Library and information services computers were in use as early as 1960s. It was first used in the preparation of author and subject index of Indian Science Abstracts in the year 1967 in the library and information centre of INSDOC (now NISCAIR). But in the developed countries computers were known to have been used as far back during period of world war-II.

Stages of Library Automation

The process of library automation has many stages of mechanization of work in order to managing the different functions of the library. The stages of library computerization may be listed as follows:

Stage I – Study of Internal Operations

This stage belongs to the study of internal work flow and sharing of catalogue of functions.

Stage II – Retrospective Conversion

In this stage all the holdings of the library needs to be converted facilitating for access to local resources and thus establishing OPAC.

Stage III – Facilitate to Access of External Resources

This stage is meant to provide access to resources like online data exchange, online resources (OPAC), web resources, and document delivery services.

Stage IV – Developing a System

A system is needed to be developed which work globally and inter-operatability of services and developing digital libraries.

An integrated library automated software is meant to operate all the aspects of library functions (except the intellectual works like classification) such as acquisition, circulation, serials control, cataloguing, financial administration, report generation etc. Each aspect of function is known as module. The following is a list of modules that should be included in library automation software:

Aquisition

- Circulation Control

- Serial Control
- Cataloguing
- Reservations and short loans
- Inter library loans
- OPAC
- Specialized service facilities (CAS, SDI)
- Document storage and delivery
- International format
- Web-services

Each module will adhere to different functions related to the activities in that area. The general functions include indifferent modules may be studies here under:

Acquisition : In this module the utilities that must be added or included are i) Ordering, ii) Receiving, iii) Claiming, iv) Accounts, v) Order/Receiving enquiries, vi) Accessioning, vii) Bill processing, viii) Payment and ix) Report and statistics.

Circulation Control : Among all the house – keeping operations, circulation is the most important module for any automation software for libraries. Utilities in this module may include the following: i) User privileges setting, ii) Issue, and Return, iii) Renewal, iv) Reservation, v) Over-dues calculation, vi) Reminder and recalling notices, vii) Borrower and reservation enquiries, viii) User management, ix) Patron self services and x) Reports and statistics.

Serial Control : The module should have basic capabilities such as : i) Order placement, ii) Renewal of subscriptions, iii) Receiving and Claiming, iv) Binding Control, v) Cataloguing, vi) Enquiries about arrival of issues, vii) Reports and statistics.

Cataloguing : Catalogues are the complete lists of the holdings of the library (both print and electronic media), which are generally arranged either in alphabetical or in any other systemic sequence. In the context of library catalogue is the list of books and other resources and therefore, the cataloguing software module should have the following: i) Support to standard communication format, ii) Shared cataloguing, iii) Authority control, iv) Using stand protocol, v) Output generation, and vi) User Services.

Access Related Services

These modules totally belongs to the accessbility of different services on computer environment. These modules should deal with such aspects related to i) On-line access (web OPAC), II) Publicly access interface (OPAC), iii) Web/Remote accessibility and iv) Gateway services.

Miscellaneous Services : The library automation software should also possess modules with the capabilities to perform the additional functions such as: i) Inter-library loan services, ii) System administration, iii) Report and statistics generation, iv) Analysis of statistics, v) Digital Media Retrieval Services System, and vi) Support Metadata harvesting.

Other Services : The software should also have additional modules related to outreach services. These modules should facilitate to automate the processes required for i) Deliver materials to differently able patrons who cannot physically visit the library, ii) Create patrons interest profiles, iii) Initiate easy delivery and return of items, and iv) Deliver community information services.

Important Library Software Packages

There are quite a few library software packages that are being widely used in India. Some of them are commercial packages and some packages are open source software available free of cost. Every software has got its own merits as well as demerits. A right software is needed to be chosen as per the requirements of the individual libraries. Some of the prominent library automation packages are explained here under.

Libsys : It's widely used software in South Asia for library automation, developed and marketed by Libsys Corp., New Delhi (now located in Gurgaon) and written on C and C++ language platform and available for system using ORACLE and SQL server as end back RDBMS. It provides support Linux, UNIX, NOVELL and Windows operating system on server side and any version of Windows on client sided and also provide graphical user interface. Its bibliographic database based on MARC format; also accept USMARC, OCLC etc. data standard. So it has great flexibility to import/export bibliographic data in MARC or Non-MARC formats (Retrospective conversion). In the resource sharing environment it follow Z39.50 protocol. Libsys has following modules for automation:

- Acquisition;
- Cataloguing (CCC and AACR with revised);
- Circulation;
- Serial Control;
- OPAC; and
- Article Indexing.

Alice for Windows (AfW) : Alice for windows is the product of Softlink in 1983 (Brisbane in Australia); in India through Softlink Asia (New Delhi) in 1996 and its' integrated Library automation software package. This software markets with various names Embla in Iceland, Alice elsewhere in Europe, OASIS in South East Asia and Australia, Annie in America. It has four distinct versions – Public library, Special library, Academic library and School Library versions. The software also grouped in three different modules sets –

1. Standard set : this set consists Management; Reports and utilities; Circulation; and OPAC

2. Advance set : including standard set other

addition is Acquisition; Periodicals; Journal indexing; Multimedia and Web inquiry.

3. Special set : addition to standard and advance set, it includes Reservation; Inter Library loan; Patron self checking; rapid retrospective conversion; Multilingual features, self Circulation and Union catalog.

It has following modules:

- Acquisition
- Management
- Circulation
  - — Periodical
  - — Journal Indexing
  - — Multimedia
  - — Subject authority
  - — Web enquiry
  - — Book hire
  - — Multilingual
  - — Patron Self Checking

A part that AfW has some sub modules like, Union Catalogue, ILL and library services. It support USMARC format for bibliographic records and LC & DDC for classification number. AfW facilities for importing data from CDs, other library software and databases.

SOUL (Software for University Library) : One of the most State-of-art integrated library management software is developed by INFLIBNET under UGC patron and first version of SOUL1.0 release during CALIBER 2000. It is suitable for MS-SQL and My-SQL and International bibliographic format MARC 21, AARC-2 (R), MARCXML beside UTF-8 and UTF-16 and for resource sharing on network it follows NCIP2.0 and SIP2.0 protocol.

It has server client based architecture and support data exchange through ISO 2709 standard. Recent version (SOUL2.0, 2009) has following modules:

- Acquisition;
- Catalogue;
- Circulation;
- OPAC
- Serial Control; and
- Administration

VIRTUA : Virtua developed by VTLS (Virginia Tech Library System) Inc., Blacks berg (Virginia), has corporate office in USA and many countries of India and its' first vendor of library automation, which got ISO certification in 1997. Virtua is UNIX, Linux based server windows based client application software. The base of virtua software is RDBMS, Server/Client architecture, Warehousing of Database, Unicode supporting, Rapid Development tool, and ATM Network Modules are available in virtua –

- Acquisition and fund accounting
- Cataloguing
- Circulation
- Serial Control
- OPAC
- Statistics and Reporting
- Chameleon Gateway

The basic feature of Virtue is the working efficiently of different standards of MARC, like USMARC, UKMARC, CANAMARK, SWEMARC etc. and also facilitates switching of keyboard (script left to right or right to left).

KOHA : KOHA is an open source web-based Integrated Library management system, which was created in 1999 by Katipo Communication Limited of Wellington, New Zealand for Horowhenua Library Trust (HLT) in Levin near Wellington, and first installation of the software came alive in january 2000 and release under GPL public license in July 2000 with using open source tool (My-SQL, Perl and apache) under Linux platform, Telnet communication branch but will work on Windows with installation of series of additional modules and operable in English, Arabic, Spanish and French with other languages being developed and translated by the community members. Backend data of catalog stored in MARC and accessible through Z39.50 or SRU (search/ retrieve URL). Benefits with KOHA is – easy access of information due to effective search and issuing of items, alert to remind for services, it brings together (Staff and user) can work effectively to achieve the goal.

The key features of the software is Open source/ free downloaded software; Customizing facility of Web-based interfaces; Fully supported to MARC 21 and UNIMARC; Circulation and borrower management; Containing all essential working modules; Support Z39.50 protocol for server and client for data interchange; and Enhancing to patron services like: online reservation and borrower purchase suggestion support.

Modules, which are included in the software –

- Acquisition;
- Circulation;
- Cataloguing;
- Serials;
- OPAC;
- Patron management;
- Branch management and
- Reservation.

SLIM21 : System for Library Information and Management, is a product of Algorhythms Consultants Pvt. Ltd., Pune. This was first designed and developed in the year 1988 and being updated continuously. SLIM21 is capable for Unicode and can handle data in almost all Indian scripts also. It is multi-user, multi-tasking integrated library software working on a single machine or in a client-server multi-platform environment.

Basic Modules of SLIM21 are:

- Cataloguing OPAC
- Acquisition
- Circulation
- Serials control
- Security solutions (RFID)

Enterprise Modules

- Web based OPAC
  - — Wet Proposals
- SDI
  - — CAS (Bulletin printing)
- Usage of Statistical Analysis.

NEWGENLIB : New Gen Lib is an integrated library management system developed by Verus Solutions Pvt. Ltd. Domain expertise is provided by Kesavan Institute of Information and Knowledge Management in Hyderabad. NewGEnLib version 1.0 was released in 2005. In the year 2008, NewGenLib was declared Open Source Software. The latest version of NewGenLib is 3.0.4 R1 released in 2012. Many libraries across the globe (mainly from the developing countries) are using NewGenLib as their Primary integrated library management system.

NewGenLib has following main modules:

- Acquisitions
- Technical Processing
- Serials management
- Circulation
- Administration
- MIS Reports
- Task to do today (daily scheduler)
- OPAC

Some advanced functional features

1. Android mobile and tablet capable
2. Integration with Twitter helping send messages of transactions directly to users' Twitter accounts.
3. Flexibility of defining own search field in OPAC
4. Enhanced contents and interactive OPAC like Availability of Book jackets, Google preview, Comments/Book review, Tagging, Favorite reading list, etc.
5. Zotero complaint OPAC
6. RSS feeds in OPAC
7. Faceted Browsing (Refining search results)
8. Suggestion for other books in the rack
9. RFID supports
10. Provision for frequently used predefined templates along with freedom of defining own customized data entry templates in Cataloguing.
11. Configurable SMS system – a proof of transaction.
12. Integration with Gmail or paid mailbox account. This enables automatic sending of email to patrons during issue/return.
13. Enhanced Report Module for generating in easy format with a provision for wide customization.
14. Provision for integrating with Vufind SOPAC (Ex: OPAC of the Library of Bangalore University)
15. Catalogue can be harvested through Google site map, and thus the visibility of the library can be further improved.

E-GRANTHALAYA

e-Granthalaya : It is a library automation software from National Informatics Centre, Department of Electronics & Information Technology, Ministry of Communications and Information Technology,

Government of India. The software has been designed by a team of experts from software as well as Library and Information Science discipline. The software can be implemented either in stand-alone or in client-server mode where database and WebOPAC are installed on the server PC while the data entry program is installed on client PCs. The software provides LAN/Web based data entry solutions for a cluster of libraries where a centralized/Common database can be created with Union Catalog output. The software provides Web OPAC interface to publish the library catalog over Internet/Intranet. The software runs on Windows platform Only. UNICODE Compliant, thus, supports data entry in local language.

e-Granthalaya was started as an in-house project at 'Karnataka State Centre of NIC, Bangalore" and first version of the software was designed for the Public Libraries in the State. Later, NIC HQs 'Library and Information Services Division' took over the designing of the software where library professionals were involved in the designing process and, thus, improved the software with enhanced user interface and simplify the work-flow of library functions so that it can suit all kinds of libraries.

Features

- Runs on Windows Platform Only (Win XP/vista/7/Server 2003/2008)
- Provides Local/LAN/WAN based Data Entry Solution
- UNICODE Compliant, supports data entry in local language
- Module – Wise Permission to the software Users
- Work-flow as per Indian Libraries
- Retro-Conversion as well as Full Cataloguing Modes of Data Entry
- Authority Files/Master tables for Authors, Publishers, Subjects, etc.

- Multi-Vol, Multi-Copy and Child-Parent Relationship pattern
- Download Catalog Records from Internet
- Z39.50 Client Search Built-in
- Exhaustive Reports for Print
- Export Records in CSV/Text File/MARC 21/MARC XML/ISO:2709/MS ACCESS/EXCEL formats
- Merger databases of eG3 into Single Database
- Common/Centralized Database for N Number of libraries, minimize data entry
- Main/Branch Libraries Acquisition/Cataloging
- Print Accession Register
- Search Module built-in with basic/advance/boolean

Parameters

- Library Statistics Reports
- CAS/SDI Services and Documentation Bulletin
- Updated Regularly with enhanced Features
- Compact/Summary/Detailed Reports Option
- Generate Bibliography
- Data Entry Statistics Built-In
- News Clipping Services Built-in
- Digital Library integration with uploading / dowloading of pdf/html, etc. documents
- Micro-Documents Manager (Articles/Chapter Indexing)
- SERIALS Control System for Subscription with Auto-Generate Schedule
- Budget Modules with Bill Register Generation, manages Multi-Budget Head
- Import Data from any structured Source
- Well exhaustive Web Based OPAC Interface with separate Membership module

REFERENCES

- Bisson, C. Open-source Software for Libraries. University of Michigan: ALATechSource., 2007.
- Brown-Syed, C. Parents of Invention: The Development of Library Automation Systems of the Late 20th Century, N.Y., Libraries Unlimited Inc., 2010.
- Clayton, M., & Batt, C. Managing Library Automation. USA: Gower Publishing Ltd., 1992.
- Conover, P.R. Technology Projects for Library Media Specialists and Teachers. New York: Linworth, 2006.
- Engard, N. Practical Open Source Software for Libraries. Oxford: Chandos Publishing, 2010.
- Head, J.W., & McCabe, G.B. Introducing and Managing Academic Library Automation Projects. USA: Greenwood Press, 1996.
- IgLesias. Problems and Failures in Library Automation. N.Y.: Idea Group, 2013.
- Information Today Inc. Director of Library Automation Software, Systems and Services. Pennsylvania: State University, 2004.
- Kochar, R.S. Library Automation : Issues and Principles. New Delhi: APH Publishing, 2007.
- Lancaster, F.W. Problems and Failures in Library Automation. New York: Read Books, 2008.
- Lass, A., & Quandt, R. Library Automation in Transitional Societies: Lessons from Eastern Europe. Oxford : University Press, 2000.
- Library and Information Technology Association (U.S.). Open Source Software for Libraries: An Open Source for Libraries Collaboration. University of California: LITA, 2002.
- Pandey, P. Recent Advances in Library Automation. New Delhi: Mahamaya, 2010.
- Pier, C.B. The Librarian's Guide to WordPerfect 5 (Supplement to Computers in Libraries). N.Y., Information today, 1990.
- Reynolds, D. Library Automation : Issues and Applications. New York: Bowker, 1985.
- Singh, B. Software Packages for Library Automation. New Delhi: Pushpanjali, 2008.

- Sunil, M. Open Source Library Automation Software: Features and Capabilities. New Delhi: LAP Lambert Academic, 2013.
- Webber, D., & Peters, A. Integrated Library Systems: Planning, Selecting and Implementing. New York: Libraries Unlimited, 2010.

8

Library System Analysis and Design

One of the most exciting activities in the information system field is the design of a new computer based system. It is a creative and labour intensive task. It is creative because here we build a new set of information processing procedures similar to that of an architect designs a new building, requiring human thought and aspects of creativity. Thus library system analysis and design requires imagination and human thought. A system is made of a number of components (parts) and activities. A system needs to be developing a sufficient understanding to document it. We, therefore need to study what constitute a system and how to document it. For this a number of different approaches are used, descriptive techniques are to be developed. The clear understanding of these help to conceptualize a system. It needs detailed listing of decisions, transactions, information flows, and functions, in a top-down fashion. Thus a system first requires an analysis of components and activities and then requires designing of the proposed new system.

The System Concept

In computer jargon a system is a group of parts that are integrated for the purpose of achieving some objectives. The following are the three key characteristics of the system:

1. A system is a group of parts, with more than one element. For e.g., a steering wheel is not a system but it is a vital for a familiar system called automobile.
2. A system has integrated parts. A logical relationship must exist between parts of a system. For e.g., mechanical and electronic systems such as washing machines and VCRs have elements (parts) that work together.
3. The system has a common purpose of achieving some objectives. It is designed to accomplish one or more goals. All system elements should be tied together and controlled so that the system goal is achieved. For e.g., a computer is a group of integrated parts that have common purpose of performing operations called for in the programme being executed, qualifies to be a system.

Library : A System

According to S.R. Ranganathan library is a trinity of books, readers and staff. It is a trinity of elements called : Documents (Books, Periodicals etc.) Users (Readers, customers) and Personnel (Man-power). All the activities in the library revolves among and around these only. Thus library work includes work with books and work with readers. These are performed by the library personnel. The work related to the documents can be further divided as job related to organisation (classification, cataloguing and maintenance etc.) and retrieval (when required). The work related to users can be divided as circulation (registration, lending etc.) reference (both reference work and service, documentation work and service, information work and service). The work related to staff can be divided as manpower recruitment and management etc.

The main challenges in library and information Science is to enhance optimizing outputs, upgrading skills and efficiency, reducing inputs & costs, increased speed, etc. In the Library and Information science filed like any other field in human activity modern technology has its sway. Library and Information Systems are being influenced by telecommunication, micrography, reprography, audio-visual technologies throughout the world.

Library computerisation needs to be implemented only after analysis and then designing the system. It varies from one library to another library. Based on the requirements of each library, the necessary system is developed. This is what is known as System Analysis and Design.

Developing a Computer Based System for LIS

Computer based programmes and systems are not usually overnight creations. Computer hardware will not automatically begin to bring output results to satisfy user needs. It is the people who must first go to create a series of steps called "Programme" for a personal computer. It is people who put computer to work. It is people working together determine processing need, provide input data, design processing procedures, select hardware and software, while computer programmes use the processed data (output). Some of the people are data processing specialists who create programmes, some of them are desks assistants and secretaries who enter the data. Some of them are managers who use the output. But all are equally essential in the creation of a successful system. However there are people who buy prewritten software programmes. They must also need to identify packages that meet their needs. All the people involved in the activity must understand the following step-by-step processes used to identify and develop specific improvements in the computer based information system.

Step 1 : Defining the need

To create a new programme or system or to improve or modify an existing one, people first have to recognize that a problem or need exists. This problem or need may result from changing operating conditions, managers, employees of departments affected by changing conditions, and data processing personnel often participated in requirements session until the problem has been defined and specific study goals have been outlined. These goals should then be put in writing and approved by all concerned. (This first step can not be by passed even if a software package is used to put the computer to work. After all, how can people identify and select a suitable package if they don't have a clear understanding of exactly what is it, that they want it to do?)

Step 2 : System Analysis

After users and specialists have identified the need for specific changes, a study team gathers and then analyzes data about current processing operations. The people on this team may be selected for the offsetting talents they can offer. At least one member usually represents (and has a knowledge of the information needs of) the departments affected by the study. Another is a system analyst – an information specialist who's knowledgeable about the technical aspects of analyzing, designing, and implementing computer based processing systems. And a third may be an auditor who can see that proper accuracy and security controls are built into a new system.

Data Collection

The team's first job is to gather data about current processing operations. These facts must be accurate, up to data, and sufficiently complete because they become the input to later study stages. Gathering such data can be difficult because a system may cut across several departments and involve many people using dozens of documents. Furthermore, accurate written notes detailing exactly what's done may be missing. Procedure descriptions often exist, but they may not reflect the most current methods. Thus, a number of data gathering tools and techniques must often be employed. Among these are interviews and observations, questionnaires, and system flowcharts.

Flow Chart Preparation

A system flowchart is a diagram that shows a broad overview of the data flow and sequence of operations in a system. The emphasis is placed on input documents and output reports. Only limited detail is furnished about how a workstation or machine converts input data into the desired output. Standard symbols are used in all flowcharts to clearly record and communicate information. Although the input/output (I/O) symbol may be used to show any type of media or device, it's often replaced in system charts by other symbols whose shape suggests the particular medium or device being used.

Preparing flowcharts can help the study team gather data on current operations. Beginning with source document inputs, each operation step is charted, suing the proper symbols. Files and equipment being used are identified, the processing sequence is described, the departments involved are located, and the output results are shown. The arrows connecting the symbols show the direction of data flow. The main flow is usually charted from top to bottom and from left to right. Notes within the symbol further explain what's being done.

Analyzing the Findings

After the data about current operations have been gathered, the team members must then analyze their findings. System analysis is the study of existing operations to learn what they accomplish, why they work as they do and what role (in any) they may have in future processing activities. In analyzing the current system, it's necessary to identify the essential data and procedures required for a new approach. It's also necessary to pinpoint current weaknesses and problems so that they will not be carried over to the new system. As part of this process, the system flowchart can be a helpful analysis tool. (It's risky for people and organizations to try to bypass this system analysis step even though they expect to buy a software package).

Step 3 : System Design

System design is the process of creating alternative solutions to satisfy the study goals, evaluating the choices and then drawing up the specifications for the chosen alternative. Design usually beings after the study team has analyzed the current procedures. Since many factors have a bearing on the design process, it can be a challenging task. For example, the design team must consider the personnel and financial resources for the organization the different procedures that can often be used to carry out a single operation, and the many equipment choices that are available to perform a given processing job. Also, the team must consider how changes made in one application or department will affect related applications. A proposed improvement in a billing system, for example, might require a redesign of accounts receivable and inventory control procedures.

Steps involved in designing an information system

1. The first step in the system study is to clearly identify the particular problem to be solved or the task to be accomplished. Managers, departmental employees, and data processing personnel jointly participate in determining the problem and setting system goals.
2. The second step involves system analysis. After the

problem has been identified, a study team works closely together to gather and then analyze data about current data processing operations.

3. The third step is system design. After analyzing the procedures currently being followed the people in the study team must then cooperate in the design of any new systems or applications that may be required to satisfy the need. As a part of the system design phase, people must settle on the most feasible design alternative to achieve the study goals. And they must prepare new design specifications that include the output desired, the input data needed, and the processing procedures required to convert the input data into the output results.
4. The fourth step is programming analysis. The new system of applications may be turned over to one or more programmers. These specifications are then broken down into the specific input/output, calculating, logic/comparison and storage/retrieval operations required to satisfy the need.
5. The fifth step is programme preparation. At this stage one or more programmers translate or code the required operations into a language and form acceptable to the computer hardware.
6. The sixth step involves the implementation and maintenance of the system or application. People must first make sure that the coded programme(s) is checked for errors and tested prior to being used on a routine basis. After programmes appear to be running properly and producing correct results. Change over to the new approach is made. The cooperation of the many who may be involved in the preparation of input data and the use of results is needed at this time if the new approach is to be successfully implemented. Finally, implemented systems and programmes are usually put to

continual change and must therefore be maintained. This modification for improvement must be a cooperative effort between those served by programme and those responsible for maintaining it.

After the team members have settled on the approach they consider best to meet the study goals, they must then prepare new design specifications. These specifications include the output desired, the input data needed, and the purpose procedures required to convert input data into output results. (When people complete the system design step, they are in a position to identify and then select software packages that meet their needs. For example, they can now see if the package output is suitable, if the files created by the package output is suitable, if the package accepts the necessary input data and if the files created by the package are acceptable in terms of size and content. If a satisfactory package can be purchased, the next two study steps may be skipped and if suitable software is not available, custom programmes must be created)

Mapping of System Tasks

A sequence of means-end relationships which link the more abstract objectives of the system user to successively more concrete and specific goals, comprises the mapping of system tasks. During the development of this sequence of means-end relationships, the design statements being to sound like description of discrete tasks performed by the system elements. A task is composed of a set of actions performed by the people (physically or intellectually) and/or by machines in order to reach specified objectives.

THE PROCESS OF DESIGNING

1. Feasibility Study

A feasibility study must be a set of general

statements that in effect present the opinion of the investigator about whether anything useful can be accomplished by further work. It can indicate the general types of services the user expects to obtain from his system.

The results of a feasibility study provide the first statement of technical and managerial guidance to be used in making plans for subsequent design work.

2. Design Format

The format of the design itself require an analysis before it is determined. The first piece of information needed to select an appropriate format are the users to which the design is to be put. The designing format should be specified precisely. A clear format will significantly reduce the communication problem at all stages.

3. System Elements

Data : An information system provides information which is the essential function. Data must be according to system tasks and it must be expressed in a language which is common to the users and designers of the system.

Personnel : In an information system, people not only use the output but also form the component of the system. As the monitor of the system, they inject information and as the user, they use the information from the system.

Display : It refers to any presentation of data to people by means of equipment. Display form the major interface between the user and his system. Timeliness of the display has to do with the needs of the user. Information needs must be analyzed in the terms of time.

Equipments : Engineering units comprise to form equipment element. Equipments should be capable according to environmental conditions. These must be compatible with information system. Equipment should be reliable as reliability of data is a particular problem for information system because of the number and complexity of transformations to which they are subjected.

Retrieval : This element is responsible for organising and obtaining access to sets of data and it is a critical element of the information system.

4. User Requirements

In general, information system can have only following goals –

- To communicate
- To process data
- To control environment and resources.

But the design of any information system starts with the specified user requirements and explanation of proposals to achieve them. The user's resources in terms of time, money and adaptability also constraint the design.

If the design process is to be iterative, the statement of user's requirements, objectives and resources becomes a primary input to the decision on design contamination.

5. Determination of system task

System task should be determined considering the following questions:

- What are the tasks?
- Where and why is each task performed, and where are the resources which are manipulated?
- Who is to perform the tasks?
- How is each task performed?

An information system will usually be required to accomplish a number of these tasks. Any system designer may select the appropriate set for the particular system under consideration.

- Planning to obtain resources.
- Planning use of resources.
- Assessing the environment

- Assessing one's own resources
- Manipulating one's own resources
- Assessing system status
- Changing system status
- Interfacing with other systems
- Protecting the system's capability to accomplish its mission.

6. System Elements Requirements

When all the tasks are analyzed, each element is required to handle. The element must now be constructed so that it can perform actions. The element is required to "know" when it should start and stop operating and when it needs maintenance. Actually, mechanisms and procedures are required for activating the elements to accomplish the system tasks.

7. Integration of System Elements

All the elements must be integrated according to system requirement and correct designing.

8. Evaluation

At the end of design process, total design must be analysed to determine whether the system as specified can perform all the tasks assigned to it.

System Installation

Whom the system is designed, installation is to take place. Installation means the phase in which physical components of the system are placed in their operational environment and in conjunction with the user's personnel, both are readied for the assumption of operational responsibility. Now the system component operation begins but the starting and completion points of the installation phase for an information system are much less determinable than is generally realized by typical users and administrative agencies.

System installation phase can be divided into

following steps :

1. To instruct the users in the characteristics of the system.
2. Trial use of the system by the users in a given period.
3. Testing and verification of system design.
4. To detect and correct the errors found in system operations.
5. To develop the operational system capability.

When the system installation takes place, time spent in installation varies according to the nature of system, its size and complexity.

For any information system, this phase is the difficult phase as it has tremendous pressure on the developers to demonstrate that they have successfully met their commitment on schedule and users also go through the pressure of new system. At the same time, due to complexity a trouble-free installation is unknown.

Development Process Nature

An information system requires on-going maintenance if it is to be kept at maximum performance. However, the sophistication of computer and information technologies are such that a question remains as to the capability of the user to maintain an information system with an in-house staff after the system attains an acceptable operational performance level.

Evolutionary Development Strategy

It is recalled that a strategy of evolution in information system development calls for the installation of a low-cost, minimal operational configuration. A strategy of evolution means that a relatively small group of developers with the assistance of the user's in-house technical personnel can initiate the first modest operational system configuration. The initial operation of the system is not terminated by design in an evolutionary development strategy. Existing budgetary and financial management practices are incompatible with the concept of system evolution. These are based on traditional hardware development concepts, such as unchanging requirements, predetermined and fixed completion dates, and predetermined and fixed budgets.

Importance

Importance of installation phase can be restated as–

1. Testing and verification of system design concepts in an operational environment.
2. Accomplishment of psychological acceptance of the system by the user, and
3. The development of an operational capability.

Feed Back

Any minor or major improvement cannot be accomplished without the provision of formally defined procedures whereby the results of system tests, system evaluations and pre-operation excercises are transmitted from the users to the developers and feedback may require attention to procedures new design concepts.

System Testing

System testing refers to experimental measurement of system performance in a credible setting involving an adequately large complex of the new equipment, and data-processing facilities of the object system. So that the results can be used to make generalizations regarding current and future system effectiveness. System testing should serve as the empirical conscience of system design throughout the life cycle of the object system. When over-all system requirements are first drawn up, system testing should be part of the formal requirements and test support should be integrated into the operational features.

Once test performance results start coming in, the empirical data gradually replaces the educated guesses and systematically observed performance levels provide the groundwork for new hypothesis involving proposed design changes. At any point in time, the operational specifications should include the latest and most valid test performance results together with scheduled design changes and the hypothesized improvement in performance.

Useful and valid system performance measures are frequently hard to establish and may constitute a stumbling block for, system testing.

Methodology

The basic tools for system-testing may be subsumed under three generic categories : the collection and analysis of digital data, simulation, and experimental design.

The collection and analysis of digital data

Ideal digital data collection should fulfill following requirements :

1. Maximum capacity and flexibility
2. Reliability and economy
3. Regenerative capability

Simulation

Simulation as a basis for the test and development of man-machine and computer-based systems has had an erratic history. The close affinity between system testing and simulation follows the commonsense injunction that system testing should use the most realistic operational setting possible, within economic and time constraints. At any stage of simulation findings should be subjected to the empirical corrective of the next evolutionary level of testing.

Experimental Design

Experimental design is too often a neglected area. Experimental methods in computerized settings and associated statistical techniques are rarely recognized as essential tools requiring former indoctrination for personnel responsible for data processing and operational procedures in object systems. Experimental design indicates the close kinship between training and testing.

System Evaluation

It is desirable, if not almost inevitable, that the users of system themselves evaluate its operations. They do this some times formally, sometimes informally.

When we say that system evaluation is conducted, it is conducted essentially without the aid of system. If the system is going to be used in evaluation, the designer must consider the tasks associated with recording and evaluation on the same level as any other system task and must design the mechanisms for their accomplishment. These include, in computer-based information systems, additional data storage requirements, procedures for conducting both operational and evaluation programmes during the same period, the selection of tasks to be observed in actions and eventually the determination of evaluation criteria.

Management Problems in the Development Process

Developing the information system, problems arise as following:

1) The widespread lack of familiarity of managers and administrators with the development process for information systems;
2) The use of an irrelevant model of hardware system development for the management of the information system development process; and
3) The incompatibility between existing management organization and administrative procedures and the unique nature of the information system development process.

The major management problem areas which are the result of the less deterministic nature of information system and the contemporary information system state of the art may be listed as follows:

1. The identification of all software products to be acquired.
2. The types of specialized skills required to produce information system items.
3. The lack of a commonly accepted set of terms to identify information system items.
4. The problem of distinguishing between "research", "development" and "production" in the software development process.
5. The difficulty of establishing appropriate relationships and sequencing information system items among themselves and with related items so that an integrated system can be built.

REFERENCE

- Augero, C. and Conford, T. Developing Information Systems : Concepts, Issues and Practice, London : Macmillan, 1993.
- Bala Krishnan, N. Impact of Information Technology on Library Science. InMalwad, N.M. et. Al. (ed.). Digital Libraries (Papers Presented at the SIS'96). Bangalore. New Delhi : New Age International, 1996, pp.115-118.
- Becker, Joseph and Hayens, Robert M. Information Storage and Retrieval: Tools, Elements Theories. New York : John Wiley, 1967.
- The Blackwell Encyclopaedic Dictionary of Management Information Systems. Ed. By Davis, Gordon B. Oxford: Blackwell, 1999.
- Burch, J.G. and Strater, F.R. Information Systems : Theory and Practice. California : Hamilton, 1974.
- Hicks, James. Management Information Systems. 3rd ed. Minneapolis: West Publishing, 1993.
- Houghton, Berhard (ed.). Computer Based Information Retrieval System. London: Clive Bingley, 1968.
- Kashi Rao. V; Sheela Devi and Abraham, J. Role of Computers and Communication Technology. In Library and Information Science Management Environment (LISME) : Need for a Policy. In Chopra, M.S. (ed.). Library Information Technology in Modern Era : Libraries and Librarians in New

Millennium. New Delhi : Commonwealth, 1999.

- Lancaster, F.W. and Sandore, B. Technology and Management in Library and Information Services. London : Library Association, 1997.
- Kendall, Kenneth E. and Julie, E. System Analysis and Design. 6th ed. New Jersey: Prentice Hall, 2004.
- Mahapatra, P.K. and Chakrabarti, C. Redesigning the Library. New Delhi: Ess Ess, 1996.
- McLeod, Raymond and Schell, George. Management Information Systems. 8th ed. New Jersey : Prentice Hall International, 2000.
- Prakash Chander, New Technologies and Developments in Library and Information Science. Jaipur: Mangal, 1996.
- Sharma, C.K. Modern Library Systems. Agra : Y.K., 1990
- Viswanathan, C.G. Elements of Information Science and Technology. 2nd ed. Lucknow : Print House, 1986.
- Webber, D., and Pters, A. Integrated Library Systems: Planning, Selecting and Implementation. California : Libraries Unlimited, 2010.
- Woodall, Jack. Rebuck, K.O. and Voehs, F. Total Quality in Information System and Technology. New Delhi : Vanity, 1998.

9

Library Services and Computers

Library computerization needs to be implemented only after analysis and then designing the system. It varies from one library to another. Depending upon the requirements of each library, the necessary system is developed. This is what is known as System Analysis and Design (SAD).

System Analysis and Design (SAD)

Before computerizing the specific aspects of library and information services, there is need for identifying the areas of study, justification of the project, and factors relating to change.

Before a system is developed we should follow a life-cycle known as System Development Life Cycle (SDLC).

Analysis : In analysis we determine and define the problems and opportunities related to library and information system and organizational processes. System analysis is simply the work of analyzing systems.

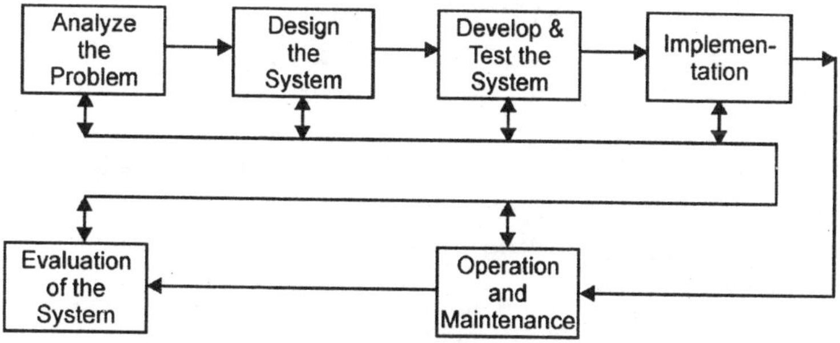

Fig. 32. System Development Life Cycle

To analyze means to study carefully seeking out the essential components, and to set down and describe the result of the work in an orderly and intelligible fashion. System analysis is concerned with methodology.

System analysis can be carried out by fact finding. Fact-finding begins at the analysis desk after a complete and thorough review of all the information that already exists about the area to be investigated. Several techniques are available to the analyst during fact finding including interviewing which provides the library staff who are going to use questionnaires which will help in the analysis of the system, and then the observation. Analysis is a very important step in the SDLC because it sets the platform for the appropriate system to be developed. Without system analysis there is danger of designing and implementing systems which do not meet the user's needs, because of lack of identification of the user's needs.

Designing : Designing of a system is done after the analysis. Designing involves the information outputs such as methods of outputting through paper, on screen catalogue (COM) which includes cassetted microfilm and microfiche of the latest output device like speech synthesizers. Inputs like structures programme language to be used and the necessary programme to be developed. Hardware and software aspects are also to be taken into consideration to support the information system.

Developing and Testing the System

After designing the input and output there is need for the system to be developed and then tested. The writing of software is necessary to support the system and test its accuracy. The testing of hardware and operating software is also done.

Implementation

Conversion of old system if any into the new system developed and providing the training and assistance to the user staff in the new system is also necessary. The implementation phase of a project covers the period from the acceptance of the tested design to its satisfactory supported by the appropriate users and operations manual.

Operating and Maintenance

System after being implemented has to be operated. If not it will become useless. The second aspect is that the system needs to be maintained, including correction of faults which arise during the operation of the system.

Evaluation

The last aspect of the life-cycle deals with the assessment of how well the system was developed and how well it operates.

The steps in the cycle are not necessarily discrete or a one-time process. Rather the SDLC can be iterative, evolutionary and overlapping. The cycle passes from one to another up to the last serially, but if any problem arises in the middle the system should be flexible.

Flow Charting

Flow charting is a diagrammatic representation of a logical solution to a problem. It is a pictorial representation of a sequence of instructions that uses boxes of different shapes. These boxes are connected by solid lines having arrow marks to indicate the flow of operation that is the exact sequence in which the instructions are to be executed. Generally an algorithm (sequence of instructions designed) is first represented in the form of a flow-chart and the flow-chart is then expressed in some programming language to prepare a computer programme. The advantage in this approach in programme writing is that while drawing a flow chart one is not concerned with the details of the elements of programming language, so he can fully concentrate on the logic of the procedure.

Since the flow chart is pictorial any error in the logic of the procedure can be detected more easily than in a programme.

Once the flow chart is ready the programmer can forget about the logic and can concentrate only on coding the operations in each box of the flow chart in terms of the statements of the programming language. This will ensure an error-free programme. Flow chart hence is a good tool to assist the programmer.

Flow Chart Symbols

Flow chart uses boxes of different shapes to denote different types of instructions. Only a few symbols are needed to indicate the necessary operations in a flow chart. These symbols have been standardized by the American National Standard Institute (ANSI). The symbols have their own function. Below are some of the symbols:

System Model for acquisition

Acquisition involves acquiring of library material for the sake of users. It includes selection and then location of the material and to procedure them.

The basic function of acquisition system includes receiving recommendation of items to be purchased and to ensure that they are not duplicated, preparing order notes to be sent to book sellers, claiming for the orders not sent by the book-sellers, accounts maintenance, accessioning facility and to update the statistics.

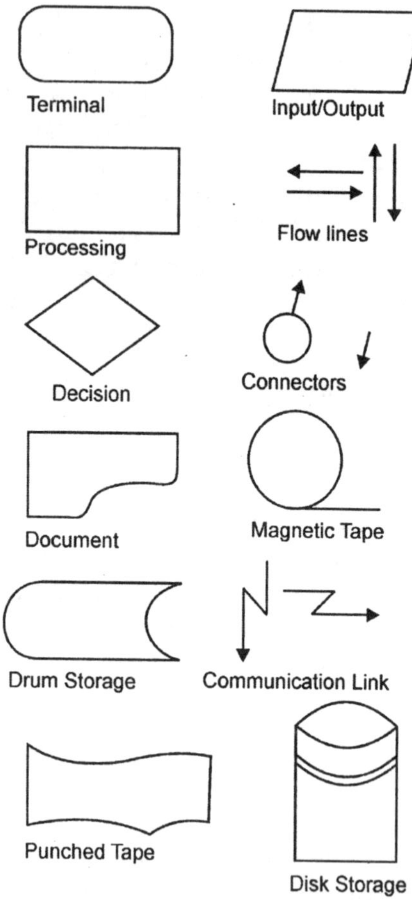

Fig. 33. Flow Chart Symbols

An ideal acquisition system which would be on-line must include:

- The ability to search via a variety of access points, the library's own Bibliographic file to determine the status (e.g. on order but not yet received) of any particular item.
- The ability to search a file of book-seller's details in a predetermined order, a performance to determine which book – seller would be able to supply a given item immediately or supply a given item at the lowest price.

- Access to status notes on all titles from all major book-sellers to see whether a given title is out of print not yet published or whatever the case may be.
- The ability for an authorized operator to place an order on on-line directly to the book seller and to adjust the library's financial files as appropriate.
- An item on order if available to be dispatched by the book seller within 24 hours and the book seller's inventory status to be adjusted.
- The ability to provide detailed financial information in a variety of ways.
- The capability of retrieving potentially useful titles from an external database which could be used for selection purposes within the library.
- The maintenance of a comprehensive file giving the library complete information of all items on order or in process and to alert the library staff when expected items do not arrive.
- The ability to deal with all the financial transactions and adjust the files accordingly.
- The ability to accommodate a variety of materials including monographs serials government documents. Blanket orders gift and exchange materials audio-visual materials etc.

In India due to the slow automation in library services and the book-sellers, there is still very little impact in the computerization of acquisition system.

Files : Various files are to be maintained to carry out the above functions. A file to store catalogue of the whole library. Order file containing elements like order number, requester supplier, discount offered, Performance etc., can be maintained in the supplier file.

With the help of the necessary files various programme modules are developed, by a large number of packages. But there is need for a system to be developed that is relevant to the particular library. Depending upon the acquisition section various files are developed. One file that is necessary is the vendor file which carries all the details of the vendor. Another one is the book request file which helps in the acquisition section for requesting of books. Accession file helps to find the holdings of the whole library and in a detailed manner. Accounts file contain all the details of money that is at the disposal for the acquisition section. The total amount of allocation for the year, amount to be spent on various materials like books, serials and other non-book materials and other items.

Many programmes are required to be developed for acquisition system depending upon the need of the library. But some programmes are common, like: A vendor file that gives details of the vendors such as their address code number, telephone numbers etc.

For all the files necessary programmes are developed and merged to get the requisite output.

Another programme which helps in the preparation of acquisition list from the order file.

One more programme that generates the account file and balance of amount from the order file and accession file.

VENDOR FILE

System for Cataloguing

Cataloguing according to Charles Ammi Cutter who wrote in 1876 should enable a person to find a book of which either the author, the title or the subject is known and to show what the library has by a given author or a given subject or in given kind of literature.

When developing a computer-based system it should be able to serve all the purposes similar to various catalogues. Computerized catalogue will minimize the

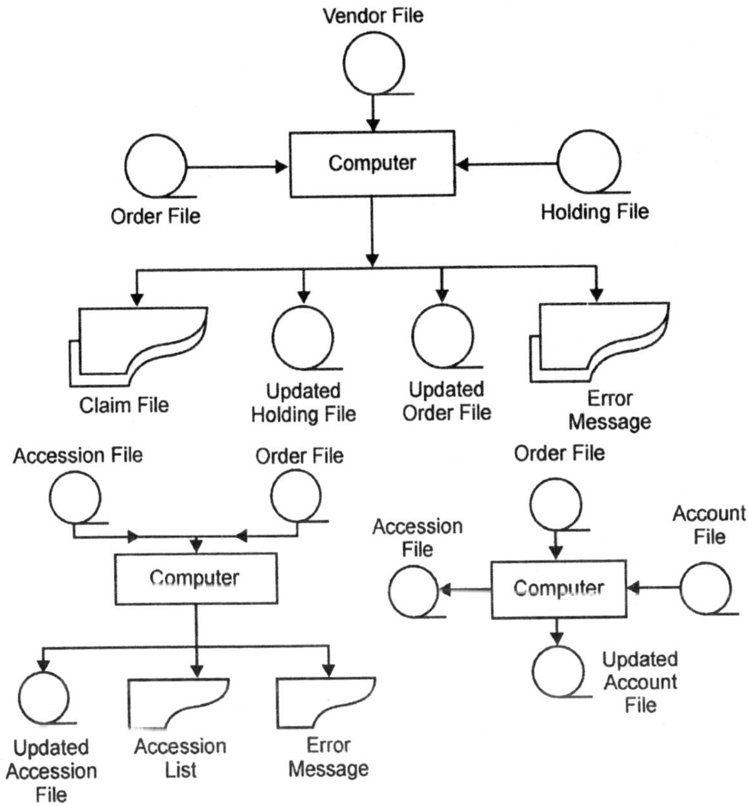

Fig. 34. Acquisition Flow Chart

labour intensiveness, time consumption, data entry etc. Book cards and spine labels can also be produced by computer.

MARC Project

A study by a panel of experts published in 1964 reported the feasibility of automation of its bibliographic processess and envisaged access to its content through computer consoles rather than through extensive card and book-form catalogues. The MARC (Machine – Readable Catalogue) that followed established and tested a standard format for exchange of bibliographic information in a machine readable form.

In the year 1967 a revised and advanced version of the MARC began to be used. The revised version is known as MARC II. In the same year the British National Bibliography began its work on the development of a MARC system in the United Kingdom.

MARC follows AACR-2. The entry contains author/title and LC subject headings and descriptive data. It also carries Library of Congress and Dewey Decimal Classification number and other identification numbers. Gradually several countries began developing their own MARC systems.

MARC Format is a standard format for the representation of bibliographic information in machine readable form. The MARC record involves three elements:

1. The record structure
2. The content designation
3. The data content of the record.

A MARC format is a set of codes and content designators defined for encoding a particular type of machine readable record. This format contains specifications for encoding data elements needed to describe retrieve and control various types of bibliographic materials. This format is extended to books serials, cartographic materials, music and audio visual materials.

Segment Control Word	Record Label	Director	Control Fields	Variable Data fields

Organization of the Record Structure

Segment Control Word (SCW) has the value of 0,1,2 or 3 as given under.

0 record begins and ends in this segment

1 record begins but does not end in this segment

2 record neither begins not ends in this segment

3 record ends but does begin in this segment.

The record label is a fixed of 24 bytes and information is held at fixed position within the field. The information content of each character position is given below

	Character Position
Record length	1-5
Record status	6
Implementation codes	7-10
Type of record	7
Class of record	8
Blanks	9-10
Indicator count	11
Subfield mark count	12
Base address of data	13-17
Encoding level	18
Blanks	19-20
Directory map	21-24
Length of data	21
Length of starting character Position	22
Blanks	23-24

Example of record label :

01543	n	a	m	tb	2	2	00205	f	ff	4	5	tt
1.5	6	7	8	9-10	11	12	13-17	18	19-20	21	22	23-24

Record length given in the character positions 1-5 is the length in characters, of the record label directory and all data fields including blanks, sub fields indicators etc.

Record status (character position 6) is maintained for file maintenance purposes like :

n - new record

c - changed record

d - deleted record

f - confirmed cataloguing in publication record

p - increase in encoding level

Implementation codes i.e., type of record (character position 7) like:

a - language material printed
b - language material manuscript
c - music printed
d - music manuscript
e - cartographic material printed
f - cartographic material, manuscripts
g - principal audio – visual media
h - microforms
i - sound recording non-musical
j - sound recording musical
k - Pictures designs and other two – dimensional representations
1 - machine readable data file
n - special instructional materials
0 - kits

Implementation codes : Class or record (Character position 9) like

a - analytic
c - collections
m - monograph
s - serial

Indicator count (Character position 11)

Subfield mark count (character position 12) is always a dollar sign.

Base address of data (Character position 13-17)

The base address of data in a typical example can be calculated as follows:

Record label	24 Characters (bytes)
21 Directory entries with 12 Characters each	252 characters (bytes)
Field terminator	1 Character (byte)
Total	277 Characters (bytes)

Directory

The directory is a sequence of data elements each consisting of 12 characters each. Each element refers to corresponding data field appearing in the record.

A directory entry comprises three parts.

Tag	Length	Starting	Character Position
1 3	4 7	8	11

Tag : A tag is a three digit code that defines the bibliographic function of the data field to which it applies.

Length of Data Field : This length is represented by 4-character positions which logically allows data field of up to 9999 characters of length

Starting Character Position (SCP)

The SCP is the displacement of the first character of the data field relative to the first character.

Every record contains a main record directory and related data fields. The directory terminator ends the director which may consist of single main record directory or a main directory followed by one or more sub-record directories.

Control Fields

Fields 001-009 are defined as control fields. Control fields have no indicators and no sub-fields.

Variable data fields : The variable data fields contain the bibliographic information. This includes:

- A full bibliographic description, together with main

entry headings as the one required by AACR-2.

- A set of subject data including Dewey Decimal Classification, Library of Congress Classification, Library of Congress Subject Heading and PRECIS subjects indexing information including identification of numbers (e.g. national bibliography numbers, alternative ISBNs) and codes identifying aspects of the item (e.g. language, physical material)

Dbase software package helps in the catalogue card production which is a tedious and time taking job for the library professionals. Catalogues should be in a position to print all record in data file, on screen viewing of individual records as and when necessary an option to print card sets to disk rather than to the printer of the screen and creation of a record which is on the same lines as that of MARC or MARC convertible record.

Systems for Serials Control

Serials include publications which are issued at regular intervals and intended to be continued indefinitely. Serials include journals newspapers, annual reports, advance or progress serials etc. Serial control system is complex because of a variety of publications, their frequency delay in publishing, supplements and various other constraints involved with the serials.

In order to design a system for serials control all these constraints are to be taken into consideration. Serials control monitoring system should be able to work in these areas:

- Monitoring periodical receipts of whether they are being received in time or not
- To keep track of subscription of renewal warning.
- Reminders to vendors for issues overdue/not received.
- To give a list of duplicate missing and special issues.
- About bound volume areas.

- To process the various important articles.
- Circulation of serials.
- Bindery management.

Preparation of various lists like

- List of periodicals received/cancelled during a specified period.
- List of journals subscribed/exchange/gift
- List of holdings (with their status on shelf, binding, circulation etc.) by subject, title etc.
- Keeping track of the amount spent on subscription, binding etc.
- Estimation of the budget for the next academic/ financial year
- Menu driven which should be user friendly.
- Flexible in nature

Files

Following files may need to be maintained to carry out these functions:

1. **Master file :** Bibliographic description of all titles held in the library collection (current, cancelled, stopped etc.)
2. **Order file :** Order details of journals newly subscribed/renwed.
3. **Account file :** Available funds, committed funds, money spent, etc. (subjectwise).
4. **Master holding file :** Holding details in summarized format of back volumes in the library
5. **Supplier file :** Details of vendors/agents/publishers
6. **Receipt file :** Receipt of current issues as and when received
7. **Exchange file :** Detail of journals received on exchange
8. **Index file :** Appropriate index files for fast searching

by approach elements like subject, title, term, ISSN etc.

An automated serials system may need the following programmes:

- Serials data input/modify
- Order processing
- Reminder processing
- Receipt
- Query (catalogue search, order status, holdings)
- Report generation

Special libraries are predominantly using these computer-based serial control systems as compared to the academic and public libraries. Computers were first used to assist in the 1960s with most of them based on batch-processed and using punched cards. But some libraries have started using on-line and real time systems for the serial control which helped in faster development of these areas.

A vendor file that gives details of the vendor similar to the acquisition system.

Flow Chart

Necessary programmes are developed and merged to get the necessary output.

Another programme is to process the order file which helps in the sending of reminders for the serials not received and to send claim notices.

System for Circulation

Circulation is an activity that is concerned with the personal contact of the library staff with the users through a system to give away the materials available in the library. It includes both charging and discharging of books. Computers are being used for circulation purposes in the US since 1960s and in the UK in late 1960s.

Computer based circulation systems are used only

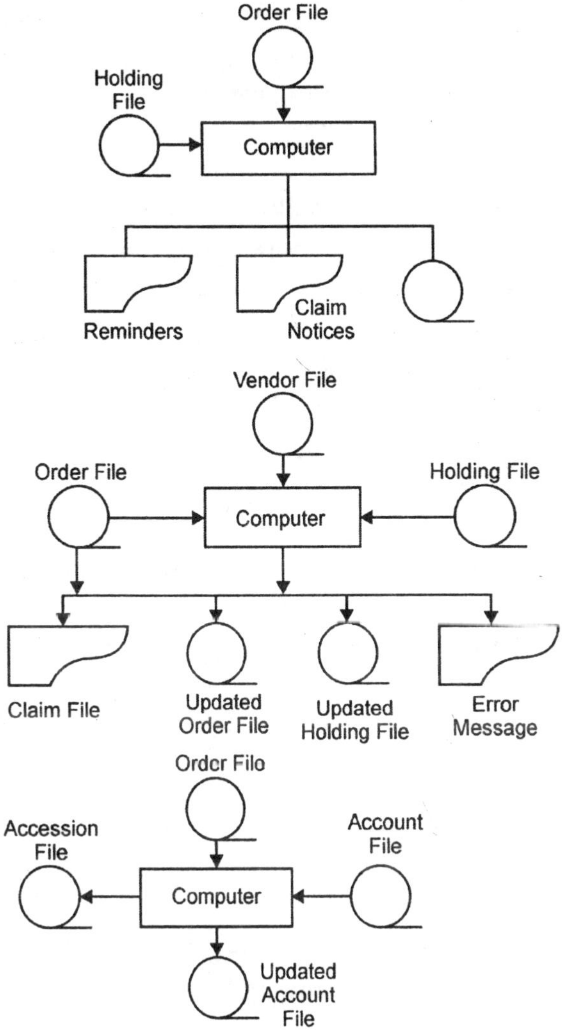

Fig. 35. Accounts Flow Chart

in libraries where the charging of book is very large. But small libraries also started using the computers to improve efficiency and better service to users.

Circulation

Manual Circulation system are typically routine in nature with a high degree of labour involvement. It is mainly concerned with the clerical function of keeping track of documents taken out of the library by the user i.e. charging & discharging overdue control records and associated file maintenance activities.

Some of the tasks, an automated circulation system can carry out, are given below:

- Recording the issue & return of book.
- Preparing of overdues & recall notices.
- Updating the record file.
- Reservation of books and maintenance of inter-library loan about a borrower.
- Searching the borrower record to find information about a borrower.
- Maintenance of statistics regarding the number of books issued returned and in other variety of forms.
- Provision for printing due date slips automatically, generating orders for lost books or addition copies and printing mailing labels for remote borrowers.

Circulation system are designed to record and manipulate the following kinds of information:

(a) Information about borrower name, address, telephone no. identification no., category etc.

(b) Information about the document (call no., identification no. etc.)

(c) Information about the transaction (due date, date or loan or time of loan etc.)

The important files to be maintained by an automated circulation system are user file, issue file, return file and reservation file.

(i) User File : It stores details of all eligible borrowers of a library including number of books permitted to be borrowed, period of loan etc.

(ii) Issue File : It will store details of books currently on issue. For charging an item, the Patron Identification

Number (Pin) and Document Identification Number (DIN) are identified to the system (through OCR or by some other means which are eventually validated by the system for their correctness.)

(iii) Return File : It is essentially an archival file containing details of returned documents. As in case of charging even in discharging the PIN and DIN are identified to the system. System automatically generates files of overdue charge also.

(iv) Reservation File : It contains details of the documents and borrowers who have placed their claims for them. It is usually practices in libraries to maintain the holds queue on first come first serve basis.

Upon the discharge of an item, the system should produce a notice to be sent to the patron at the head of the queue. If the patron does not claim the item within specified time the system should automatically send the notice to the next patron in the queue.

Methods of Inputting Identification Numbers

Patron Identification Number (PIN) : To have effective circulation control system each member of a given library must be assigned an individual number. It is known as Patron Identification Number (PIN). It can be any one of the following:

(a) Roll number or registered numbers assigned by the library.

(b) Social security or insurance number, if any.

(c) Name.

Document Identification Number (DIN) : Every document of a given library must be assigned an individual number. It is known as Document Identification Number (PIN). It can be any one of the following :

(a) Call Number

(b) Accession Number or ISBN

(c) Serial Number (when is different from Accession No.)

(d) Any other code such as author, title code.

The early batch processing off-line system gave away to real-processing turn key and on-line systems. Several new devices started to be experimented in circulation control like, pens, wards etc.

The circulation is mainly based on the processing system. If we have a batch processing system, the processing is done in a batch mode with records of items issued and dispatched being recorded on to the paper tape or magnetic tape and then processed in the evening. The drawback with this is the reserved materials cannot be tracked so currently. The other available systems are turn key systems, which are on-line and real time. Turn key system is a system where the hardware and soft ware are supplied as an integrated package, with on line and real time as soon as an item is issued or returned the relevant files are instantly updated and the most current information is immediately available.

There is need for large number of files which has to be maintained like document which has the details of the documents of holdings of the library, user file which has the details of the members, reservation file where the members reserve a document of their interest etc.

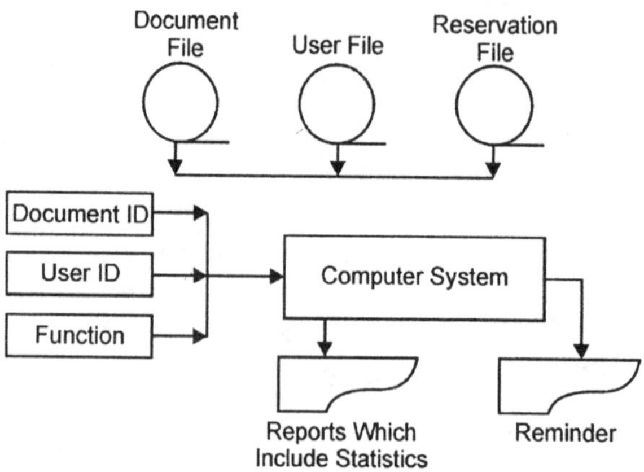

Fig. 36. Flow Chart for Circulation

Common Communication Format (CCF)

It is the ordered or standard form for creating bibliographic records and also for dissemination of exchanging of records between two or more organizations. In April 1978 there was UNESCO General Information Programme (UNESCO-PGI) on International Symposium on Bibliographic Exchange Formats held at Taormina, Sicily; after the Symposium and result was that UNESCO-PGI had created an ad hoc group for the establishment and maintenance of Common Communication Format and first edition of CCF was published under the editorialship of Peter Simmons and Alan Hopkins in 1984 and its second edition was published in 1988 with two volumes these are CCF/B and CCF/F and after that many countries have started creating and sharing their bibliographic records in CCF format. It was the execution of ISO-2709 and contains following structure:

a) **Record levels :** every CCF structure begins with 24 character fixed record label, which contains data elements.

b) **Directory :** Directory contains tables of variables of 14 characters entries.

c) **Datafields :** it contains of Indicators, Subfield Identifier and Datafields Separator.

d) **Record Separator :** the record separator is the final character of the CCF record.

The CCF was designed to provide structural format for three major purpose, these are as follows :

a) To provide accessibility for the exchange of bibliographic information among the group of information agencies.

b) To permit the use of single computer software for the creation and dissemination of bibliographic information among the various information agencies.

c) Acts as a standard for sharing of Bibliographic information with internationally accepted structured format.

Radio Frequency Identification Device (RFID)

Radio Frequency Identification Device (RFID) is the very fast growing technology for increasing efficiency of any organization. It is one of Automatic Identification Devices (Auto ID) such as Bar Code, Magnetic Tapes, Smat Cards, Biometrics, etc. which automatically identify objects. RFID were successfully opted by many libraries and using it for many reasons, some of them are: for document security, circulation, time saving, error free, reduces manpower, self check-out and check-in, etc. libraries began using RFID technology to replace their magnetic tapes and bar code systems in late 1990s.

Components of RFID

- Tags
- Antenna
- Reader
- Server

Tags

RFID tags are the heart of any RFID system, which can be fixed inside a book's back cover or directly on it. Each paper thin tags contain an engraved antenna and a microchip with a capacity of at least 64 bits which stores bibliographic information. There are mainly three types of tags: "read only" "WORM" and read/write tags.

Antenna

An antenna produces radio signals to activate the tag and read and write data to it. An antenna acts as a channel between the tags and the reader which control the systems data acquisition and communication. The electromagnetic field produced by an antenna can be constantly present when multiple tags are expected continuously. The RFID antennas connected to the readers emit power and data from the server and to the tags.

Reader

RFID readers are composed of a radio frequency module, a control unit and an antenna to interrogate electronics tags via radio frequency communication. The reader power an antenna to generate an radio frequency (RF) field. When a tag passes through the field, the information stored on the chip in the tag is interpreted by the reader and sent to the server, which in turn communicates with the integrated library system.

Server

The server is the important part of any RFID system. It acts as a communication gateway among the various components of RFID system. It receives information from one or more of the readers and exchanges information with the circulation database. It includcs a transaction database so that reports can be produced link between the computer and your library automation system.

Advantages

1. Self issue return : The use of RFID reduces the amount of time required to perform circulation operations. It facilitates self circulation. Information can be read from RFID tags which are much faster than barcodes.

2. High speed inventorying : An advantage of RFID systems is their ability to scan library books on the shelves without removing them. A hand-handled inventory reader can be moved rapidly across a shelf of books to read all of the unique identification. Using wireless technology it is possible not only to update the inventory but also to identify items which are out of proper order.

3. More security : It provides more enhanced security system to library sources with real time monitoring system. It has an interface between the exit sensors and the circulation system to identify the items moving out of the library.

4. Less manpower needed : It automates library systems which enhance library working and services which ultimately reduces man power and error free work.

5. Increase in staff productivity : With the help of automated library system the productivity of staff were increased.

6. Reduce repetitive jobs : Eliminate respective works by automating the library and its services.

7. Less staff injures : With the help of RFID system it reduce the repetitive stress injuries caused by sustained and repetitive motion mainly connected to circulation duties especially.

Disadvantages

1. High Initial Cost : The major disadvantage of RFID technology is its initial cost. As we all know that libraries are the non profit making organizations which are fully depending on their parent institution for funding so it's very difficult for the libraries to collect such amount and adopt RFID technique.

2. Accessibility to compromise : It is possible to compromise an RFID system by wrapping the protected material two to three layers of ordinary household foil to block the radio signal.

3. Removal of exposed tags : RFID tags are typically affixed to the inside back cover and are exposed for removal. This means that there would be problems when users become more familiar with the role of the tags. In Indian libraries it is a major challenge to keep the tags intact.

4. Exit gate sensors : While the short range readers used for circulation charge and discharge and inventory appear to read the tags 100 per cent of the time the performance of the exit gate sensors is more problematic.

5. Reader Collision : The signal form one reader can interface with the signal from another where coverage overlaps. This is called reader collision. On the way to avoid the problem is to use a technique called time division multiple accesses.

6. Tag collision : Another problem readers have is reading a lot of chips in the same field. Tag clash occurs when more than one chip reflects back a signal at the same time which confuses reader.

7. Lack of standard : The tags are used by library RFID vendors are not compatible even when they conforms to the same standards because the current standards only seek electronic compability between tags and readers.

Management Information System

Library managers need to prepare budgets, account, large number of reports etc. Therefore the statistical information needs to be collected and presented.

Word Processor Packages

There are various sophisticated packages available nowadays for every maker of a microcomputer. At the bottom of the range word processors may offer basic facilities like storage and production of standard documents to which minor changes are made, draft, documents which can quickly and easily be amended, lists catalogues etc. which are amended at intervals.

The top word processors like Word Perfect come close to desktop publishing in the function which they provide. Depending upon the requirements, library managers can choose wide range of packages that are available.

Desktop Publishing

Desktop Publishing (DTP) is a new microcomputer users package. It is possible to produce documents in a professional way with appropriate hardware and software. Word processors, spread sheets and data base packages are therefore an essential part of DTP. Depending precisely on what has to be printed the field of DTP is normally associated with microcomputers rather than mini- or mainframes.

DTP more normally is associated with (WYSIWYG) what you see is that you get approach. What you see on the screen is what you get in print.

Accounts and statistics

Daily accounts are maintained which is a routine task. Spending of money is done which has to be accounted for. For this necessary software packages can be used. Spread sheet package like Lotus 1-2-3 can be very good for account and statistics. Statistics help the manager to plan the future taking the past into account. Spread sheet is an alternative method for statistical analysis and administering its budget.

Spread sheet programme consists for matrix of boxes on cells into which the user enters data . They allow to present graphs, bars, diagrams, etc.

REFERENCES

- Adams, R. Information Technology and Libraries : A Future for Academic Libraries. London : Chapman and Hall, 1986.
- Boss, R.W. Library Manager's Guide to Automation. 2nd ed. New York : Knowledge Industry, 1984.
- Burton, Paul F. and Patrice, J. Howard. Information management Technology : A Librarian's Guide. London : Chapman and Hall, 1991.
- Daniels, A. and Yeats, D. Basic System Analysis. London : ELBS, 1992.
- Hunter, E.J. Computerized Cataloguing. London : Bingley, 1985.
- Kochar, R.S. Library Automation: Issues and Principles. New Delhi: APH Publishig, 2007.
- Kumar, P.S.G. Computerisation of Indian Libraries. New Delhi : B.R. publishing, 1987.
- Lauden, Kenneth C. and Lauden, Jane Price. Management Information System : A Contemporary Perspective. New York:

Macmillan, 1988.

- Lancuster, F.W. Problems and Failures in Library Administration. New York: Read Books, 2008.
- Rowley, J.E. Computer for Libraries. 2nd ed. London : Bingley, 1985.
- Tedd, Lucy A. An Introduction to Computer Based Library System. 2nd ed. London : John Wiley, 1985.
- Vashisth, C.P. (ed). Computerisation and Library Networks. Delhi : ILA, 1991.
- Wilson, K. Computers in Libraries: an Introduction for Library Technicians. New York: Haworth, 2006.

10

Information Services and Computers

Information is heard and seen everywhere. One is puzzled to which information is relevant and which is irrelevant. Information useful to one is useless to another and vice-versa. There is information explosion or boom taking place these days. Providing the useful information to the user is information service. The two words, data and information are often confused. Data is unorganized piece of information while information is something that is organized.

The need for information is multidimensional. There is need for it in education and research. Students need it to pass their examinations. Teachers need it to impart education. Researchers are the maximum consumers of information. Similarly professionals like medicos, lawyers, engineers, managers, executives, bureaucrats, need current information to update themselves in pursuing their professions.

Depending upon the need information services are offered by libraries. Due to the bulk of information being generated and used by the people there is need for computers to be used for the information services.

Computerization of information services can be utilized by the users of the library. In house information storage and retrieval system can be developed which is limited to the resources available in the library. Computers can be put to use for having access to the external databases on on-line or buying a database and use it for library purpose.

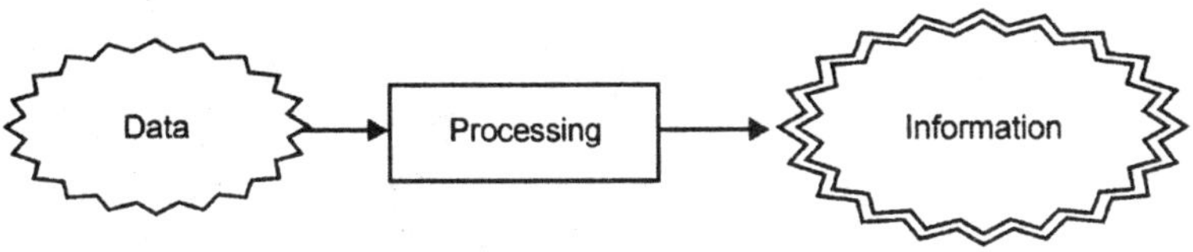

Fig. 37. Transformation of Data

Creating a local database inside the library serves many purposes. Local database may be developed, for e.g., for the doctors, lawyers, engineers, managers, executives, etc. of a particular area. This kind of local database helps in many ways to the users. Public libraries can develop such types of databases. Depending upon the various constraints and requirements numerous options are available to the designers and implementers of local information retrieval systems.

Current Awareness Services (CAS)

People who use information can be made aware of their surroundings by a variety of ways like personal contacts, telephone calls etc. Library and information staff tried different approaches to keep their users abreast about the latest developments like production of information bulletin, running on SDI (Selective Dissemination of Information) service and producing evaluating reports.

Due to the information explosion and the volume of scientific and technical information being generated it cannot be traced by the individuals easily. There are many reasons for this, first, due to the rate of new information coming out in the market and secondly due to interdisciplinary nature of information and thirdly the information started coming in a variety of documents and formats.

Straues et. al. defines "current awareness as the establishment of the system for reviewing publication immediately upon receipt, selecting information pertinent to the programmes, of the organization served, and recording individual items to be brought to the attention of those persons to whose work they are related. It involves a combination of processes including the selection of pertinent information from periodicals, books, pamphlets, patents, reports in fact, anything of serious content that is received".

Current awareness service is usually in the form of a publication which is confined mostly in a particular subject area and sometimes to the related areas. Services help the users to abreast themselves about the recent or latest developments in their areas of interest.

Different types of current awareness services commonly practiced are contacts by journal service which duplicates the contents of journals in a broad subject area e.g. physical sciences. In a library, say a public library, the services may be restricted itself to the journals subscribed by the library. Another type of service is research-in-progress-bulletins, which implies that whatever research is in progress it is published in the form of bulletins. This will appraise the scientific personnel about the research in their field of interest. Newspaper clipping service is another type of current awareness services. The above services are all done manually.

Selective Dissemination of Information (SDI)

Computers, making advent in the 1950s, started to be used by the current awareness services also. Hans

Peter Luhn, a computer scientist in 1961 proposed a project to use it in current awareness service.

H.P. Luhn defined SDI service as "that service within an organization which concerns itself with the channeling of new items of information, from whatever source, to those points within the organization where the probability of usefulness in connection with current work or interests is high.

Luhn's system has the following features as described in his definition of SDI:

1. To channel the new information irrespective of the source to user.
2. Matching of user profiles with the new documents of information.
3. Usefulness of information is the objective of SDI to the organization which should be treated at high priority.
4. The necessary feedback is taken to update and modify.

SDI service has four phases, namely, selection, notification, feedback and modification. Selection phase includes the input of the SDI system consisting of profiles of users interest, usually produced by librarians or information scientists and the documents descriptions which are generally indexed. The vocabulary of both these profiles need to be on the same lines so that matching becomes easy and accurate. Notification includes the items selected for an individual user to be notified. Feedback is an important part of SDI system because it helps the library or information centre to analyze the answer of the user and to ensure their system working. The last phase is the modification, it can be changed in the interest of the user or the changes that are done after the feedback from the user. Feedback and modification are the ones which make SDI system unique, as compared to the other current awareness services.

SDI which started as a service for only a particular organization has changed these years to a versatile service in the information dissemination. H.P. Luhn's definition of SDI needs to be changed taking the present developments in the current awareness services.

Components of SDI System

(i) User profile or search profile : A user profile is a list of terms which collectively characterizes the technical & scientific interest of an individual group or an organization. The profile generally consists of keyterms which reflect individual interest. They are organized by logical relations.

(ii) Document profile : A file of computer readable bibliographic records which could be searched with reference to specific criteria laid down by the user of the system.

(iii) Computer system (Hardware) : In the earlier stages computers were costly and not available at an affordable price for libraries and information units. Therefore they tried to utilize computer facility available elsewhere on a rental or sharing basis. But now a days most of the medium sized libraries have their own in-house dedicated system.

(iv) Software : There are two alternative approaches, the first one to develop inhouse software. The second is to identify commercially available package which can be run on in-house computer system.

(v) User – SDI System Inter-face : It is the junction between the user and the SDI system.

(a) ***Notification*** **:** When there is close match between the terms in user profile and the terms in document profile the details of the document matched are usually sent to the user. This is called as notification or output.

(b) ***Feedback*** **:** Feedback is an instrument of response which is provided alongwith the notification and is used by the recipient of notification to inform his opinion or reactions to the information centre.

(c) ***Modification*** : The profile of the users can be modified by the information centre depending upon the feedback.

Document Delivery : Use of full text CD-ROM ensures supply of full text of references immediately after the receipt of request by the user.

Translation Facilities : As and when a request is made for translations, document delivery section will take up the work, thus solving the problem of foreign language.

Evaluation of the SDI System : Once implemented the information system should be evaluated at periodical intervals. The evaluation process compares the operational system with the design goals and objectives.

User profile construction is the most important part of the SDI system. It involves the user to be asked to give his needs. Then, the user is asked to give the list of title of his interest and organizations in whose work he is interested, etc. In addition to the above interests he is also asked whether he wants the information to be broad or specific. All the above information helps in the construction of user profile. This makes SDI service a different one as compared to the other current awareness services.

User of SDI service is requested to fill in a questionnaire containing all the above information with the help of which user profiles are constructed.

The user profile is similar to a mathematical expression with user Boolean operators AND, OR and NOT.

The expression A and B means a set that contains elements of both A and B.

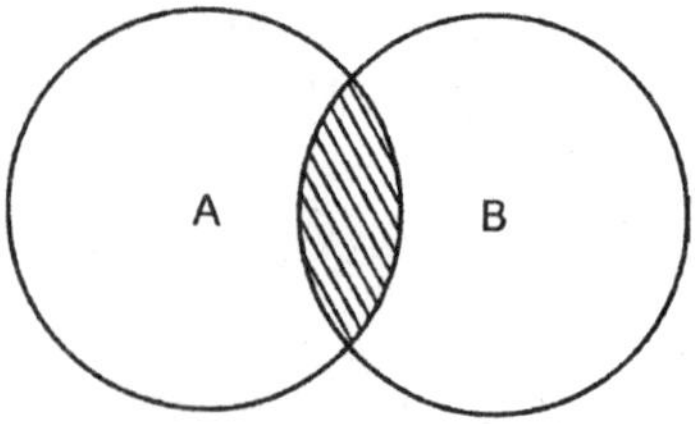

Fig. 38. A and B

The expression A or B means a set that contains elements of A only, B only or both A and B.

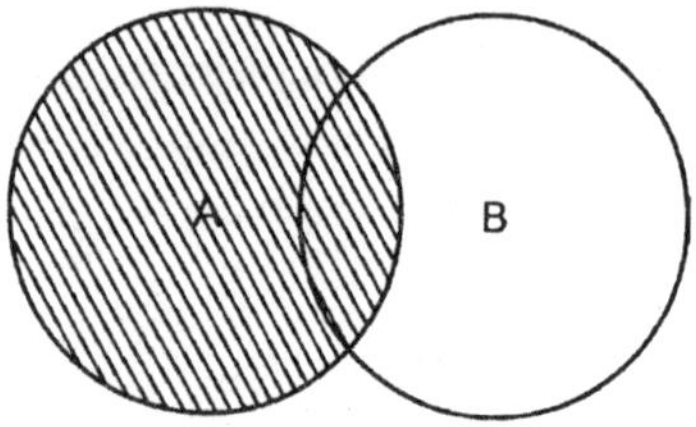

Fig. 39. A or B

The expression A not B means a set that contains elements of A which are also not elements of B.

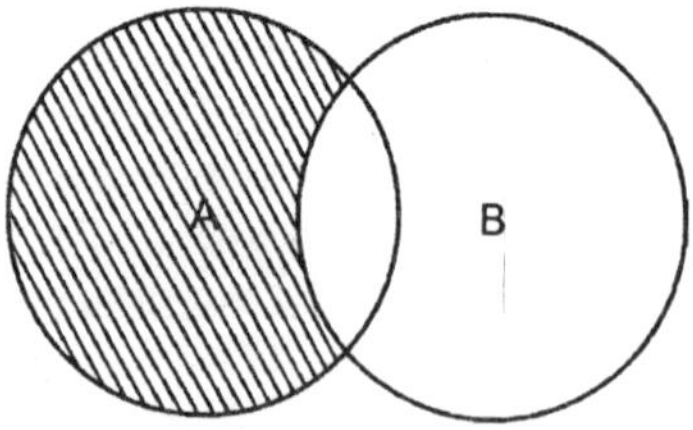

Fig. 40. A or B

With the help of the above operators it is possible to build user profiles accurately as an expression.

With the advent of computers the SDI services are being computerized. The following are the different types of computerized SDI services.

(a) Batch SDI : Batch SDI : Batch SDI is also known by the term offline SDI. Here, the operator or the staff of the information centre searches on behalf of the user. The requirements of many users are combined together in 'batches' and the database is searched. The processing time is minimized in this type of SDI service.

(b) Online SDI : Online search programmes make use of inverted files which provide direct access to any portion of the file. This provides case of access similar to the opening of the dictionary in the portion of the book that contains the entry. The inverted file structure is useful in an interactive multiple user searching.

(c) CD-ROM Based SDI : CD-ROM have more storage capacity. With such a storage capacity and rapid retrieval, the optical disc storage technology has tremendous impact on libraries. The total number of databases available on CD-ROMs are increasing rapidly. Around 60% of the databases have abstracts, 30% contain reference information and 10% are full text databases.

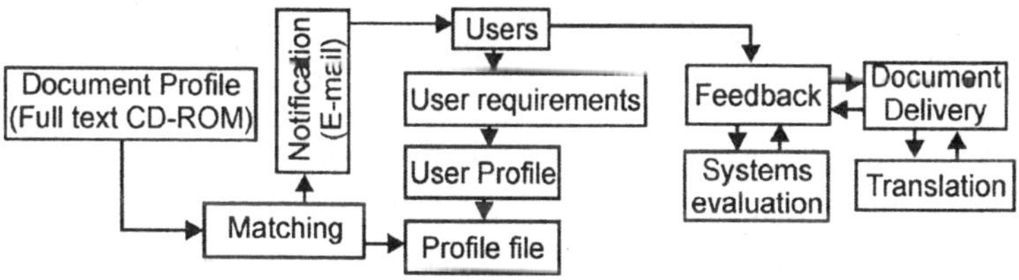

Fig. 41. Schematic diagram showing the model SDI system

SDI has changed since its inception in 1950s. The age now is of computer-readable document databases available in the market. Organizations can subscribe to these databases and then install a SDI system. This helps in the learning of research work done elsewhere by any information scientist. Buying a database is an expensive affair, but this is feasible for an organization having large number of users. The information dissemination centres started functioning particularly in USA and then with on-line vending of these information dissemination centres cater to others. Thus, enabling users to have access to these centres via telephone lines in a conversational way. The searching capacities have become instantaneous rather than taking days or even months in some cases. One more development is that, if a user gives a profile of his to the centre and then the centre after matching his profile with the database and the output is sent to him regularly.

Information Systems

Information systems are systems which are developed for a specific purpose. They may be in a broad field like life sciences or in a narrow field like toxicology. Here the emphasis is on specificity. Irrespective of the source of information databases of the field of interest are developed and are put to use by on-line, off-line or by buying the databases on popular CD-ROMs. The necessary information is searched by the users through communication channels and feedback is given to the producers.

The advent of computer in information processing has made it possible to develop international information systems. The central agency or the phases where the main centre is present acts as a receiving point of information from all the member countries, where processing is done and the processed information is distributed to the users. Taking this concept IAEA is the first one to have succeeded in its attempt to develop Global information system called INIS in the field of Nuclear Science.

INIS : In 1970, sponsored by the International Atomic Energy Agency, Vienna, INIS was launched. The member states participating in the cooperative venture contributed their share to the central-pool in Vienna.

The salient features of INIS are :

1. Information retrieval system is international in nature and it includes all the nations who are usually advanced in nuclear capability.
2. There is proper communication channel between member-states and central agency and hence it is cooperative in venture.

3. The system is more for decentralization than centralization.
4. The member states need to follow standard rules while preparing their input of information.

INIS Operation : Each participating country has a designated centre which is responsible for identification and selection of documents published within their country and for the preparation of bibliography in a standard format. This input is sent to the headquarters at Vienna, where INIS has its own thesaurus for subject indexing. The input is checked, corrected and transferred into machine-readable form. There are various products of INIS (given below) which can be obtained by the participating countries.

- NIS magnetic tape
- Atomindex
- Cumulative index
- INIS on-line service
- INIS non conventional literature on microfiche.

The processed information at thc INIS is distributed in all the above forms.

INIS magnetic tape can be had from INIS by the participating countries. This is prepared from the necessary input provided by the member countries.

INIS Atomindex is an announcement and abstract journal which is bimonthly. It contains personal author index, corporate entry index, subject index, conference index and other indexes.

Cumulative index is issued twice a year consisting of five parts.

INIS literature comes out both in conventional documents through normal channel and non-conventional literature in microfiche.

The member countries can have access to the INIS on on-line directly.

India is a participant in the INIS since the beginning. The Library and Information Service at Bhabha Atomic Research Centre, Mumbai is the national centre responsible for INIS activities. Thus, the Indian nuclear scientists are having access to the world nuclear science literature.

AGRIS : Information system on Agricultural Science and Technology was developed on the lines of INIS. This became operational from 1975. This system was sponsored by the Food and Agricultural Organisation of UN. Like INIS this is also a cooperative venture. The participating countries are about 114 in number and with 14 international institutions.

AGRIS Operation : AGRIS operates very much similar to INIS. Each member country has a centre which collects the information on Agricultural Sciences and Technology and then that information is processed and distributed in various forms to the participating countries. AGRIS products are given below:

- AGRINDEX
- Agris tapes
- Cumulative indexes

Both the AGRINDEX and AGRIS tapes are monthly containing detailed bibliographical information of the documents in Agricultural Sciences and Technology. Abstracts of AGRIS are available on magnetic tapes and microfiche.

Agricultural Research Information Centre of ICAR acts as the national centre for India. About 3,500 bibliographical entries are passed onto AGRIS database as Indian input every year. This centre receives AGRIS magnetic tape updated every month. A computerized SDI service is operational at this centre which has around 200 profiles.

United Nations Educational Scientific and Cultural

Organization (UNESCO) Science and Technology Policy Programme

UNESCO was established in 1946 which is a specialized agency of United Nations concerned with the information needs. Its main objectives at the time of its origin was to encourage intellectual cooperation among the members nations, increase the growth and development of member nations, promote peace, human rights and cultural cooperation. It provides assistance to member's nations to rebuild their libraries destroyed during world war-II and its continuing effort for the development and growth of Documentation, Libraries and Archives of the member's nations.

With rapid growth and development of Information Communication Technology it's very difficult for libraries to adopt new trends and technology with this in view UNESCO has started Communication and Information Sector in 1990, its main aims are:

1. Universally accessibility of Information or Ideas.
2. Accessibility to Information Communication Tcchnology for all.
3. Promote the cultural diversity in the world of information networks.
4. It provides financial assistance to many national and international projects.

There are many information Networks of UNESCO, some of them are:

1. MEDLIB-Internet Based Virtual Library
2. APIN – Asia and Pacific Information Network
3. JOUNET – Global Network for Education in Journalism
4. UNAL –UNESCO network of Associated Libraries
5. NFOYOUTH – International Information and Data Exchange Network on Youth

UNESCO Intergovernmental Programmes

Presently UNESCO runs two programmes in the field of information and communication, these are:

1. Information for all : It acts as a platform, for planning and Implementation of :

a) Conservation and Preservation of Information.

b) Universally accessibility of Information.

c) Contribution of entire member Nations in the creation of new knowledge and its effective and efficient Dissemination.

d) It promotes common strategies, methods, tools for building of Information Society and;

e) Education for all.

2. International Programmes for the development of Communication (IPDC) : The main aim of IPDC is to promote media pluralistic and growth and developments in the modes of media in the developing countries, because media play a very vital role for the growth and development of any nation. It gives assistance to the projects which enhance press or media freedom and pluralism, development of community media, etc. it provides guarantee every people to express their views without exclusion and discrimination.

National Institute of Science Communication and Information Resources (NISCAIR)

Formerly known as Indian National Scientific Documentation Centre (INSDOC) it is a body of CSIR and it was established with the support of UNESCO in 1952 for providing information related to science and technology for any users of India with following objectives:

a) To collect and disseminate all the scientific periodicals which may be useful for the country.

b) Reference services to their users.

c) Informs intellectuals regarding to their information needs.

d) Provides photocopies facilities to the Country Scientists which they need information.

e) Translates foreign scientific materials which are available in other languages.

f) Acts as a repository of published and unpublished materials.

g) Acts as a medium through which the worker of the nation to be known to the rest of the globe.

In September 2002 INSDOC merged with National Institute of Science Communication (NISCOM), another body of CSIR and renamed as National Institute of Science Communication and Information Resources (NISCAIR). The main objective of NISCAIR is to collect and disseminate information from the different institutions of the nations and foreign nations.

Main activities of NISCAIR :

a) Publications of various Scientific/Research Journals

b) Publication of various scientific Books and Magazines.

c) Publication of CSIR News and CSIR Samachar.

d) Collection of Published and non-published scientific materials.

e) Information collection and dissemination services.

f) Creation and maintenance of different databases.

g) E-Publishing such as Indian Science Abstracts, Medicinal and Aromatic Plants Abstracts, the Wealth of India, Raw Materials Series, etc.

h) Human Resource Development such as Training Programmes, orientation courses, etc.

i) Consultancy services which includes design, development and automation of libraries, editing, designing and printing of publications

j) Financial Assistances.

k) Literature search services, content abstract and reprographic services.

l) It is national center for assigning ISSN number for those serials which are published in India.

User Education : Microcomputer is being used for user education in a large number of libraries and information science departments. The user education uses computer-aided learning as an application. Different methods are used for users education within library and information schools. In some a preliminary course of interaction is given and then reinforced by suitable software which assesses how much the student has learned and retained. In other cases, instruction is provided by the programme with or without relevant questions. Such programme can be used as a refresher course or a specific course of instruction programme can be developed in-house to suit particular applications. Department of Information Science, University of Strathclyde used dBase to provide computer-aided learning programme, leading on from the general to the specific area.

Expert systems are being used in the user education in LIS and the computerized libraries. Expert system shells are a potentially useful tool, since they can be built with advice and help screens with relatively little difficulty, and can also monitor the user's progress through the various parts.

The library of the University of Waterloo in Ontario has developed a system to simulate the services of a reference librarian, primarily using expert system techniques. The various modules provide advice and instructions on query negotiation (clarifying what the user wants), use of specific reference tools, classroom instruction on library techniques.

These packages or expert system techniques help in the reference queries to be answerable at a faster rate as most of the queries are simple, but numerous are time consuming.

REFERENCES

- Bunch,Allen. The Basics of Information Work. London : Bingley, 1984.
- Brown – Syed C. Parents of Invention: The Development of Library Automation Systems in the late 20th Century. California: Libraries Unlimited, 2010.
- Burstein, Jerome, S. Computer and Information System. New York: Holt, Rinehart and Wilson, 1986.
- IgLesias. Problems and Failures in Library Automation Hershied : Idea Group, 2013.
- Houghton, Bernard (ed.). Computer Based Information Retrieval System. London : Clive Bingley, 1968.
- Kumar, P.S.G. Computerisation of Indian Libraries. New Delhi : B.R. Publishing, 1987.
- Meadow, Charles T. Text Information Retrieval System. London: Academic Press, 1991.
- Mohanti, T. Library Services and Computers. New Delhi : Alfa, 2009
- Rowley, J.E. Mechanised in-house Information System, London: Bingley, 1979.
- St. Clair, Guy and Williamson, Joan, Managing the New One-Person Library. 2nd ed. London : Bowker-Saur, 1992.
- Vickery, B.C. and Vickery, A. Information Science in Theory and Practice, London : Butterworths, 1987.
- Williams, H.L. Computerised Systems in Library and Information Sciences, London : ASLIB, 1982.

11

Information Retrieval System

The present era is often called as era of 'Information Explosion'. It is so because of the huge amounts of information that is being generated in a variety of formats in a variety of resources. As there is loads of information available, it is very difficult to locate and identify and disseminate the desired information. If one tries to get the information by a single term, there is too vast amount of information available on-online as well as in databases. In order to find the desired information from such a huge collection, we need a system which can facilitate the retrieval of desired information easily.

With the advent of computers, it became possible to store large amounts of information, and finding useful information from such collections became very easy and convenient. With computers around people realized that they could be used for storing huge quantity of information and at the same time mechanically retrieving the desired information. The field of 'Information Retrieval' was born out of this necessity.

The term 'Information Retrieval' was first coined by Kelvin Mooers in the year 1948 but gained popular in the 1960s only when computers were introduced for Information Management. Initially term retrieval was used for dissemination of bibliographic information stored in the local database. Now a day's modern information retrieval systems deals not only with textual information, but also deal with multi-media information such as audio, video, images etc.

Modern information retrieval systems are able to retrieve bibliographic items, and also the exact text that matches a user's search criteria from a stored database of full texts of documents. Information retrieval systems are originally meant for text retrieval. Since they are also dealing with textual documents, modern information retrieval systems therefore not only deal with textual information but also with multimedia information comprising text, audio, images and video. While many features of conventional text retrieval systems are equally applicable to multimedia information retrieval, the specific nature of audio, image and video information have called for the development of many new tools and techniques for information retrieval. Thus, modern information retrieval systems deal with storage, organization and access to text, as well as multimedia information resources.

Objectives of Information Retrieval System

The main objective of Information Retrieval system is to retrieve users required information from the database. It may be the exact information or the objects containing the information which may exactly or partially match user's queries. The search results may be indexed or bibliographic details that match the queries. Thus database is very important for any retrieval system as it contains required information either in abstract form or in full text form. In an information retrieval system the term "relevant" is used to represent either exactly or partially the needed information. Now days, databases are the store house of information, in which information is stored in indexed form. When users needs that information the given keywords were matched with the indexed information of the database and the needed information is retrieved from the database. The information retrieval system acts as bridge between the information creators and the users.

Components of IRS

There are mainly three basic components of Information Retrieval Systems, these are : i)user queries, ii) Database and iii) Search and Retrieval System.

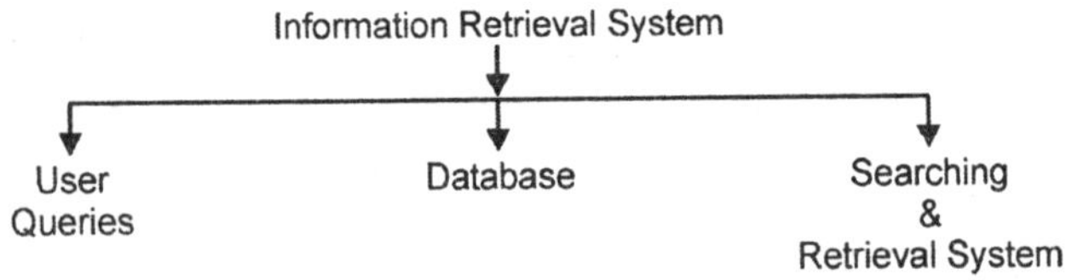

Fig. 42. Information Retrieval System

User Queries

User queries are very important for any Information Retrieval System. Without it IRS will be unable to search anything. The IRS are designed only for their users. The retrieval process begins with a user query. The IR systems are usually designed for a group of users. Users are considered to have certain queries or information needs, and when they put forward their requirement to the system, the system should be able to provide the necessary bibliographic references of those documents containing either the required information, or the actual text in the case of a full-text retrieval system. There are information retrieval systems which provide the user with the information directly rather than just the citations, or the abstract or the full text.

An Information Retrieval System locates and presents information to the user, based on a query presented to the system. A query may indicate precisely the characteristics of information to be retrieved, or it may express as approximation of information need, indicating merely an initial guess as to the characteristics of the information to be retrieved.

Database

For any information retrieval system database is very important. The word data is refers to collection of facts, ideas, words, symbols, etc. The computer manage data according to their hierarchy. Database is simply a computer based record maintenance mechanism. There are many software packages which manages data. These are called database management system (DBMS), in which data is acquired, analyzed, processed, stored and disseminated as per user's needs or queries.

The system is designed to take-in information and information sources acquired for the specific purpose of serving user groups. The selection of information and other sources is based on this objective of serving them. A database has a logical and physical organization. It is an arrangement based on the users' approach. The main purpose of a bibliographic database is to collect and collate standard bibliographic information, assign index terms and abstracts for technical papers, monographs, etc. In case of full text databases, the complete text of document is made available along with bibliographic details.

A search in a print index restricts the user to chosen keywords or index terms that can be combined in relatively limited ways. A search in an electronic database generally allows freedom and allows to define more precisely the hierarchical and proximal relationships the terms should have.

Searching and Retrieval System

When users need any query, they have to enter some string of words in the database search interface. The database breaks the string of words into keywords and then the database management software match the keywords with the indexed keywords in the database. While searching for information in a database, users may approach with some keys. For a bibliographic database, such keys can be name of the author, title, ISBN, subject keywords, etc. In a non-bibliographic database, these keys will depend on the nature of the database concerned.

In a bibliographic information retrieval environment, searches can be divided into two main classes: *known item search* and *unknown item search*. A known item search is the one where the user knows something about the item being sought. This may be any key like author, title, publisher, ISBN, and so on. An unknown item search is the one where users are not aware of the existence of any document that may solve their problems. Users do not know whether or not any such item exists that can meet their information requirements.

Kinds of Match Searching

There are three kinds as far as the searching of match process is concerned. These are i) Exact Match Search, ii) Best Match Search and iii) Partial Match Search.

i) Exact Match Search : In exact match search, the search engine will only match query terms exactly. It does not allow for truncation, wildcards, or stemming. Exact Match option is nowadays available in Internet based databases to retrieve more relevant information. Phrase search can be characterized as exact match search, where a phrase is given at the search query that searches whole phrase.

ii) Best Match Search : In best match search, the search engine will match query terms closely, if not exactly. It may allow for truncation, wildcards, or stemming. Best Match search is performed, when exact match could not fetch sufficient number of relevant information. Best match search constructs a tree-structured self-organizing map, where each level of the tree consists of a separate, progressively larger self-organizing map. The search for the best match then proceeds level by level, at each time restricting the search to a subset of units that is governed by the location of the best match in the previous, smaller level. The map is taught one level at a time, starting from the smallest level. The best match search can be done even more quickly if the data set is relatively small: the location of the best match in the previous level can be tabulated for each input sample.

iii) Partial Match Search : A partial match is one that matches one or more characters at the end of the text input. But it does not match all of the regular expression, although, it may have done so had more input been available. Partial matches are typically used when either validating data input, checking each and every character as it is entered on the keyboard. When searching texts that are either too long to load into memory or even into a memory mapped file, or are of indeterminate length, for example the source may be a socket each character is checked. Some information retrieval systems perform partial match search.

When the user's keywords match with the database indexed keywords then the user gets output in the form of relevant information. For any IRS there is searching and retrieval system which search and retrieve users queries. Information retrieval system is designed to retrieve the documents or information required by the user community. It should make the right information available to the right user at the right time. Thus, an information retrieval system aims at collecting and organizing information in one or more subject areas in order to provide it to the user as soon as asked for. Thus, an information retrieval system serves as a bridge between the world of creators of information and the users of that information. The information resources are processed, indexed and stored in an appropriate way. The user interacts with the system through a user interface. The user queries, submitted through the interface are matched with the index and the matching items are retrieved. A number of activities are involved in the processes of information processing, indexing, matching and retrieving.

Information Retrieval Process

The retrieval process begins with a user query. A user with an information need interacts with the information retrieval system through the user interface and submits a query. A query may contain a simple keyword or a phrase, or may contain more than one keyword or phrase combined with some search operators. The retrieval system matches each search term with the inverted index file, and retrieves the matching items. Although this is the basic process in an information retrieval operation, the specifics of each of these activities may be quite complex and depend on the retrieval system, or the retrieval engine, as they are now called. A number of tools may be used in many stages. For example, vocabulary control tools like thesauri, and machine translation tools, may also be used in the indexing and retrieval processes.

One can see information retrieval systems everywhere: Web search engines, library catalogs, store catalogs, cookbook indexes, are just few examples only. Information retrieval (IR) is also called as Information Storage and Retrieval (ISR) or Information Storage, Analysis and Retrieval (ISAR) or Information Organization and Retrieval. It is the art and science of retrieving from a collection of items a subset that serves the user's purpose.

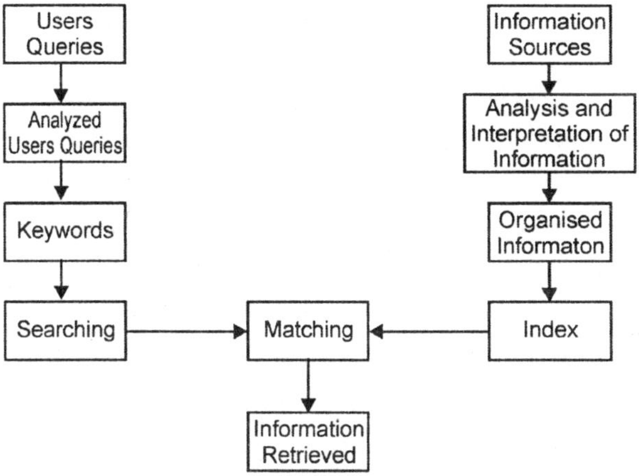

Fig. 43. Information Retrieval Process

Main Function of Information Retrieval System (IRS)

There are several functions of an IRS. Some of them are :

Identifying the Information Sources

The main function of IRS is to identify the information sources through which the information may be acquired in the database. A database is an organized collection of related sets of data that can be accessed by more than one user by simple means and can be searched to reveal those that touch upon a particular need. Examples of bibliographic databases: Medline, ERIC, BIOSIS, LISA, ISA, etc. A database is designed to take-in information and information sources acquired for the specific purpose of serving user groups. The selection of information and other sources is based on this objective of serving them. It has a logical and physical organization. It is an arrangement based on the users' approach. The main purpose of a bibliographic database is to collect and collate standard bibliographic information, assign index terms and abstracts for technical papers and monographs, etc. In case of full text databases, the complete text of document is made available along with bibliographic details. The resources may be classified according to present and future needs of the hosting institution and their users.

Retrieve Information Requested by the Users

Retrieval of information from the database as requested by the users and make the maximum utilization of the database is the main aim of IRS. Retrieval in the sense is the final results related to users queries which the users get. IRS interfaces basically perform two major functions: (1) they allow users to search or browse an information collection, and (2) they display the results of a search, and often allows users to perform further tasks, like sorting, saving and printing the search results, modifying the search query, etc.

Right Information to Right User at Right Time

The IRS matches the user's queries to the database and retrieves most relevant results in less time. The involvement of computers and database management systems and tools were increasing day by day and make IRS more effective and speedy. Any one from the globe can retrieve their needed information easily and effectively.

Acquire, Analyze, Store and Disseminate Information

The IRS acquire information from the external and internal sources. After that they analyze the information to make it more usable and store it in the database for preparation of index and when users need information it simply disseminates it. Originally the term information retrieval was used to mean retrieval of bibliographic information from stored document databases. Since they were also dealing with text databases, they are called text retrieval systems. Modern information retrieval systems deal with multimedia information comprising text, audio, images and video. While many features of conventional text retrieval systems are equally applicable to multimedia information retrieval, the specific nature of audio, image and video information have called for the development of many new tools and techniques for information retrieval. Modern information retrieval systems deal with storaging, organizing and provide access to text, as well as multimedia information resources.

Searching user's queries in the database

When any users enter a query in the database, the search interface search as all the available or indexed information in the database and match it with the indexed information. If the user's keywords match with the index then the IRS retrieve the information as output. A Search interface is the means by which information is transferred between the user and the computer and vice-versa. It is an important component of an information retrieval system since it connects the users to the organized information resources. Search Interface is the most commonly used tools for finding information on the database. There are three main components of a search engine: (1) the spider, i.e., the Program that automatically collects information about the index file on the database, (2) the index that stores information collected by the spider and (3) the search engine software and interface with which the users interact to conduct a web search.

Features of Good Information Retrieval System

A good and proper IRS must possess the following features:

Fast Dissemination of Information

With the involvement of computers the speed of access and dissemination were rapidly increasing day by day. The data management software makes database more effective to acquire and disseminate information. Due to the rapid growth and developments in information communication technology it is bridging the gap between the users and the information sources. Within seconds any one from any part of the globe can easily access their needed information. The role of IRS in the field of information retrieval is increasing day by day.

Filtering of Information

The IRS filters information and thus provides the needed relevant information to the users. Now a day's many databases put some privileges so that users can access full text or all information. They facilitate uers to get authorized and relevant information related to their needs and uses.

Relevant Information to the Right user at the Right Time

The IRS provides relevant information to the right user in a very less time. With the involvement of Computers and Database Management System (DBMS) the IRS is a very fast search interface. Due to the natural searching facility it accepts smooth search through which normal users can easily search the database and get their information.

Searching

The IRS and Database management system (DBMS) together provide quick searching techniques with many layer of search interfaces. Users can put many layer of search for a single term to get most relevant output. Most IR systems are based on the principle of indexing and searching. Typically, documents are represented by a set of index terms (keywords) appearing in the documents. A user's need is represented by a query, which may be a Boolean expression or simply a list of index terms. The retrieval process is modeled as a match between documents and a query.

Economical and More Accurate

On comparison to manual databases the IRS are more economical and more accurate. It is only one time investment and needs upgradations only. IRS system is one time investment and after that it acquire, access and retrieve more and more information on comparison to traditional retrieval systems.

Access to other relevant information

In IRS users get a list of relevant information which matches to their queries. It is upto the users what kind of information they want. Now a days many IRS provide external links to their users so that they can access external information as well, which is basically not possible in the databases.

Latest Information

The IRS contains latest information along with their basic information as the availability of internet makes it easier to update.

Feedback

Many IRS have two way communication systems. They not only provide information but also take users feedback time to time, so that in future they may provide better services to their users.

Artificial Information Retrieval System

A conventional information retrieval system is normally based on matching the search and the index terms. It retrieves items that match the search terms only. Since user search terms and index terms may differ in a number of ways, conventional information retrieval systems often fail to produce the desired results. They may produce unwanted materials, or may some times fail to produce the relevant materials.

Intelligent information retrieval systems use techniques such as those used in artificial intelligence and expert systems field, as well as natural language processing techniques to overcome the problems of conventional information retrieval systems that suffer from term matching. Such systems aim to use expert techniques, on the line of the actions of human experts, in finding information relevant to a user need. As a result they are more resource intensive. They are quite expensive to build and maintain, and often have applications in a limited subject domain.

Information retrieval systems were basically designed to deal with bibliographic information and would allow users to search the collection using some keys like author name, keyword, etc. With the advent of online information retrieval systems, search techniques and user interfaces became more sophisticated. Side by side use of vocabulary control tools for indexing and searching bibliographic databases became more common. The same practices were followed in case of CD-ROM databases. Subsequently the connotation of information retrieval also changed and first came full text and then multimedia information retrieval which called for more sophisticated indexing and retrieval techniques. Although the basic nature of information retrieval remained the same, in the sense that retrieval was done through the inverted index files. More sophisticated techniques for the creation and organization of index files are being developed.

The nature of information access and retrieval changed drastically in the recent past. With the advent of the World Wide Web and digital libraries, search engines brought significant changes in terms of sophistication in indexing and searching. Users now a days can get access to information through a number of channels, and the underlying information retrieval systems vary significantly in terms of the features and facilities. Moreover, more and more challenges are now being faced by the information professionals as far as the information processing and retrieval activities are concerned.

REFERENCES

- Bates, M. Understanding Information Retrieval Systems : Management, Types and Standards. USA: Auerbach Publications, 2011.
- Bezboruah, T., & Gogoi, R. Information Storage and Retrieval Systems: Basic Design and Implementation. New Delhi: LAP

LAMBERT, 2011.

- Chowdhury, G.G. Introduction to Modern Information Retrieval. 2nd ed. London: Facet, 2004.
- Chowdhary, G. Text Retrieval Systems in Information Management. New Delhi: New Age International (P) Limited, Publishers, 2009.
- Kowalski, G. Information Retrieval Systems: Theory and Implementation (The Information Retrieval Series). USA: Springer, 2013
- Kowalski, G., & Maybury, M. Information Storage and Retrieval Systems: Theory and Implementation (The Information Retrieval Series). USA: Springer, 2000.
- Tyagi, N. Information Retrieval System. New Delhi: VDM Verlag, 2011.

12

Telecommunications and Networking

The rapid growth of telecommunications led to the creation of new methods of computer-based library systems. These developments enable the user to sit before a personal computer and have access to the information at a far-off place. Any communication via electrical or electromagnetic media, including radio, television, telegraph or telephone is known by the word telecommunications. In the computer field application of this term is meant to the transmission of digital data between remote computers over a telephone system. The linking of computers along with telecommunications have made the networking usage to the maximum extent.

Network is the term used between a system of computers connected by transmission channels. Network cannot be classified rigidly as one overlaps over the other, and often data flow from one kind of network into another.

The main benefits of computer networks are:

- Resource Sharing
- Enhanced Performance

- Improved Reliability & Availability
- Modular Expandability

Varieties of Networks

Networks can be grouped to four categories. They are :

Local Area Network (LAN)

It is a communication channel that spans a limited geographic area. Data is transmitted from one computer to another digitally over the channel (twisted pair wire, co-axial cable, or fibre-optic cable) at speed currently ranging from 1 million to 16 million bits per second. A LAN is typically confined to a single building or a single department in a building. They may consist of a mix of microcomputers, minicomputers, mainframe computers and various kinds of stand-alone video-display terminals (VDTs). Local area networks do not need telecommunication channels as they are limited to one area only.

All local area networks transfer data in digital form at a high speed and have low implementation cost.

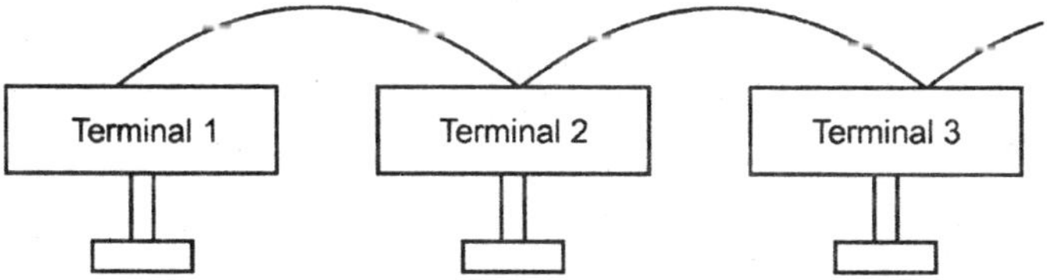

Fig. 44. Local Area Network

Special Interest Network (SPIN)

SPINs are usually within the same city, state or region and are tied together via telephone lines. There are many kinds of SPINs. Community conferencing systems and electronic bulletin board systems, for example, are SPINs by another name.

Metropolitan Area Network (MAN)

It connects the computer system and other resources and some times local area networks to a range from 5 to 50 km. It uses high speed data transfer medium like Fiber Optics.

The main reason for even distinguishing MAN as a special category is that a standard has been adopted for them, and this standard is now being implemented. It is called DQDB (Distributed Queue Dual Bus). DQDB consists of two unidirectional buses (cables) to which all the computers are connected as shown in figure.

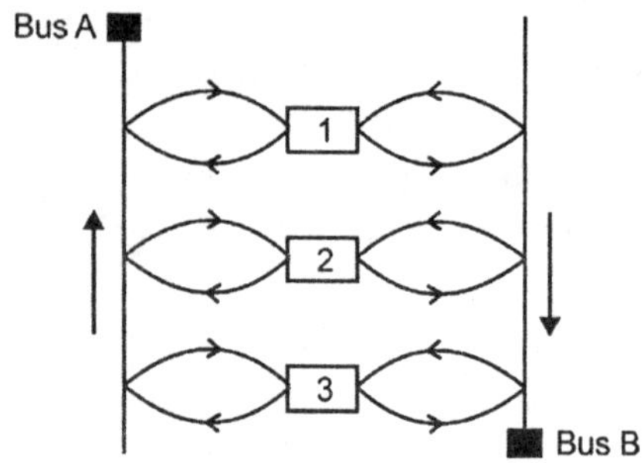

Fig. 45. Metropolitan Area Network

The dual bus helps the transmission of data in both directions simultaneously. Data going up uses bus A and data going down uses.

Wide Area Network (WAN)

They are bigger networks with dedicated telephone lines or satellite links and broadcasting. WANs are also called Long Haul Networks (LHNs). Wide area networks can either be point to point type or broadcast type. In a point to point type network, the source and the destination machines are connected to each other via several intermediate routers. In most WANs, the network contains numerous cables or telephone lines, each one connecting a pair of routers. Here the collection of machines intended to run user programmes (i.e. application) are called hosts, and the hosts are connected by a communication subnet. The job of subnet is to carry messages from host to host, just as the telephone system carries words from speaker to listener.

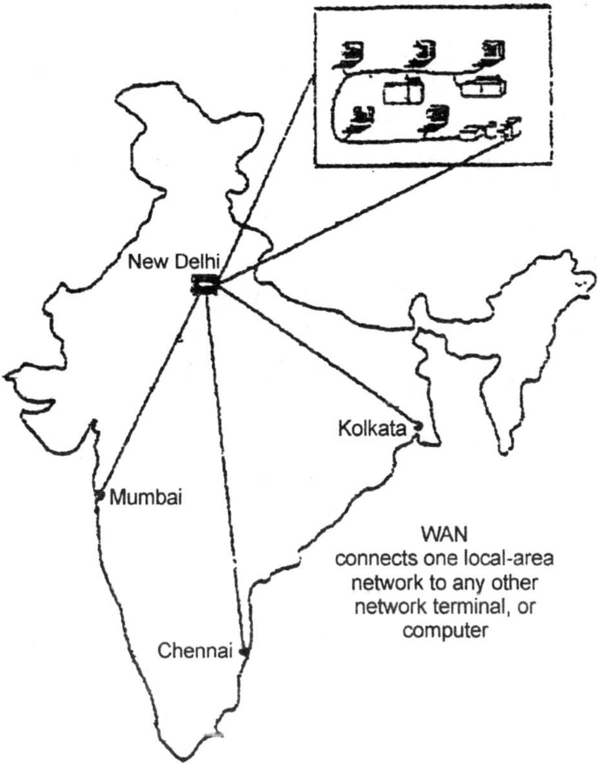

Fig. 46. WAN connects one local-area network to any other network terminal or computer

A second possibility for a WAN is a satellite or ground radio system. Each router has an antenna through which it can send and receive. All routers can receive the output from the satellite, and in some cases they can also receive the upward transmissions of their fellow routers to the satellite as well.

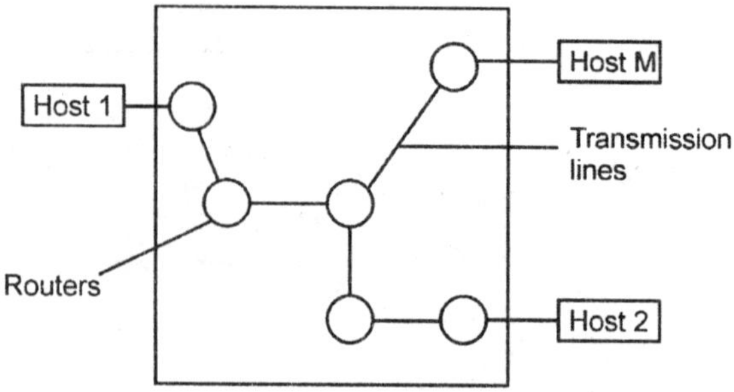

Fig. 47. Routing

The best example for Wide Area Network (WAN) is the British Library Wide Area Network (BLWAN) which is operated by BL Computing Telecommunications Directorate. This enabled terminals and computers within the British Library to communicate more easily with each other and have access to other services as well.

Routing

When data is to be transmitted between two remote machines using intermediate machines, certain routing techniques (such as routing algorithm in the intermediate machine) have to be applied. The intermediate machines may be termed as one of the following:-

1. Repeaters
2. Bridges
3. Routers
4. Gateways

1. Repeaters : A repeater receives the incoming signal, repeats it or amplifies it and retransmits the transformed signal. This is necessary when the transmission lines run over longer distances, the signal tends to weaken (the technical term is attenuate) and disact due to "noise" on the line. Repeaters regenerate the weakened data signal back to its original strength and they are used to extend the length of a single network. A repeater does not simply amplify the signal, it would also amplify any noise that may have been introduced into the digital message.

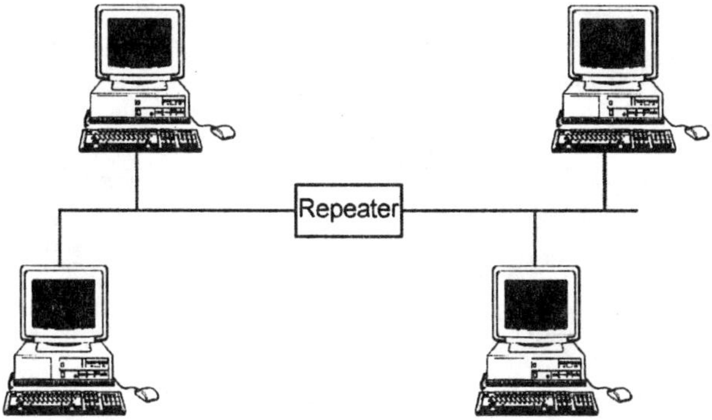

Fig. 48. A repeater connects two network segments

2. Bridges : A bridge is a device that is used to connect two networks so that they are able to perform as one. A bridge can also be used to connect two networks that use the same technology, such as the Ethernet network. One of the main functions of the bridge is to partition one large network into two networks which subsequently increases the performance of the network.

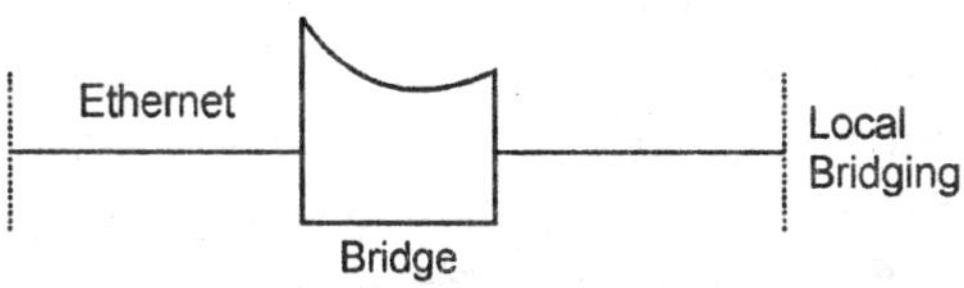

Fig. 49. The Bridge

3. Routers : Routers are used to connect two networks together that may be either the same or a different type of network architecture like network topology. It does this by maintaining a routing table to identify the optimal path to use in traversing the interconnected network.

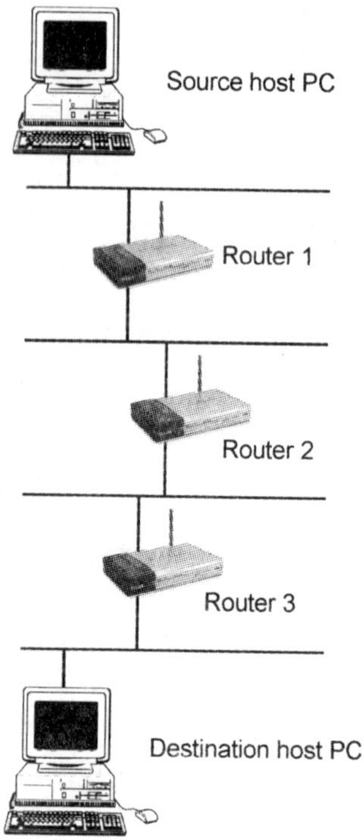

Fig. 50. The Route

4. Gateways : Gateways are even more complicated interconnection devices. It is one of the several types of communication servers. Gateway is software, the term is sometimes used also to refer to the computer that is dedicated to the task. The two machines that have to transfer data between themselves may have different operating systems of their transport protocols may be different. It is then the job of the gateway to connect such machines.

Routing Techniques

Computer networks may use one of the following routing techniques :

1. Circuit switching
2. Message switching

3. Packet switching

1. Circuit Switching : In circuit switching there is a dedicated communication path between the sending and receiving devices. The dedicated path is a connected sequence of links between switching nodes. A conventional telephone network where a dedicated path is set between caller and the called party for the duration of a telephone call is an example of circuit switching.

2. Message Switching : Message switching is an alternative switching technique, where it is not necessary to establish a dedicated path between the sending and receiving devices. In message switching the sending device appends the destination address to the message and passes it to the network, the message is then passed through the network from one node to another till it reaches the intended destination. Each switching node receives a message, stores it briefly and then transmit it to the next node. Examples of message are electronic mails, computer files, telegrams.

3. Packet Switching : Packet switching combines the advantages of message and circuit switching. Packet switching is functionally similar to massage switching, in which data is transmitted in block, stored by the first switching node it meets in the network and is forwarded to the next subsequent downstream nodes until it reaches the destination.

Network Configurations

An important aspect of any Network (LAN, SPIN, MAN or WAN) is the path or route that the data take when these are being transmitted from one location to another. This is referred to as network configuration or topology. Several different network topologies exist, each with its own advantages and limitations.

Star Network : Star network derives its name from the fact that there is one central controller (usually a computer) which has communication channels radiating outward. Each one is connected to a separate device such as a terminal or another computer. For two devices to send or receive data from one another, the data are routed through the central controller. These networks are typically found in cases where a large-scale central computer is connected to many terminals. The reliability of central controller becomes the main issue in star networks, because when it goes down, the entire network fails.

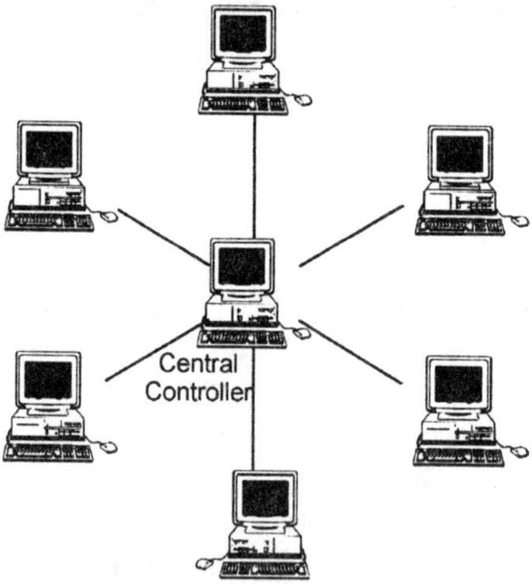

Fig. 51. Star Network

Hierarchical Network : Hierarchical networks also known as tree networks, consist of a central computer to which several other computers or nodes are connected. Each node in turn, has devices, such as terminals connected computerally. Each node acts as a star network. So a hierarchical network is essentially a multi-level star network. Nationwide organizations with divisional and regional stations are hierarchical networks.

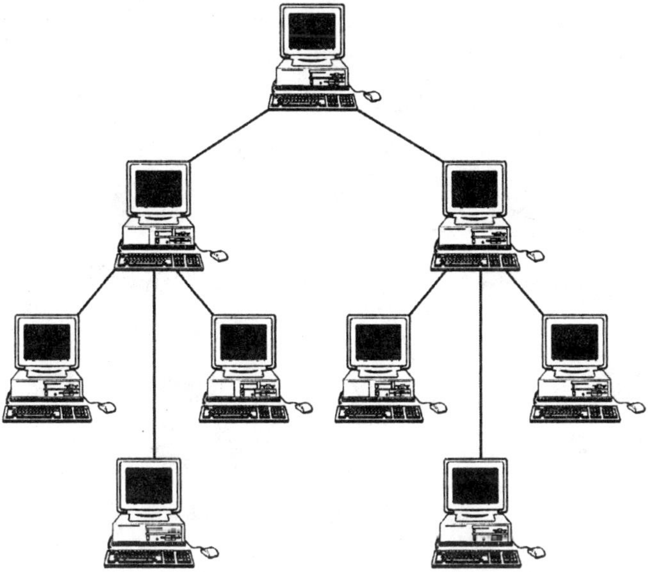

Fig. 52. Hierarchical Network

Ring Network : A ring network is a completely closed loop. A single communication channel with devices connected to it, runs through a building or office until the end of the channel connects bulk to the beginning. There is no central controller here unlike in Star Network.

Bus Networks : A bus network is a single communication channel routed along a path in which various devices can be attached. In this networking adding or taking off one computer from the bus does not disturb the system operation or the rest of the network.

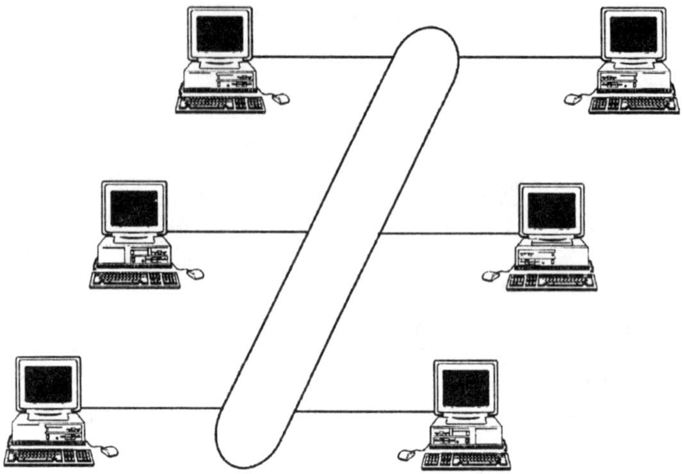

Fig. 53. Ring Network

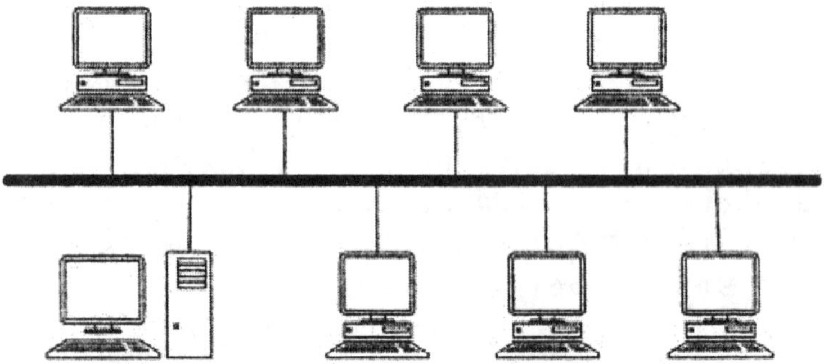

Fig. 54. Bus Networks

Computers for Network : Library staff and other information personnel have their terminals connected to various devices helping them to have access to the outside world. In order to link the terminal to the host computer system there are various components which are necessary for the system.

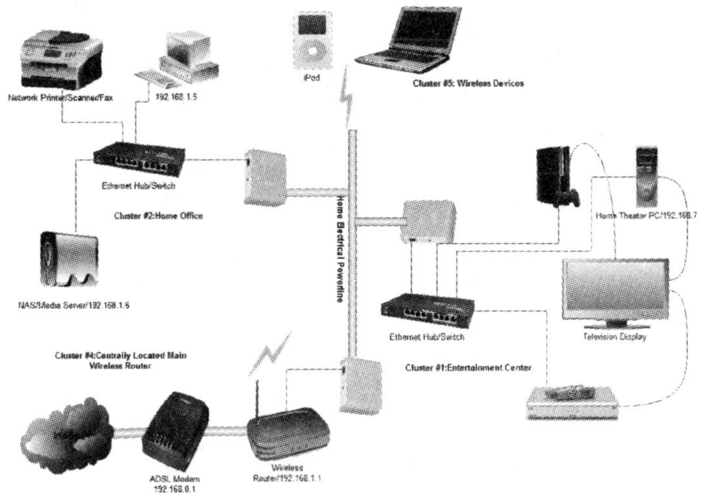

Fig. 55. Components of Network

Telephone Line : The ordinary telephone lines we use in our day-to-day life are only meant for voice transfer from one place to another. They are hence called voice-grade connections.

The telephone in the library or information centre was designed not to carry microcomputer signals but human speech. Likewise, the telephone lines that connect your phone with the central switching office were meant for your voice.

In phones the signals are electrical. Human voice is converted into electrical signals by microphone in the telephone hand-set. The electrical signals are converted back into double sounds by the miniature speaker in the ear-piece of the hand-set. Every line you speak the voice signals are converted into electrical signals and are then transmitted and are then converted back into audible sounds by the miniature speaker.

Two basic kinds of electrical signals are used in telecommunication analog and digital. The sound we hear consists of frequencies measured in cycles per second or

Hertz (Hz). Audible sound has a spread of frequencies-vibrations of the air against your eardrum-from about 25 Hz-20,000 Hz. The current on the wire would vary just as you hear sound continuously. This is called analog signal transmission.

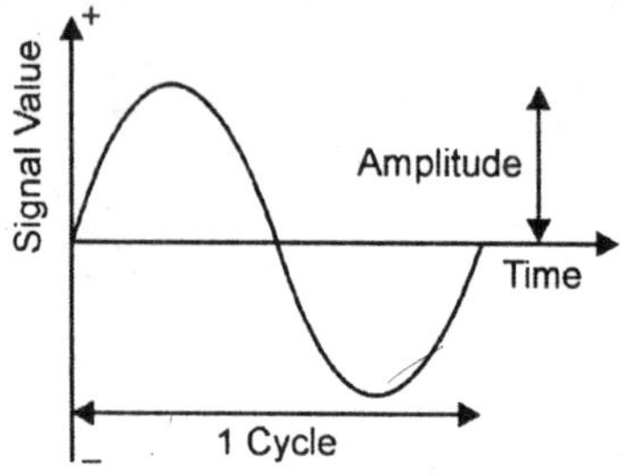

Fig. 56. Simple Analog Signal

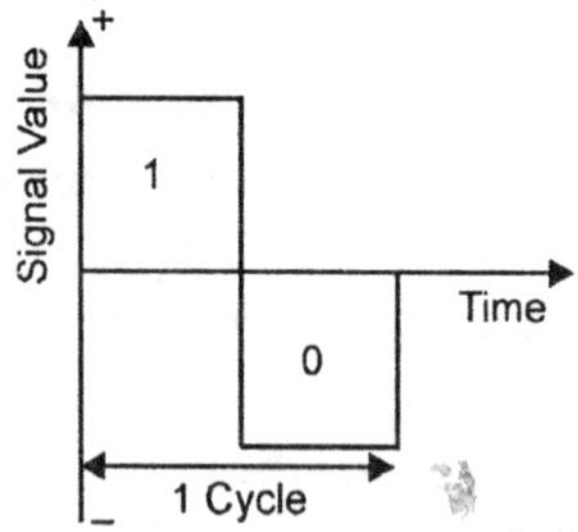

Fig. 57. Simple Digital Signal

The second method of sending signals is digital signal transmission. This means that stream of on/off pulses is sent. The personal computer works with digital signals. These pulses are called bits and a group of bits put together are called bytes. The phone lines send analog signals whereas computer works with digital signals. So, if we want the computer data to be sent through telephone lines then it is necessary for us to get them converted into analog signals and then once again into digital when it reaches its destination computer. This is possible only by a converter called Modem, an acronym for modulation/ demodulation.

Modems : The modem is the crucial link between

the microcomputer and the telephone network. The basic specifications of a modem is its rate of transmission, also called its baud rate. This is the speed at which information can be sent back and forth.

In many of the cases baud rate of modem can be through of as the equivalent of the number of bits (ons and offs) that can be sent each second. Thus, 300 baud is approximately 300 bits per second, which is roughly equivalent to 30 characters per second or about 350 words per minute.

The next important feature of modem is their different types. They are acoustic-coupled, direct-connect and auto-answer (sometimes referred to as answer/ originate) modems. All auto-answer modems are also direct-connect, but not all direct-connect modems can auto-answer. There are some very sophisticated devices called smart or intelligent modems that can do such things as store files in memory for later transmission to another machine, which the smart modem dials up on cue from its own internal clock.

Acoustic-coupled modems use as ordinary telephone hand set to send and receive signals. These are generally limited to 110/300 baud and are less convenient to use than direct-connect modems.

Direct-connect modems plug in directly into telephone. The signals exchanged are clean as outer sounds are eliminated.

Auto-answer modems are usually able to auto-dial, which means that one can select a phone number, type it on PC rather than using a telephone.

Synchronous/Asynchronous Transmission

In synchronous modems bits of information are transmitted continuously, that involves counting and timing of characters which is generally used for faster transmission rates. Here both the sending and receiving devices must be on the same schedule as it were, in order for the information to arrive in intelligible fashion. The disadvantage with this is the high cost factor involved.

In asynchronous transmission modems information is sent at random intervals with start and stop bits for each batch of information. These are simple and are used usually when terminals access remote computer systems.

Simplex, Half-duplex and Full duplex Communication

In *Simplex mode*, the communication channel is used in one direction. The receiver receives the signals from the transmitting device. A typical use is to gather data from a monitoring device at a regular interval. The simplex mode is rarely used for data communication.

In *Half-duplex mode*, the communication channel is used in both directions, but only in one direction at a time. This requires the receiving and transmitting device to switch between send and receive modes after each transmission. The analogous example of this mode is the old wireless system (Walkie-Talkie).

In *Full-Duplex mode*, the communication channel is used in both directions at the same time. Typical example of this mode of transmission is the telephone in which both parties talk to each other at the same time.

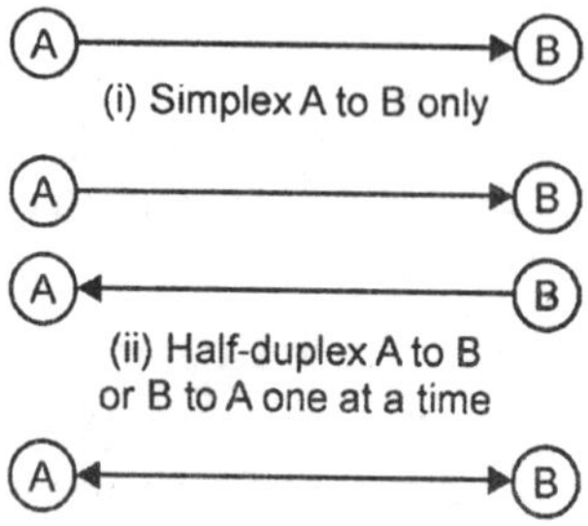

Fig. 58. Communication Channels

Software for Network

By and large there are two types of software for a personal computer. They are : (i) Text telecom software and (ii) Graphics telecom software. There is a third one also which handles both text and graphics simultaneously.

Telecom software that handles text can further be divided into general terminal programme, smart or general terminal programme, electronic mail programme, bulletin board, software and computer conferencing software.

General terminal programmes are common programmes that are supplied along with the modem. Smart or general terminal programme are smart in the sense that they can do more and make things easy for a user and they are expensive. They may cost you as much as word processor package or an accounts package.

Micro to Mainframe programmes are designed to communicate with specific kinds of mainframe computers. These programmes may also be called as terminal emulators. Since they mimic the communications behavior of a specific brand or configuration of terminals.

Electronic mail programme is a computer-based message system that is used primarily for the automatic transfer of information from one person to another. Most of these programmes allow one to dialup another computer and send your message to a pre-specified electronic address. Some electronic mail and terminal programmes have built-in error checking protocols.

In addition to the above software the future programmes will be called Executive Management Station Software, Electronic Publishing Software, Telemarketing Software, Network Management Software and so on.

REFERENCES

- Burkett, J. Library Information Networks in the U.K. London: ASLIB, 1979.
- Collier, Mei. LAN : The Implications for Library and Information. London : BL, 1984.
- Forouzan, B. Data Communications and Networking. New

Delhi : Tata McGraw-Hill, 2013.

- Hallberg, B. Networking : A Biginner's Guide. New Delhi: Tata McGraw-Hill, 2013.
- Kaul, H.K. Library Networks: An Indian Experience. New Delhi : Virgo, 1992.
- King, G.V. (ed). Telecommunications and Libraries: A Primer for Librarians and Information Managers. New York : Knowledge Industry, 1987.
- Kurose, J. Computer Networking : A Top-Down Approach. New Delhi: Pearson, 2012.
- Russell, D. Principles of Computer Networking: Cambridge University Press, 1989.
- Tedd. Lucy A. An Introduction to Computer Based Library System. 2nd ed. London: John Wiley, 1985.
- Vashishth, C.P. (ed.). Computerisation and Library Networks. New Delhi: ILA, 1991.

13
Library and Information Networks

The increasing popularity of computers and their explosion of use has created a situation where it is no longer simply enough to process data on one computer. The need frequently arises to share data and resources between many computers. Network is the term used among a system of computers connected by transmission channels.

As networks become widespread, its use has also became more difficult. Networks have brought many advantages to companies and enterprises. It resulted for minimizing costs, sharing expensive peripherals between many users. Thus networks while making a large number of users increases the utilization of resources at only marginally increased costs. A computer network can eliminate dependence on a single resource, resulting that the failure of a single computer is no longer to halt the working of the organization. Because there will be several other machines or servers that can perform the same task.

Types of Computer Networks

Computer networks come in many shapes and sizes. The size and complexity of the network is the characteristic often used to distinguish one network with the other. Networks can be grouped into three categories – Local Area Networks (LAN), Wide Area Networks (WAN) and Special Interest Networks (SPIN).

Local Area Networks (LAN)

LANs are the most common type of telecommunication network. It is a network that spans a small geographic region. Devices or nodes in a LAN are generally never beyond a few kilometers. They are generally owned by a single organization and contains not more than a few hundred nodes. The cabling between the nodes is typically installed and owned by the organization that manages the LANs. Data transmission speed is in the range of 10 mb/s. However, with the use of fiber-optic links, these speeds are constantly increasing.

A larger categories of networks, is commonly known as Metropolitan Area Networks (MAN). A MAN typically covers a larger geographic region than LAN. Otherwise, they are no different from LANs.

Wide-Area Networks (WAN)

WANs are the largest of the discrete networks. They often cross the boundaries of state and even country boundaries to create a single network for larger organizations. The costs associated with such networks are usually high, as the cable invariably has to be leased from inter exchange carries, also known as "long-distance carriers". Several intercontinental fiber optic connects are now available. They are often used on larger data pipes (150 Mb/s to 1.5 Gb/s).

The best example for WAN is the British Library Wide Area Networks (BLWAN) which is operated by the British Library computing telecommunications Directorate. This enables terminals within the British

Library to communicate more easily with each other and have access to other services as well.

The concept of connecting various networks together in order to provide a frame work for integrating the advantages of multiple network. Such integrated web of networks is often known as inter-networks.

Computer networks are becoming more prevalent and necessary elements of many activities of the society. They are available in homes, business, schools, R & D agencies, libraries and governmental organizations.

Some International Networks

The first real computer network was built in 1950s at the Lincoln Laboratory of Massachusetts Institute of Technology. In 1964 a large commercial computer network was built by IBM for American Airlines. There are several networks operating at present.

ARPANET

In 1971 the Advanced Research Project Agency (ARPA) created ARPA Network (ARPANET). They created this network to connect military installations and universities. Packet-switching was the technique used then. In 1983 it was divided into two separate networks. The Defence Data Network (DDN) and a new ARPANET. Today ARPANET is completely phased out paving way to Internet.

INTERNET

The Internet is a worldwide internetworks of computer and communication networks. It connects a variety of computers with distinctive software and hardware. These computers internet worked to allow them to communicate by translating messages into a mutually understandable language, referred to as communication protocols, such as TCP/IP, HTTP/IP etc. Internetworks are multiple networks connected in such a manner that data can pass between the various networks. The internet is the only current global-scale-internetwork. Internet was possible due to developing suite of communication protocols that was formed as a result of the ARPA research. Its strengths are in fast and simple scalability, although as local area networks have expanded into the global internet. It is now being touted as the information superhighway of the future.

Now Internet connects millions of people worldwide and offer tremendous amount of information that can be shared. It allows users to transfer files between incompatible computers, send messages across the globe, and log into databases thousands of miles away. Internet provides many services, such as E-mail and Telnet.

INTERNET is going to celebrated its forty fifth anniversary in 2014.

Today, the INTERNET is a partnership by consent between the burgeoning number of networks (7 crores of networks worldwide) and with 90 crore hosts. This consenting partnership offers across to more than 240 crores of users, which is growing steadily.

The library and information community must be able to articulate its vision of the evolution of its services involving the information infrastructure at the national and international levels.

TELNET

Telnet allows one computer to communicate with another computer. It allows Internet users to log into other intranetworking computers to access online databases, electronic library catalogues and other information services. In order to improve the effective utilization of internetwork services other information products such as WAIS, GOPHER, World Wide Web (WWW) are made available to the user community.

Initially in India Internet was accessible through some of the networks (such as NICNET, ERNET,

INDONET, etc.) to a small group of academic and government users. It is now being used effectively for commercial applications as well. Various interfaces makes it possible to access text, graphics, sound and full motion videos via, Internet.

Networking : Indian Scene

Ever since India attained independence, due recognition is being given to the vital role of library and information services. The vast proliferation of information on one hand, and the varied and complex needs of users on the other, resulted for the development of an effective system for information transfer. As a result, a fairly good infrastructure for library and information transfer. As a result, a fairly good infrastructure for library and information services has been developed, such as National Libraries, a Network of Public Library services through legislation, documentation centres, and information systems in various disciplines.

Several institutions such as Bhabha Atomic Research Centre (BARC) at Bombay and the Indian Council of Agricultural Research at New Delhi, are already functioning as centres for inputting and accessing data for the international databases, such as INIS and AGRIS. Collaborations with several other global information programmes and databases, such as UNISIST, ASTINFO, APPINESS and DIALOG. Computerized information services are available in several libraries. Since Information Centre at Bangalore is already providing computerized bibliographic information to teachers and researchers in the country.

The concept of networking in India goes back to the creation of various committees and their submitted reports. Several committees were appointed to look into the issues related to Library and Information Services and to come out with necessary recommendations. Sinha Committee (1959), Ranganathan Committee (1965), etc.

were amongst the earliest submitted. In July 1984 Planning Commission headed by Dr. N. Seshagiri recommended to the Government the need for modernization of library services and information activities in the country in the Seventh Plan 1985-90, which also emphasized on the interlinking of library system.

NISSAT convened a meeting in Calcutta under the chairmanship of Director-General, CSIR and discussed about. V. A. Kamath report about automation and networking in the city of Kolkata. Accordingly NISSAT commissioned CMC Limited to work on the feasibility study of Calcutta Library Network (CALIBNET). The report was completed in 1989.

In 1988 DELNET (Delhi Library Network) case was also discussed and henceforth CMC Limited once again did the feasibility study and submitted their report in 1990 resulting in creation of DELNET. Similarly INFLIBNET (Information and Library Network) was worked out and its office was opened at Ahmedabad in 1991.

There are many more proposals on the lines of Calcutta and Delhi networks in the cities like Madras, Pune, Bomay and Bangalore. Regional networks like Northeast India, are also very much in the offing. Some of the networks are discussed below.

NICNET

NICNET is a government data network of National Informatics Centre, New Delhi. It was set up to link government departments for decision optimization. National Informatics Centre (NIC) was established in 1975. NIC established NICNET in 1977 having regional nodes at New Delhi, Pune, Bhubaneshwar and Hyderabad, 32 nodes at state and union territory levels and 700 earth stations at districts headquarters.

This network helps flow of information among all

these nodes. The information flow varies from agriculture, water resources, customs, media, socio-economic conditions, to auditing elections, etc.

INDONET

INDONET is a commercial computer based network commissioned by the Computer Maintenance Corporation Ltd. (CMC), with nodes at Kolkata, Bombay and Chennai, which are connected to other cities like Ahmedabad, Bangalore, Delhi and Pune. The centres are expected to link to many more. This is used in the export of software, maintain common interest database like stock exchange and foreign currency conversion rates centrally. The Bombay node of INDONET is connected to the international gateway of Videsh Sanchar Nigam Limited. Thereby facilitating entry to public data networks of other countries.

ERNET

The Education and Research Network (ERNET) is a project of the Department of Electronics, Government of India. It connects a large number of teaching and research institutions in the country. It has nodal centres at the five Indian Institutes of Technology (Bombay, Delhi, Kanpur, Kharagpur, Madras), Indian Institute of Science (Bangalore) and National Centre for Software Technology, Bombay and the ERNET group at New Delhi. It is a general purpose academic network, over a hundred Indian academic institutions are on the ERNET Email network. They are reachable by E-mail by users of all major academic networks in the world over. ERNET uses TCP/IP link from Bombay to UUNET, USA over a largest line operating at 64 KBPs links from 1992. This facility has improved communication of thousands of scientists and technologists within India and with their counterparts all over the world.

VIKRAM

It, is a packet-switched public data network

established by Department of Telecommunications. The initial network would consist of 8 switching nodes and 12 remote access points with its network management centre at Delhi. This network has a potential for several applications for independent corporate bodies, computer facilities, banking industry, airlines, and transport sector.

INFLIBNET

Information and library network is a project initiated by University Grant Commission. It was set up in 1991 in Ahmedabad.

It is a computer communication network for linking libraries and information centres in all the universities, deemed universities and institutes of national importance, UGC Information Centre, R and D institutions and Colleges.

CSIRNET

Council of Scientific and Industrial Research (CSIR) is planning to set up a computer communication network for exchange of information among its 40 or so research centres. The CSIRNET would help in organizing indigenous online database services on subjects such as drugs, toxicology, food technology, medical plants, electronics, physics, chemistry and other areas. It would provide electronic mail and have access to international databases through networking.

All the above networking projects are general data/ information network services.

CALIBNET

National Information System for Science and Technology (NISSAT) took the responsibility of initiating CALIBNET (Calcutta Library Network) with the main objective of resource sharing. CMC Limited was given this task to be done. About 50 libraries in Kolkata were covered by this network.

In this networking adding of records is done by only

one library and hence the swing of duplication of work and valuable manpower. The cost of hardware being high, it is reduced to a large extent by sharing.

DELNET

DELNET (Delhi Library Network) was also initiated by NISSAT. DELNET had the objective on the lines of CALIBNET. They were the promotional sharing of resources by users to the maximum extent, to reduce unnecessary duplication, development of various databases to help in the usage of libraries resources, to have access to resources at a faster pace by using modern electronic equipment, etc. Telecommunications are also playing their valuable role. It is the most successful network at the moment in our country. DELNET also had the plans to coordinate with other regional national and international networks for exchange of information.

BONET

Bombay Library Network (BONET) was inaugurated in 1992 in order to facilitate access to the resources of many libraries in and around Bombay. About 50 libraries were covered by this network. The help of ERNET was sought in the execution of this network. BONET is building a low cost library network system which can be considered for future expansion of this service outside Bombay.

Using computer facilities provided by NCST, any member of BONET can get network access. This access covers electronic mail and on-line access to remote databases, both Indian and foreign. Various networks can be set up depending upon the necessary use.

Conclusion

UK, USA and other developed countries are far more superior in the computer communication technology. They are claiming to deliver books via phone lines from computerized libraries. The end of the traditional library and the arrival of library without walls is being made possible by the developments in communications, electronic texts and optical storage systems and superior database research systems.

The British Library, London has put its entire catalogue covering four million or so items dating from the dawn of printing to the present day on the computer. People can now have access to the British Library Automated Information Service via terminals.

India is still far-off from the big claims of the developed world in computer communications. Various attempts are being made for the development of networking in India.

REFERENCES

- Balakrishnan, Shyama. Networking and the Future of Libraries. New Delhi: Ess Ess, 2000.
- Bazzewski, Philip et. al. Tricks of the Internet. Curus : Sams Publishing, 1994.
- Burke, J. Richard. Network Management: Concept and Practice : A Hands-on-Approach. New Delhi: Pearron, 2011.
- Dhawan, K.S. Online Cataloguing Systems. New Delhi: Commonwealth, 1991.
- Ferouzen, B. Data Communications and Networking. New Delhi : Tata-McGraw-Hill, 2013.
- Fox, F.A. et. al. Introduction to Digital Libraries. Communication of the ACM, 38(4)m pp, 22-38.
- Gopal Krishan. Digital Libraries in Electronic Information Era. Delhi: Authors Press, 2000.
- Gopal Krishan. Technological Feature of Library and Information Science. Delhi : Authors Press, 2001.
- Houghton, Bernard and Convey, John. Online Information Retrieval System. London : Clive Bingley, 1984.
- Jacobson, L. Robert. Desk Top Libraries. The Chronicle of Higher Education, Nov. 10, 1995.
- Kanungo, S. Making Information Technology Work. New Delhi: Sage, 1999.
- Pandian, M. Paul and Jambhekar, Ashok. Internet for Libraries and Information Centres. New Delhi : Tata-McGraw Hill, 2011.

- Rai, A.N. Communication in the Digital Age. Delhi : Authors Press, 2000.
- Pendall, Grunk. Unlocking Data Content, Byte, Sept. 19, 1993, pp.3
- Samulson, Pamela Copyright and Digital Libraries Communication of the ACM, 38 (4), pp.15-21.
- Shukla, R.K. Automation of Libraries and Information Centres. New Delhi : Concept, 1995.
- Singh, K.B. and Singh, D.K. Digital Libraries : Challenges of the 21st Century, In Vyas, S.D. (ed.) Excellence in Information Technology, Jaipur: Rajasthan, 2000, pp 163-176.
- Suryadevara, Sanjay. The Internet-Joining the Gobal Information Superhighway, Business Standard, Aug. 19, 1995.
- Vickery, B. and Vickery, A. Online Search Interface. Journal of Documentation, 49 (2), 1993, pp 103-187.

14

Internet and Library Services

In this information age, the elemental process is communication. Recipient's state of knowledge is alerted by informative communication. Information gamut is felt everywhere. Presently technology has been a marvelous tool to have access to governmental information, grey literature, trade reports, technical reports, etc., and other unpublished, yet to be published the electronic journals. This tool has enabled us to communicate between anyone, anywhere in the world without any discrimination of status. This tool is nothing but the talk of the present world "Internet".

The Internet is a collection of networks, a giant agreement among thousands of computer systems to connect together. Internet is the network of 'networks' spread worldwide. It connects people world wide to have access to remote databases, allow personal communication, and group discussion.

In other words, Internet is another telecommunication network. Majority of connections for the Internet run on standard telephone lines. The concept behind the internet is 'Resource Sharing'. Internet paves the way to Universal Availability of Publication (UAP). Researchers from all corners of the earth are finding that their work is thriving in a network environment-immediate access to the work of colleagues and a vital library of millions of volumes of paper-afford them the ability to incorporate a huge amount of knowledge hither to unthinkable.

Internet has the philosophy of sharing information (mail, documents, programmes, data, graphical and the perspectives, dominate how the system work today). The development of Internet goes back to 1960's with the establishment of ARPANET of Department of Defence (DOD), USA.

Internet Connection

Basic requirements to get into the Internet are:

i) Computer

ii) Modem

iii) Communication-link (Dial up or lease line access)

iv) Password or login address.

In India, Internet connection can be had through the following:

1. ERNET : The Educational and Research Network (ERNET) implemented by Department of Electronics (DOE) of Government of India has over 400 organizations connected within India and neighbouring countries. These institutions are mainly academic and research organizations, non-governmental organizations and to a limited extent private and international organizations. Several backbone sites support ERNET, covering DOE (New Delhi), IIT (Madras), IISC (Bangalore). IMTECH (Chandigarh), VECC (Calcutta), IUCAA (Pune), NCST (Bombay) and University of Hyderabad, which enable organizations located at different geographical locations to access various services of Internet.

2. NICNET : The National Informatics Centre (NICNET) supported by the Planning Commission, connects 700 earth stations, with links to all district headquarters and a number of public sector undertakings. NICNET has become an important network facilitating decision-making in the government.

3. BSNL (Bharat Sanchar Nigam Limited) : It acts as the gate keeper to Internet connectivity.

Internet Access Services

The Internet has enabled global connectivity of computers and develop various tools and techniques for networked information provision and access. The various services offered by the Internet are as follows:

1. Gopher : Internet Gopher was developed at the University of Minnesota. It is a menu driven application that allows the users to access data residing on multiple hosts and servers as a distributed document delivery system. Gopher actually goes out, gets the information that one wants, and puts the information on the computer.

2. FTP : File Transfer Protocol (FTP) is used to transfer files from one computer to another across the Internet. The files of different types like text, binary or compressed can be transferred by using different modules of FTP. Most of the academic institutes make available material on their systems, which they think might best interest to others. FTP access is granted to everyone under the user name 'anonymous' using the E-mail address as the password.

3. Veronica : Veronica is a search tool that allows one to quickly scan Gopher space for particular files and directories. It is a programme that one can access through Gopher. Veronica not only find files and directories, but also get those files and directories and places them on the temporary Gopher menu for browsing.

4. WAIS : The Wide Area Information System (WAIS)

is a full text indexing software that is used to index large text files, documents and periodicals. Its application allows the user to search text, sound or images from a single interface located anywhere on the networks. A bibliography of WAIS related articles is available via anonymous FTP.

5. Newsgroup/Usenet : There are thousands of Usenet sites all over the world that collect and send information to other usenet sites. Usenet is a set of machines that exchange articles stacked with one or more universally recognized tasks called newspapers. Newsgroup is another way to meet people in cyberspace. The basic building block of usenet is the newsgroup which is a collection of messages with a related theme.

6. Archie : Archie is an indexing tool which can be used to search and download files via FTP. It is actually a collection of servers on the Internet. All of the Archie servers talks to each other and they pool their information into a huge global database that is periodically updated.

7. Telnet : Telnet is a simple programme created by the NCSA that uses the communication protocol of the Internet TCP/IP to provide a connection onto another computer. One can use Telnet in huge databases to do research or even Telnet can be used in libraries around the world to check if they have a certain book that one is looking for.

8. World Wide Web : The World Wide Web or WWW is a client server based distributed, hypertext, multimedia information system on the Internet. WWW servers can publish text and graphics including sound and video.

Gopher and WWW are mostly limited to publishing of text. Both these solutions are client-server based. The users have to install WWW and Gopher software in their machines.

Web uses a protocol called HTTP (Hypertext Transfer Protocol). The Web server maintain information in the

'Web pages' which are all the text marked with HTML (Hypertext Mark up Language) tags. HTML has tags for providing references to other Web pages, which can be on the same server or any other server on the Internet irrespective of the geographical location. The location of documents or Web pages is specified by the URL (Uniform Resource Locator).

WWW today has become the most popular information service and is associated with accessing and browsing information resources on the Internet.

Internet Resources

1. Online Catalogues : Internet provides access to catalogues of far located libraries and one can come to know the availability of the particular information in particular library. Catalogues of many libraries are available on Net.

2. Databases : Vast and in-depth information is present in databases, available on Net. Through Internet, one can get access to different databases of any library. In this way, Internet is an ocean of information.

3. Discussion groups : Discussion on a desired topic or required can be done on Internet. Various newsgroups, discussion forums are available on Net which provides information on a particular subject-field.

4. E-mail : E-mail facility is available on the net for quick communication. It communicates and passes the message within seconds. There is no effect of area on the time taken in sending the e-mail.

Services of Internet

1. It enhances the ease and speed of communication through e-mail.
2. It provides common platform like list serves for discussion and these type of common platforms are considered as electronic vehicle. These electronic vehicles include using the internet to share

information on any subject of interest.

3. Internet is supportive towards reference services of any kind, because it searches all the databases available on the net. To satisfy the user needs of difficult queries, it conducts co-operative approach.
4. It exploits the catalogues of libraries which are not available locally and may offer access or search.
5. Regarding SDI services, it gather information from users to create their SDI profile.
6. It makes locally produced databases available to the remote users.
7. It evaluates competing online-systems for the purpose of selection.
8. It does various library related functions like inter-library loan verification, requests, document delivery, and consortial file sharing e-journals, image data, and text files of FTP and WWW sites, cataloguing, books-journals ordering.
9. It produces homepages of libraries so that information regarding thc library, its resources and services can be made available through out the world.
10. It provides the connecting facility among the libraries.

Advantages of Internet

- It is an agilitarian to a fault.
- Individual's wealth, state, power do not have much significance.
- Much high quality, professionally produced information already exists and is on the increase, relevant for research, education, business and entertainment.

Disadvantages of Internet

Besides advantages, it has some disadvantages also

which are as follows:

- Seems to be virtual mess
- It is difficult to navigate through.
- Difficult to control non-productive use
- Information source of doubtful quality
- Lack of single protocol, lack of uniformity, lack of proper indexing etc.
- Lack of expertise to use the technology
- Slow response line
- Poor quality of data and poor organization of the information, one may get lost in the Net
- Noise in Telecommunication.

Even then, the rapid growth in the utility and functionality of the Internet is amazing. Internet is now growing at a much faster rate than our knowledge of using its resources. People by and large are using Internet for :

- Problem solving
- Accomplish task
- Create resources etc.

Impact of Internet on Library Services

As the library is meant for providing information and due to information explosion, fast information services are required. Internet is working to make the work easier and reduce the time lag in providing the information even if it is located somewhere at far. Basically Internet services provide the networking by connecting with other computers, including library catalogs, moving files and texts, sending and receiving e-mail, searching of databases even for. Some of the other functions are read news from many different sources, software finding. Internet has not only helped in accessing the information but also introduced new ways for storing, moving, finding and communicating the information among themselves and users. Internet has opened various options for reference and public services. As various dictionaries, census information and CIA World Fact Book are available from numerous websites, so ready reference service can be provided at greater speed.

OCLC (On-Line Computer Library Centre) has established a very distinctive service called Persistent Uniform Resources Locator (PURL). This service is meant to aid libraries and other organizations in maintaining consistent user access to web pages that may change physical location, when the URLs (Uniform Resource Locators - the web address of a document) of an institution has been registered with the PURL service. Software freely distributed by OCLC helps web managers to keep track of any subsequent address changes so that the user who returns to a URL that has been changed will be seamlessly routed to the new URL.

As Internet is providing assistance in reference service, it has another aspect also. It is increasing pressure on reference librarians due to availability of electronic versions of information sources to stay current with Internet resources. Reference libraries are working as 'intermediaries' in the information seeking process. This is how the Internet is changing the nature of traditional refrence interaction with users.

Internet has become the very important information access point, it has spread within the library community. Internet has been incorporated into different areas of library services and respective responsibilities. The designations are changing from traditional to web based titles. This effect can be seen from direct service positions to upper-level administrative jobs. Presently "Networked Information Resources Librarian", "Internet Services Co-ordinator: or "Electronic Resources Librarian" are designated to perform Internet related functions. These personnels are integrating the traditional library services into modern technological services. Various job titles are given as under:

Systems Librarian

Electronic Systems Librarian

Librarian for Internet Services

Network Services Librarian

Public Services/Reference Librarian (with emphasis on Internet resources)

Database Co-ordinator

Network Co-ordinator

Electronic Information Services Librarian

Presently the information services are composed of advanced work in computing and information science, online integrated library systems, campus networks and electronic information resources, strong public service orientation, searching electronic resources (online, CD-ROM etc.) and web administration and operations.

For proper functioning the desired qualification is that of the knowledge of information technology. Technical and public responsibilities have been distinctive traditionally due to the present status of Internet.

A major distinction can be seen in between primarily technical development and support skills and those that are used to help provide some method of organization and access to electronic resources.

The combination of simplified knowledge-technologies and the increased likelihood that professionals will enter the information market has resulted in increased professional facility with the Internet and networking resources. Professionals are providing training and support services between library and computing centre personnels. Training programmes are being offered through collaboration between the library and the computer centre. Computer centre provides the "physical access" and library provides "intellectual access".

The present need of the information seeking and providing services with the help of Internet requires proper guidelines regarding:

- Training for navigational efficiency for the information providers.
- Involvement of librarian not only in information contribution but also information organization on Internet.
- Library connectivity to Internet
- Awareness of information availability on Internet.

Library Service to Support Remote Students

In order to provide services to remote users, Southern Illinois University, Carbondale (SIUC), developed partnerships between instruction support librarians and reference librarians to create innovative services. While there has been considerable discussion about how libraries should meet the needs of remote students, little has been said about their role in supporting instructors. Instructional Support Services at SIUC, for many years affiliated with the library , have been the primary resource for instructors wishing to enhance their methods.

Digital Library

The information revolution is rapidly widening horizon of application of upcoming technology promising the accessibility of relevant information to the users on one hand and enhancing the productivity of information work and services on the other. The revolution of digitization is not instantaneous, it is likely to start with slow pace and accelerate over the time. But it is clear that the emergence of digital libraries will severely affect the traditional functions of libraries, readers, library professionals, authors, editors, publishers, book sellers etc. A digital library is popularly viewed as an electronic throughout replacing conventional archival and print media by electronic version with the inclusive sense of greater information exchange and value added professional elevations.

According the Berkeley Digital Library Project of the University of California "The digital library will be a collection of distributed information sources; producers of information will make it available, and consumers will find it perhaps through the help of automated agents".

The Standford Digital Library Project states that the "integrated digital library will create a shared environment linking everything – personal information collection to collection of conventional libraries to large data collection shared by scientists. Integrated virtual libraries provide an array of new services, uniform access to networked information collection."

Traditional libraries devote an ever increasing share of their funds to electronic services, whether in the form of CD-ROMs, on-line public access catalogue, or on-line databases. As digital storage costs go down relative to cost of library shelf space, and as electronic services become more useful, affordable, available and usable, there is a move towards the grand challenge of a World Digital Library System.

Transformation of Libraries

In case of libraries, as microform and audio-video materials took over the revolution after print media, in case of computer-communication facilities, revolution is both in the media of information and the speed of communication. Transformations may be as follows :

i) The basic innovation is that the material (books, journals, magazines, newspapers, videos, etc.) are to be stored in digital form.

ii) The secondary innovation is in communication. Communication is direct.

iii) In electronic (digital) library, material will be always copied from the master version of the work.

Characteristics

The transformational effects that digital technology brings into information system are as follows:

(a) Collections : Digital Library collection contains fixed, permanent documents. Not only that current libraries have more dynamic collections but digital environment will enable of quick handling of ephemeral information.

(b) Technology : Digital libraries are based on digital technology. The underlying assumption is that the digital libraries will contain only digital materials, may be wrong. It is likely that both digital and non-digital information material will have to coexist.

(c) Work : Digital Libraries are to be used by individuals working alone. There is work oriented perspective focusing on group of information analysts, work being done and the documents and technologies that support it.

(d) Transporting of Information : Breaking the physical boundaries of data transfers with in and outside countries. It is viewed that the support for communications and collaboration is as important as information seeking activities.

Compact data storage enables storage of conventional works in digital form. Bulk space is being converted into table top swiftly by electronic publishing. The telecommunication is facilitating the use of electronic methods to get back, browse, and connect to teleconferencing, video, text, paging, messaging etc. With the capacity to copy from master version, the mechanical aspect of publishing and printing of books and magazines will gradually disappear as soon as the replicating facility of digital library takes in.

Assumptions

In the context of digital library, four assumptions can be identified. These are :

i) It is a totally paperless system with computer networks and communication facilities.

ii) It is a supplementary facility to traditional library for better retrieval and faster communication.

iii) Any individual can have a direct link to electronic publishers, their agents, with or without librarianship.

iv) Any commercially interested organization or any individual, with or without knowledge of librarianship, having a direct access to electronic publishers can become local promotional trade agent in information service, like that of present day the ISD/STD centres, electronic typing centres.

Design of a Digital Library

Digital libraries have evolved with improved access, multimedia and the growth of world wide web.

The design of the digital library eatures two major distinctions. The system incorporates a 2-tier repository system to facilitate context management and the system incorporates an object-oriented model to facilitate the management of temporal information and exploits information extraction and deductive inference to derive implied knowledge based on the content of the digital library. The two tier repository system relieves the system manager from manually maintaining the hyperlinks among web pages. He should be temporal information manager and serve implied relations among the objects in the digital library. The motivation behind developing these knowledge processing utilities is to create a system that complements the capabilities of human beings.

Information Access Features of Digital Libraries

1. Enquiries may be either vague or specific.
2. Searching is only through indexes resident in the system.
3. Selection of titles is possible.

4. Physical availability/accessibility of the document/ information is always ensured.
5. Loss of time is only in browsing on the screen and using inefficient search tools.
6. Assistance of staff is needed less frequently.
7. Cost of accessibility may not be free.
8. Computer literacy is essential.
9. Communication is by e-mail, rarely person to person or telephone.

Digital Information Users

Users of digital information can be broadly divided into the following four groups:

a) Those who have started using the latest technology of digitized information.
b) Those who have been using these technologies and digitized information and are expanding it rapidly.
c) Those who have the fear of using new technologies for information retrieval.
d) Those who are intermixed between the above three groups, but have no training to use the technology for accessing global information.

Among all the four groups, the last one is the largest of these grups.

Digital Library and Conventional Library

Books and documents are placed on the racks in conventional library. Classified arrangement enables the user to browse through a set of documents on a subject and the related subjects. In digital set-up it is not needed because computer is capable in searching and linking various approaches automatically.

In libraries, for faster checking of availability, the catalogue is consulted. Many a times even without consulting the catalogue people go to the racks directly and browse because they know where to locate. Therefore, the minimum literacy requirement is the art of locating the books on the racks; may be without consulting the catalogue, even if a computerized catalogue is available. But, in the digital context the access is only through the computer. Hence, minimum computer literacy is essential. The loss of time due to adhoc searching is more common in libraries; and it can be expected that more time may be lost in browsing on the screen in the digital library.

Though, the nature of queries may be the same in both systems, the way in which assistance is sought from the staff changes. That is, users seek the help of the staff both in locating the materials physically as well as for checking their availability in libraries. In a digital system they may still delegate the task of checking the availability to the library staff; but may not need any assistance in locating them. The delegation of the responsibility of checking may be communicated by e-mail instead of the usual means of telephone or fax or personal contact.

Cost of such accessibility cannot be easily defined in both the systems. Though, at present, consultants charge fee for all information services, the institutions such as, public libraries, companies etc., who usually establish the facility for the sake of their obligation to their clientele, provide almost free access to them. But, Xeroxing is not free. Therefore, depending on the establishment cost of digital libraries, they may have to review their decisions regarding charging. However, the printing facility in the digital library which will be equivalent to the Xeroxing facility of the present day may not be free.

Digital Library and Virtual Library

As newer technologies are always adopted by libraries, their basic commitments are to be fulfilled. The terms digital library, electronic library, and virtual library are being used synonymously, which is not the exact case.

Digital library and electronic library may mean one and the same thing. These libraries may not be networked necessarily, but would largely contain digitized information along with print-based publications, but the virtual library is a library without walls, spread across the globe, from where one is able to retrieve the whole world of information through a properly networked workstation. Virtual library gives the impression of a big library, visited by the user.

Merits of Digital Library

- Quick retrieval and time saving
- Reliability and quality of data seeking
- Shrinking of bulk space
- High speed communication and internet working
- Increasing scope for information marketing
- Scope for knowledge augmentation
- Thrusting global consecutiveness
- Increasing resource-sharing opportunities.

EXAMPLES OF DIGITAL LIBRARIES

Alexandria Digital Library

The Alexandria Digital Library (ADL) is one of the 6 digital library projects funded by National Science Foundation, Darpa, and NASA. ADL's collection and services focus on information containing georeferences: maps, images, data sets, text and other information sources with links to geographic locations.

University of Derby Electronic Library

Main objectives of the University of Derby Electronic Library project are to store in electronic format and provide World Wide Web interface access to the wide range of information resources previously described only in printed form and to allow staff and students at Derby University, UK, to view, print or download these resources from any networked computer with access to a web browser. A Microsoft access document management system linked to a web server enables documents to be delivered across the campus. An important feature of the system is a means of tracking copyright permission seeking and management.

EARL and the UK Electronic Library

At the rollout of the People's Network begins to gather momentum and programmes of training and content creation get underway, the EARL, Consortium of UK Public Libraries and Associated Organizations in developing the UK Electronic Library, a unique resource which will deliver the national face of public library in the UK. For its development three main elements are envisaged : an Internet Resource Guide; a Guide to Resources in UK Public Libraries, and an Online Enquiry Service.

REFERENCES

- Balakrishnan, Shyama. Networking and the Future of Libraries. New Delhi : Ess Ess, 2000.
- Bazzewski, Philip et. al. Tricks of the Internet. Curus : Sams Publishing, 1994.
- Dhawan, K.S. Online Cataloguing Systems. New Delhi : Commonwealth, 1997.
- Evans, C. Internet Issues : Blogging, the Digital Devide and Digital Libraries. New York : Nova Science, 2011.
- Fox, E.A. et. al. Introduction to Digital Libraries. Communication of the ACM, 38(4), pp. 22-38.
- Gopal Krishan. Digital Libraries in Electronic Information Era. Delhi : Authors Press, 2000.
- Gopal Krishan. Technological Feature of Library and Information Science. Delhi : Authors Press, 2001.
- Houghton, Bernard and Convey, John. Online Information Retrieval System. London : Clive Bingley, 1984.
- Jacobson, L. Robert. Desk Top Libraries. The Chronicle of Higher Education, Nov. 10, 1995.
- Kanungo, S. Making Information Technology Work. New Delhi: Sage, 1999.

- Liu, L. The Role and Impact of the Internet on Library and Information Services. Washington : Greenwood, 2001.
- Pandian, M. Paul and Jambhekar, Ashok. Internet for Libraries and Information Centres. New Delhi : Tata-McGraw Hill, 2001.
- Rai, A.N. Communication in the Digital Age. Delhi : Authors Press, 2000.
- Pandall, Grunk. Unlocking Data Content. Byte, Sept. 19, 1993, pp. III.Samulson, Pamela Copyright and Digital Libraries. Communication of the ACM, 38 (4), pp. 15-21.
- Shukla, R.K. Automation of Libraries and Information Centres. New Delhi : Concept, 1995.
- Singh, K.B. and Singh, D.K. Digital Libraries : Challenges of the 21st Century. In Vyas, S.D. (ed). Excellence in Information Technology, Jaipur : Rajasthan, 2000, pp. 163-176.
- Suryadevara, Sanjay. The Internet-Joining the Global Information: Superhighway, Business Standard, Aug. 19, 1995.
- Vickery, B. and Vickery, A. Online Search Interface. Journal of Documentation, 49(2), 1994, pp. 103-187.

15
Digital Library

An electronic library is generally referred in informal conversation as a digital library. Digital library is a library in which the documents in the library are stored in electronic media formats. General libraries usually possess their collection either in printed form or in microform or in other media, where as in digital libraries the contents are stored in electronic form only. The contents in digital libraries may be stored locally, or accessed remotely through computer networks. Thus digital library is a type of information retrieval system. A digital library is potentially an organization that collects, manages and preserves rich digital collection for long depth of time. This digital content is offered to its targeted user communities.

Though term 'digital library' was first used during the 1980s, but was popularized by the Digital Libraries Initiative of NASA during the year 1994. The term 'virtual library' was initially used interchangeably with 'digital library'. But the term digital library is now primarily used for libraries that are virtual in other sense such as libraries which aggregated distributed content.

The contents that was created in the digital format is known as 'born-digital'. It must be distinguished clearly with the information that has been converted from a physical medium, such as paper, by digitizing. It should also be noted that not all electronic content is in digital data format. The term 'hybrid library' is often used for libraries that have both physical collections and electronic collections. Some important digital libraries also serve as long term archives, for e.g., Internet Archive, and some make digital information widely accessible through public libraries, for e.g., Digital Public Library of America.

The Process of Digitization

Origin of digitization comes from the word 'Digital', which is opposite of analogue, means constant or continuous data or event. The meaning of digital is expressed as a series of the digit 0 and 1. In the computer process all the data encoded only in the form zero and one only. Digitization is process to converting piece of information in bits form. Bits is a fundamental unit of information in the computer system and digitization is the process of converting physical media (book, periodical, manuscripts, images etc.) to digital form. It is the way to make it more useful and more accessibility of the source of information i.e., physical media. There are three methods for building up the digitized collection, viz.: e-resources, portal and more important method is digitization. The main benefits of the digitization is:

- To preserve rare, precious and fragile objects;
- To provide multiple user accessibility (multiple reference) at a time;
- To have more accessibility of objects;
- To provide good alternate for cease to be visible.
- To provide archival storage and security.

Materials or physical media, which may be protected or digitized are : audio, video, photographs and documents etc. There are four basic approaches from print to digital viz., scanning it as image only, OCR and retaining page layout, retaining page layout, using acrobat capture and re-keying data (data entry) for process of the digitization. The main steps for digitizing object involve:

1. Scanning objects through the scanner in appropriate format
2. Indexing of scanned objects linking them to text/ image to object files
3. Provide external storage media for storing the scanned and index file
4. Design retrieve technique like Boolean or proximity operators and wild cards for retrieve to object.

While building up a digital library and thus preserving and archiving of objects/physical media, it is highly labour and cost intensive process which include issues such as IPR, copyright and other complexities.

Tools used for Digitization

There are several tools used for digitization which include many core and peripheral systems like interlinked system of hardware, software, database and access sub system. The system may consist of a stand-alone workstation where most of the work or all the work is done on the same workstation or as a part of a network of workstations with imaging work is distributed and shared amongst various workstations. The network usually includes a scanning station, a server and one or more editing, retrieval stations, these are :

- Hardware (Scanners, computers, data storage and data output peripherals)
- Software (image capturing and image editing)
- Network (data transmission)
- Display and Printing technologies.

Scanners : scanners are the medium of importing or scanning physical media (analog media) into digitalized form (image). There are 2 types of scanners available :

- ***Vector Scanner*** **:** a type of scanner which use to scanning images on set of 'x' and 'y' coordinate. It is generally used in Geographical Information System (GIS) and other examples are – architectural blueprint, engineering drawing, maps etc.
- ***Raster Scanner*** **:** Raster scanner capture images after passing lights on objects and converted in digital form one by one. The maximum electronic images are generated by raster scanner and also used in libraries to convert print publication in electronic forms.

Some important scanners are :

Flatbed Scanners : They look like photo copying machine. Source material is placed face down for scanning and a light passed through CCD (charge-coupled device) beneath the glass plate and object passed out for scanning process. They are available in various models like prism/ planetary and right angle. Image is shown here.

Fig. 59. Flatbed Scanner

Sheet fed Scanners : In this scanners the object fed over on CCD and light source via roller, belt, drum or vacuum transport,

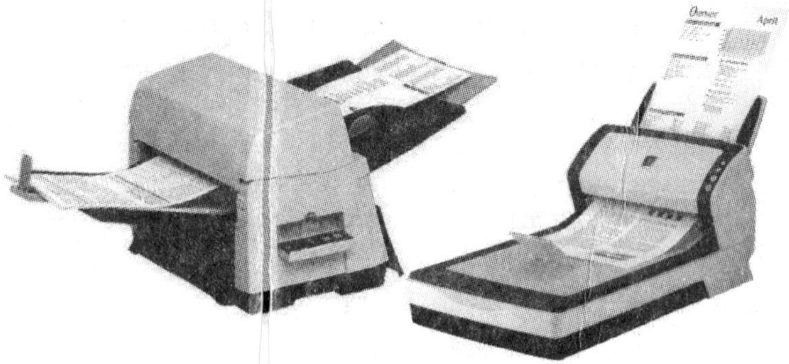

Fig. 60. Sheet Fed Scanner

Drum Scanners : In the drum scanners, the objects wrapped on a drum and high intensive light source capture the images of object.

Digital Cameras : It allows to shoot 3-D objects in digital form much like regular cameras.

Slide Scanners : Slide scanners have a slide (35mm), it only can scan 35mm transparent source material.

Micro film scanners : It used for scanning the objects in micro forms -

Video frame capture (grabber) : Video frame capture is a device which converts analog video signals in digital still frames.

Hand held scanners : according to webopedia, "A small handheld scanning device used for digitizing images. While images from a handheld scanner are considered low quality, today's technology enables full color 24 bit scanning. Depending on the scanner device type and manufacturer, handheld scanners can also define, translate, and hear printed text, and can also store and beam text to computers and other devices".

Institutional Repositories as Digital Libraries

Now a days several academic libraries are actively involved in building institutional repositories of the institution's publications, such as books, articles, theses, and other works which can be digitized or were 'born digital'. Many of these repositories are made available to the general public with few restrictions. It is in accordance with the goals of open access, in contrast to the publication of research in commercial journals, where the publishers often limit access rights. Institutional, and corporate repositories are sometimes referred to as digital libraries.

Digital archives as Digital Libraries

Physical archives differ from physical libraries in several ways. But, the technology used to create digital libraries is even more revolutionary for archives. In other words, "digital archives" or "online archives" will contain primary sources, but they are likely to be described individually rather than in groups or collections. Further, as they are digital their contents are easily reproducible and may indeed have been reproduced from elsewhere.

Large scale digitization projects are underway at Google, the Million Book Project, and Internet Archive. With continued improvements in book handling and presentation technologies such as optical character recognition and e-books, and development of alternative depositories and business models, digital libraries are rapidly growing in popularity. Just as libraries have ventured into audio and video collections, so have digital libraries.

In the past few years, procedures for digitizing books at high speed and comparatively low cost have improved considerably with the result that it is now possible to digitize millions of books per year. Google book-scanning project is also working with libraries to offer digitize books pushing forward on the digitize book realm.

Advantages of Digital Libraries

The advantages digital libraries as a means of easily and rapidly accessing books, archives and images of various types are now widely recognized by commercial interests and public bodies alike.

Traditional libraries are limited by storage space; digital libraries have the potential to store much more information, simply because digital information requires very little physical space to contain it. As such, the cost of maintaining a digital library can be much lower than that of traditional library. A physical library must spend large sums of money paying for staff, book maintenance, rent, and additional books. Digital libraries may reduce or, in some instances, do away with this. Both types of libraries require cataloguing input to allow users to locate and retrieve material. Digital libraries may be more willing to adopt innovations in technology providing users with improvements in electronic and audio-book technology as well as presenting new forms of communication such as wikis and blogs. Conventional libraries may consider that providing online access to their OPAC catalogue is sufficient. An important advantage to digital conversion is increased accessibility to users. They also increase availability to individuals who may not be traditional patrons of a library, due to geographic location or organizational affiliation.

No physical boundary : The user of a digital library need not to go to the library physically, people from all over the world can gain access to the same information, as long as an Internet connection is available.

Round the clock availability : A major advantage of digital libraries is that people can gain access 24/7 to the information.

Multiple access : The same resources can be used simultaneously by a number of institutions and patrons. This may not be the case for copyrighted material: a library may have a license for "lending out" only one copy at a time; this is achieved with a system of digital rights management where a resource can become inaccessible after expiration of the lending period or after the lender chooses to make it inaccessible (equivalent to returning the resource).

Information retrieval : The user is able to use any search term (word, phrase, title, name, subject) to search the entire collection. Digital libraries can provide very user-friendly interfaces, giving clickable access to its resources.

Preservation and conservation : Digitization is not a long-term preservation solution for physical collections, but does succeed in providing access copies for materials that would otherwise fall to degradation from repeated use. Digitized collections and born-digital objects pose many preservation and conservation concerns that analog materials do not. Please see the following "Problems" section of this page for examples.

Space : Whereas traditional libraries are limited by storage space, digital libraries have the potential to store much more information, simply because digital information requires very little physical space to contain them and media storage technologies are more affordable than ever before.

Added value : Certain characteristics of objects, primarily the quality of images, may be improved Digitization can enhance legibility and remove visible flaws such as stains and discoloration.

Easily accessible : Accessibility to the collection is very easy, as people from anywhere, anytime can desired information through Internet.

Digital Preservation

Digital preservation aims to ensure that digital media and information systems are still interpretable into the indefinite future. Each necessary component of this must be migrated, preserved or emulated. Typically lower levels of systems (floppy disks for example) are emulated, bit-streams (the actual files stored in the disks) are preserved and operating systems are emulated as a virtual machine. Only where the meaning and content of digital media and information systems are well understood is the possibility of migration as is the case for office documents.

Metadata Creation

In traditional libraries, the ability to find works of interest is directly related to how well they were cataloged. While cataloging electronic works digitized from a library's existing holding may be as simple as copying or moving a record from the print to the electronic form. Complex and born-digital works require substantially more effort. To handle the growing volume of electronic publications, new tools and technologies have to be designed to allow effective automated semantic classification and searching. While full text search can be used for some items, there are many common catalog searches which cannot be performed using full text.

Digital Library Software

Software which used for digitization of library documents (sources of information) is known as digital library software. Digital library may define as searchable collection of digital format or it may creation, organization and retrieval services over computer networks and other electronic media. A digital library is "an environment to bring together collections, services and people in support of the full life cycle of creation, dissemination, use and preservation of data, information, and knowledge." According to Donald Waters, "Digital libraries are organizations that provide the resource including the specialized staff, to select structure, offer intellectual access, interpret, distribute, preserve the integrity, of and ensure the persistence over time of collections of digital works so that they are readily and economically available for use by a defined community or set of communities.

Digital libraries have some expectation like: content management, user interface, user administration, system administration, interoperability etc. The main characteristics of digital library software are:

- Object model;
- Collection and relation support;
- Metadata and digital content storage;
- Search and browse;
- Object management;
- User Interface;
- Access control;
- Multiple language support ;
- Interoperability features; and
- Level of customization.

Some Important Packages of Digital Library Softwares

D-SPACE

D-Space is an open source digital library software, which is a joint project of HP (Hewlett Packard) Lab in and MIT (Massachusetts Institute of Technology) libraries in Cambridge and it was release in year 2002. It is freely available to research institutions and an open source system than can be customized and extended.

Some characteristics of D-Space

- It has service model for open and digital achieve for perennial access;
- Provides a platform for framing of institutional repositories, searchable collection and web retrieval.
- It also helps to make institutional-based scholarly material in digital formats.
- It is written on JAVA Platform.

Some Features of D-Space:

- BSD open source lenience
- Using qualified metadata standard (DC)
- Web based user interface
- Availability on multiplatform like – Unix, Windows, LINUX (some version)
- Field based Indexing (Metadata)
- Support Boolean, 'Nested' searching and ranked retrieval
- Full text and hierarchical browsing
- Support UTF Unicode for multilingual – documents and interfaces
- Compiles with OAI-PMH (Open Achieve Initiative – Protocol for metadata harvesting)
- Service model for open access
- Level of customization.

GREENSTONE

Greenstone open source software suits for building and distributing digital library collections for promoting digital library objective. It is produced by New Zealand Digital Library (NZDL) project at University of Waikato, headed by Dr. Ian H. Witten and sponsored and distributed cooperation with UNESCO and Human Info NGO (Belgium) under the terms of GNU Public License. Software coding is written in JAVA, Perl and C++ programming languages. It provides way to build up, maintaining and distribution of digital collections.

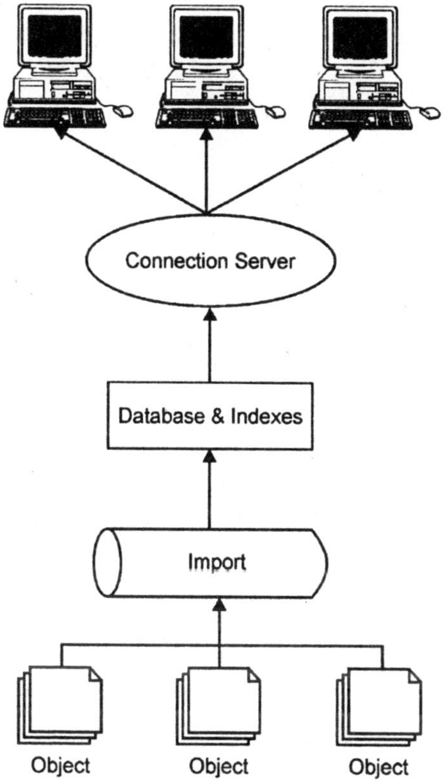

Fig. 61. Data Model for GSDL

Some Important Features of GSDL:

- Full text, field and flexible web searching
- Create access structure automatically
- Plug-in extends on system's capabilities
- Customization of collection of presentation
- Collection may contains like text, graphics, audio and video
- Support to multilanguage for user interface
- Collection support multi-formats
- Accessible via web browsing
- Supports to multi gigabite collection

- Uses advanced compression techniques
- Publication facilities of collection either Internet or on CD-ROM
- Administrative Login capabilities

FEDORA

Flexible Extensible Digital Object and Repository Architecture (FEDORA) is based upon repository management system Digit and Digital Asset Management (DAM) architecture. It began as NFS (National Foundation of Science) funded research project at Carnell University's Digital Library Research Group in 1997 and initially released under GNU Public License in May of 2003. The key features of Fedora is listed below:

- Digital objects are stored as XML-encoded files that conform to an extension of the Metadata Encoding and Transmission Standard (METS) schema.
- Behaviors defined for an object support user-supplied options that are handled at dissemination time.
- IP range restriction is supported in both the Management and Access APIs (Application Programming Interfaces). In addition, the Management API is protected by HTTP Basic Authentication.
- It provides a system-defined behavior mechanism for disseminating the basic contents of an object.
- It provides a search interface for both full text and field-specific queries across these metadata fields.
- Every Fedora digital object has a primary Dublin Core record that conforms to the schema. This metadata is accessible using the OAI Protocol for Metadata Harvesting, v2.0
- The Fedora repository system includes a Batch Utility as part of the Management client that enables the mass creation and loading of data objects.

REFERENCES

- Ali, A. Digital Libraries and Information Networks. New Delhi : Ess Ess, 2008.
- Arora, Jagdish. Building Digital Libraries : An Overview. Desidoc Bulletin of Information Technology. V. 21, No.1, 2001, p. 3.24.
- Arms, W. Digital Libraries. Messachutts, MIT Press, 2001.
- Kenney, A.R. and Chapman S. Digital Imaging for Libraries and Archives. New York : Cornell University, 1996.
- Noerr, P. The Digital Library Kit. Palo Alto : Sun System, 2000.
- Rajashekharan, K. Digital Library Basic. New Delhi : Ess Ess, 2010.
- Rhyno, F. Using Open Source Systems for Digital Libraries. New York : Libraries Unlimited, 2003.
- Singh, C. Digital Libraries : Tools and Techniques. New Delhi : Alfa, 2007.
- Smith, T.R. Meta Information in Digital Libraries. International Journal of Digital Libraries. V.1, No. 1, 1997, p. 105-7.
- Witten, I. Bainbridge, D., and Nicholar, D. How to Build a Digital Library. New York : Morgan Kaufmann, 2009.

Glossary

Abacus : The earliest device that qualifies as a digital computer. It permits the user to represent numbers by the position of beads as a rack. Simple addition and subtraction can be carried out rapidly and efficiently by positioning the beads appropriately.

Accession : It is the process of entering particulars of each book or document in the library records (i.e. Accession Register).

Access Time : It is the time taken by a computer when the data are called from the store and the beginning of the delivery of data.

Acoustic-coupler : It is a type of modem, through which sound waves (tones) are transmitted, through telephone lines.

Acquisition : It is the process (often processes) of obtaining books, serials, and other documents for the library.

ADA : A high-level programming language developed in the late 1970s and early 1980s for the United States Defence Department.

AGRIS : (International Information System for the Agricultural Science and Technology). This information system was established by Food & Agricultural Organization (FAO) of the UN in 1971. Information is collected on agricultural literature of the world through 120 national, regional and international centres. The data are processed and made available every month in two formats – printed AGRINDEX and online AGRIS.

ALGOL : (Algorithmic Language) An algebraic high level language similar to FORTRAN.

Algorithm : It stands for a set of precise steps that can solve a given problem. It also stands for the proof that the problem has no solution. In computer language algorithm expresses in various ways in clear English sentences, in codes, a structure chart, a flow-chart, etc.

Alice for Windows : Alice for Windows (AfW), an integrated library automation software package is the product of Softlink, a Brisbane based Australian company. Since its inception in 1983 in Brisbane and as Softlink Asia (New Delhi) in 1996.

Analog Computer : A computer operates on electrical signals with continuous range of current or voltage values. In contract to this digital computer is characterized by discrete current as voltage states.

Analog Signals : It is an electronic signal with continuous range of voltage values.

Application Software : It is a computer programme for a particular use designed to meet users specific needs. (e.g. salary calculation; processing of examination results, etc.0

ARPANET(The Advanced Research Projects Agency Network) : Established in 1971 to connect military installations and universities in USA.

ASCII (American Standard Code for Information Interchange) : It is a standard coding system for computers. It generally has 256 sets of 8 bits (bytes) from 0000,0000 to 1111 1111. Knowledge of the code is necessary for writing programmes.

Assembly language : It is programming language in which a source programme is converted into machine code. It is a translation programme that carries this conversion.

Asynchronous transmission : It is a mode of data communication in which each character is preceded by start but and followed by stop bit. In this transmission mode the timing of transmission is not critical.

Auxilliary memory : It is a storage unit that supplements the primary internal storage of a computer. It generally has an operating speed far slower than that of primary storage.

Bar-code reader : It is a form of machine readable input. It is very widely used in trade. The bar-code itself is a set of black lines and spaces of varying thickness, used to carry information about the nature and source of the product concerned. A bar-code reader measures the reflected light level from the bars and spaces and outputs to a processor, the corresponding signal.

Baud : It is the main unit of data transfer speed. One baud is almost the same as one bit per second.

BASIC (Beginners All purpose Symbolic Instruction Code) : It is the most widely used general purpose programme language for personal computers, developed in the late 1960s. It is still regarded as a friendly system easy to pick up and easy to extend.

Batch-processing : It is the technique by which the items to be processed in a computer must be collected into groups (batches) prior to their processing.

Bibliographic Retrieval Services (BRS) : It is a service available commercially, on a commission or rental basis, access to any number of databases. It is a New York-based Service widely marketed in Europe also (such as Dialog).

BCD : It is one of the early coding systems used in computers. It is based on the idea of converting each digit of a decimal number into its binary equivalents. Thus 1993 could appear as 0001 1001 1001 0011.

Binary Number System : A number system using only two digits 1 and 0, to represent a number, as compared with the ten digits of more familiar decimal number system. It is used to the "on" and "off" states of electrical switches.

Bits : Abbreviation for binary digit. It is the smallest unit of information a computer can store. A single but specifies a single value only. This can be either 0 or 1.

BNB (British National Bibliography): It is a weekly printed list of books published in Great Britain since January 1950. It is a classified list according to DDC.

Boolean operations : A set of operations devised by George Boolean (1815-64) which provides a mathematical procedure for manipulating logical relationship in symbolic form.

BONET (Bombay Library Network): It was established in 1992. ERNET helped in networking of libraries of Mumbai.

BUS Network : It is one of the network styles. In this network, computers are connected to one another, as that of a single line. Whenever data are to be transmitted among any two computers it is always transmitted through a fixed route (as that of city bus route).

Bytes : A basic unit of bits that represent a particular character or symbol. Normally a bite consists of eight bits. One each byte can handle (store, process, transfer) a single character.

C : A high level language.

C++ : A high-level programming language developed by Bjarne Stroustrup at Bell Labs in 1983.

CCF : Common Communication Format is a internationally accepted structure format for creating bibliographical records and for exchanging records between groups of information agencies and libraries.

Cache Memory : It is a small, but high speed memory situated between processor and main store. When computer is approached for information, the information is first transferred to the cache anticipating the demand.

CALIBNET (Calcutta Library Network) : It is a metropolitan Network of Calcutta. It is a special Interest Network.

Cataloguing : It is the process of making entries for a catalogue.

Circulation : It is the process by which a library lends books for use outside the building.

Circulation-Control-System : It is a package available to libraries for the routine of circulation of books in libraries. Software records loans, using a stock-database and a user-database. It generates over-dues information and reservations for documents.

CD-ROM (Compact-Disk/Read-Only-Memory).: It is a small disk normally 4.8 inches in diameter. It is widely used to store audio, but it is being used, increasingly, as a computer backing store, then it is called CD-ROM.

COM (Computer Output Microfilm/Microfiche) : Here, a computer system may point the output directly in a micro-format, instead of a paper output.

Configuration : The physical layout and relationship of the various components and parts of a computer system.

C.P.U. (Central Processing Unit) : It is the principal part of a computer. It is usually linked to various peripherals. It is generally in three basic parts. Main store, arithmetic logic unit; and the control unit, it actually performs all the data operations specified by the programme.

COBOL (Common Business Oriented Language) : It is a high-level programme language designed for office software. It was developed in the early 1960s. It is regarded as the most readable programme language because the instructions are written like that of simple English sentences. This makes the COBOL programme slow.

CDS/ISIS (Computerized Documentation System/Integrated Sets of Information System) **:** It is a relational database package widely used for information storage and retrieval system of non-numerical databases. It is developed by UNESCO in the late 1960s.

Compiler : It is a system software which translates a high-level language programme into machine code.

Control Unit : It is that portion of the computer's control processing unit (CPU) that selects, interprets and executes programmed instructions and directs other parts of the computer to perform the tasks required by programme instructions.

CP/M (Control Programme for Micros) **:** It is an outdated operating software. It was the main operations software until MS-DOS appeared in to early 1980s.

CAS (Current Awareness Service) **:** It is a system (sometimes a publication) for notifying current documents to users of libraries and information services. Some current awareness services are SDI, indexing service, current literature, information bulletin, etc.

CSIRNET : It is a network of Council of Scientific and Industrial Research centres.

Cumulative Index : It is an index which is built up from time to time by combining previously published indexes of the same publication into one sequence.

Data : A collection of facts in raw form that becomes information after proper organization or processing. In it data stand for information of any type.

Database : It is a large collection of data or data files. It is arranged in a file system with convenient provision for access to information. Many people use the word database to mean databank, where a databank is wider in its collection like that of a library.

dBase : It is a relational database package. It is very popular for its user-friendliness.

DBMS (Database Management System) **:** It is a software package designed to help the user work easily and efficiently with databases (including maintenance, management, and retrieval of data stored in the data base).

Data bus : It carries data in large volumes between different parts of a computer i.e., CPU, memory unit and peripheral devices (such as keyboard, VDU, printer, etc.). It is usually a set of parallel wires over which it is transmitted.

Data dictionary : The document that contains clear definitions of the data that will be used in setting up database management system.

Data Processing : Recording information by some means whereby it may be obtained immediately by some mechanical or semi-mechanical process.

DELNET (Developing Library Network) : It is a metropolitan network of Delhi. It is a special interest network.

Desktop Computers : It is a word processor with a high quality printer. Most suited for publishing work. The output of a DTP can be used directly for plate-making in printing work.

DTP (Desk Top Publishing) : It is a word processor with a high quality printer. Most suited for publishing work. The output of a DTP can be used directly for plate making in printing work.

Dialog : It is a major American host service making available, on a commission or rental basis, access to any number of databases. It is located in California, offering access to over 300 databases (such as BRS).

Digital Archives : The Digital Archive is a secure storage environment for Traditional Sources or manuscripts, so that it can be easily manage and monitor the health of your master files and digital originals.

Digital Collection: It stands for texts, images, databases, files, etc. in a digital format. It comprises documents which are in digital formats like CD-ROM Database, floppies, magnetic tapes, discs, etc.

Digital Computer : A computer which operates on discrete current or voltage. It contrast to this an analogue computer is characterized by electrical signals with continuous range of current or voltage values.

Digital Library : Library with both digital collection and traditional, fixed media collection. It also includes digital materials that exist outside the physical and administrative bounds of any one digital library.

Digital Signal : It is an electro-magnetic signal that has discrete voltage values.

Digitisation : It is the process of converting print information and other media information of the existing collection to digital form. It is the conversion of any fixed or analog media, such as books, journal articles, photos, paintings, microforms, etc., into electronic form through scanning or in fact even re-keying.

D-Space : D-Space is an open source repository software package typically used for creating open access repositories for scholarly and/or published idigital content developed by Duraspace in 2002.

E-Granthalaya : e-Granthalaya is a library automation software from National Informatics Centre, Department of Electronics & Information Technology, Ministry of Communications and Information Technology, Government of India, developed in 2003.

Electronic Mail : It is a computer based message system that is used for the automatic transfer of information. The message is stored in a central computer in a network. Each user can have access to their stored messages.

Emulator : It is a term used for making one system (computer) to make it act like a standard computer.

Expert system : It deals with the application of machine intelligence research which combines a knowledge base with suitable software to allow the user to question the system and make additions to the systems accordingly.

EBCDIC : It is an 8-bit coding system developed by IBM. It is used to represent characters in many of the modern-day computers.

EPROM (Erasable Programmable Read Only Memory) **:** It is a PROM whose contents can be erased by the user. New Information can be stored in later on.

ENIAC (Electronic Numerical Integrator and Calculator) **:** The first all electronic digital computer developed by Mauchly and Eckert around 1940.

FEDORA : Fedora or Flexible Extensible Digital Object Repository Architecture is a Digital Asset Management (DAM) architecture upon which Institutional Repositories, Digital Archives and Digital Libraries systems might be build founded by researchers at Cornell University and the

University of Virginia Library in the year 1997.

Fibre-optic cables : They are thin, flexible fibers of glass combined into a cable. These cables are used for carrying information or data of enormous quantities.

Floppy disk : It is a magnetic disk on which data can be stored. They come in various sizes (5.5, 5.25 and 8 inches) and can hold few hundred kilobytes. They are cheap, thin, and flexible. It is also called a diskette.

Flow chart : It is a method of showing an algorithm or the processes involved in a programme in block form. The shapes of the blocks show the nature of each action.

FORTRAN (FORmula TRANslation) **:** It is the first highlevel programme language developed in the mid-1950s. Because of its great numerical power it is still very widely used in science and technology.

Four GL : Fourth generation language, used in modern database query languages, spread sheet systems, graphic and system integrated with text processing.

Full-duplex : It is a mode of data communication in which both the parties have access to the transmission channel in both ways at the same time. Simultaneous two-directional transmission is possible in this type of communication.

Functional programming : In this programming pure function evaluation solve the problems.

Greenstone : Greenstone is the digital library software which was developed by the New Zealand Digital Library Project at the University of Waikato, and developed and distributed in cooperation with UNESCO and the Human Info NGO.

Half-duplex : It is a mode of data communication through a channel which can be either way, but only one way at a time.

Hardware : The physical parts of a computer system, i.e. the one you can touch, as opposed to software (operating instruction) that makes the system work.

Hertz (Hz) : It is a unit of frequency, named after German physicist H. Hertz. One Hz equals to one cycle per second.

Hexadecimal system : A number system using a base of 16. The 16 digits are 0-9 and A-F. It is commonly used as a short-cut notation for groups of four binary digits.

Hierarchical DBMS : A tree like structure representing data in DBMS.

Hierarchical Network : It is one of network styles. In this network each computer is linked with one another in a hierarchical fashion. Whenever data are to be transmitted among any two computers it is routed through the next hierarchical stage.

High-level language : It is a programme language in which each instruction is translated into machine code. The higher the level of programme language, the more suited to the needs of the programmer and the user.

Hybrid computer : Anything made out of two or more different forms. A combination of an analog and a digital central processor and analog input/output.

Information : The processed data recorded on paper or any other media which can be used for the purpose of communication or for making decisions.

IRS (Information Retrieval System) : It is a system for finding documents or the information contained in documents in a library or other collection. The methods or retrieval vary from a simple index to a computer-based system.

INDONET : It is a network with commercial purpose developed by CMC Ltd. It is an integrated information management network.

INIS (International Nuclear Information System) : This was established by International Atomic Energy Agency (IAEA) in 1970. INIS is fully decentralized computer-based information system covering the world's literature in nuclear science and allied fields. INIS Atomindex first appeared in 1970 in the printed form (monthly) and simultaneously on magnetic tape.

ISBN (International Standard Book Number) : It is a number given to every book before publication to identify the publisher, title, edition and volume number. It consists of 10 digits (0-9). The first group of digits indicates the country of origin, the second group indicates the publisher, the title, or edition of the title, and the final digit serves as the check digit. Each group of numbers is separated by a space or hyphen.

ISSN (International Standard Serial Number) : It is an internationally accepted code for the identification of serial publications. It consists of eight Arabic digits. The eighth digit serves to verify the number in computer processing.

Input devices : It is an item of hardware which has the task of accepting data in one form from outside. It codes the data into electrical pulses of a form that suites the processor. It then passes the data on to the processor. There are many types of input units such as punched card, keyboard, character readers, bar-code readers, etc.

Interpreter : It is a machine code programme used to translate the instructions of a high-level programme one by one. The same is immediately executed before the translation of the next statements.

Internet : It is a worldwide network of computers and communication networks, working as information super highway.

Integrated circuit : A small wafer of silicon material on which an electronic circuit is mounted. It is usually less than the size of a human fingernail and almost of the same thickness.

Integration : The concentration of more and more electronic circuit components and their linking on the surface of a small chip.

INFLIBNET (Information and Library Network) : University Grants Commission started this project. The computer communication network for linking libraries and information centres in universities was established in 1991.

Institutional Repositories : An institutional repository is an online archive for collecting, preserving, and disseminating digital copies of the intellectual output of an institution, particularly a research institution.

IRS : Information Retrieval System is the activity of obtaining information resources relevant to an information need from a collection of information resources.

Java : A general-purpose computer programming language designed to produce programs that will run on any computer system designed in 1995 by James Gosling and Sun Microsystems.

Keyboard : It is an input device. On its surface there are a number of keys. It holds a typewriter arrony of letters, numbers symbols, and function keys.

Key-word : It is a word indicating a subject discussed in a document. It is this word considered to be most indicative of the title and is used as an access point (i.e., key-word) of the subject content of the document.

KWIC (Key-Word In Context) : It is a method of indexing which uses a computer to permute automatically the words in the periodical articles. Thus, to group titles in which the same words occur, when index is printed. The keywords in each index line are printed in the middle of the type, thus appears under the one another in alphabetical order in a column.

K (kilo) : An abbreviation for the Greek prefix Kilo meaning thousand, in computer-related usage. K usually represents the quantity 2 to the power of 10 or 1024 bytes.

Kilobyte : Usually taken as one thousand bytes; but it is exactly equal to 1024 bytes.

KOHA : Koha is an open source Integrated Library System (ILS), used world-wide by public, school and special libraries designed, updated and maintained by KOHA Community from 2000.

Laptop computer : A microcomputer with a size less than that of desktop computer and more than that of a pocket computer. They usually weight less than 10 kg and are portable.

Libsys : LIbsys is an integrated multi-user library management software, that caters to the needs of an advanced library and information professionals managed and developed by LIBSYS Ltd in 1984.

Light pen : It is a pen or stylus with light sensor at its head. It can be used to mark a position on the VDU screen. The word sometimes is used to mean a bar-code scanner.

LISP : It is a programming language appeared in 1958 designed by John McCarthy.

LAN (Local Area Network) : It is a network linking computers and other devices within a restricted geographical area, usually not more than a kilometer or two from the central server (for e.g. campus-wide network in a university).

Logic programming : In this type of programming, the application is focused and problems are specified on a high level.

Lotus 1-2-3 : It is a spread-sheet software package widely used for statistical applications.

Machine Language : The programme of computers must be in machine code, in which all the instructions are in the sets of bits (of 0s and 1s). The machine usually accepts only these codes, which are otherwise called machine languages.

MARC (Machine Readable Catalogue) : The Library of Congress began this project in 1966 as a pilot scheme to provide an internationally acceptable standard for the bibliographic records in the machine readable forms.

MARC 21 : Marc 21 Format for Bibliographic Data is designed to be a carrier for bibliographic information about printed and manuscript textual materials, computer files, maps, music, continuing resources, visual materials, and mixed materials. Bibliographic data commonly includes titles, names, subjects, notes, publication data, and information about the physical description of an item. It was developed by Henriette Avram at the US Library of Congress during the 1960s to create records that can be used by computers, and to share those records among libraries.

MS-DOS (Microsoft Disk Operating System) : It is the standard operating software for PCs.

Magnetic disk: It is a plate coated with magnetic material on which data can be stored. They are usually flat, circular and small in size. Magnetic disks come in two types : hard and flexible (floppy).

Magnetic drums : They were the first effective form of direct access backing storage before disks appeared. They were bulky and costly.

Magnetic tape : It is a very common storage media. It uses a long plastic strip coated with magnetic material. It is usually spooled in a magnetic cassette or cartridge.

Mainframe computer : They are the largest class of computers. They can occupy an entire room and have very large data handling capacities. They are many times costlier than minicomputers or microcomputers (PCs).

MICR : It is a form of machine readable input. The characters are also readable by human beings. It is very reliable and used for clearing cheques in banks.

MEDLARS (Medical Literature Analysis and Retrieval System) : It is a database created and maintained by National Library of Medicine (USA). It contains nearly three million citations from bio-medical literature. MEDLARS is also available on on-line and it is called MEDLINE.

Mega Byte : One million byte (10^5).

Metadata : It is the data that describes the content and attributes of any particular item. It is the key to resource discovery and the use of any document. The cataloguing record (i.e. bibliographical record) is an example of metadata.

Meta Resources : Meta resources is a database of Internet resource descriptions that is made accessible through a structured and/or unstructured network service.

Microcomputer : It is Personal Computer (PC) usually used by one person at a time.

Microfiche : It is a flat sheet of photographic film sizing 105x148 mm(4x 6 inches). It bears micro images of the text of documents in horizontal and vertical rows, these images can be read with a microfiche reader. At the top of which a catalogue entry, i.e., title and other information is displayed prominently which can be read with human eye.

Micro-processor : A large-scale integrated chip which contains the entire CPU (Central Processing Unit) of a computer. It is usually a single chip.

Minicomputer : A computer that is large than microcomputer (PC) in size and capabilities and lesser than mainframe computer.

ML : ML is a general-purpose functional programming language developed by Robin Milner and others in the early 1970s at the University of Edignburgh.

Mnemonic scheme : In a library classification scheme mnemonic stands for use of symbols that they have more or less with constant meaning. In the field of computer mnemonic stands for an assembly language opcode, i.e., fairly easy to remember as the symbol related to function (e.g. LDA = Load into Accumulator).

MODEM (Modem/DEModulator) : It is a device that permits data communication over telecommunication lines. A modem converts information from digital to analog frequencies and it reverses the process when receiving data.

Multiprocessing : It is the feature of powerful multiprocessors. It allows them to work with two or more independent CPUs that have the ability to simultaneously execute several programmes.

Multiprogramming : It is the name given to the execution of two or more different programmes by the same computer. The programme shares the same hardware with the operating software responsible for allowing the machine to take different tasks from time to time.

NewGenlib : NewGenlib is an integrated library management system developed by Virus Solutions Pvt. Ltd. Domain expertise is provided by Kesavan Institute of Information and Knowledge

Management in Hyderabad, India.

NIC (National Informatics Centre) **:** NIC was established in 1975 which gave birth to NICNET for information flow.

NICNET (National Information Centre Network) **:** It is a process of NIC used for a variety of administrative purposes.

Network : A number of computer units linked by communication channels, as in the case of telephone network.

Networking : The process of creating or establishing a network of computers is called networking.

Network DBMS : A generalized type of hierarchical model in which a segment can have multiple parent segmenets.

NISSAT (National Information System for Science & Technology) : It is an information system under DST. NISSAT is responsible in developing information product and network for resource sharing.

Nodes : It is a word standing for one of the computers on the network.

Object Programme : It is a programme in machine code. It is an assembled programme that is ready to be loaded into the computer. In other words it is the result from the translation of a source programme by a language processor.

Octal number system : A number system with using the base of the octal digits range from 0 to 7. It is commonly used as a short-cut notation for groups of three binary digits.

OCR (Optical Character Recognition) **:** It is a method of machine readable input in which the characters are read by light-sensitive device.

OPAC : An Online Public Access Catalog (often abbreviated as OPAC or simply library catalog) is an online database of materials held by a library or group of libraries. Users search a library catalog principally to locate books and other material available at a library.

Optical disk : It is a disk that stores data in the form of bits in the surface. The data is read with the help of a laser or photo-cell in the head.

Optical fibre : Glass made fibres used in networking and they carry signals in the form of light.

Operating system : It is a programme that controls all the operating systems as each machine needs its own particular king of operating software. It is also called as systems software.

On-line : It is a general term for using devices and peripherals which interact directly and simultaneously with a CPU (Central Processing Unit).

ORACLE : A well known Commercial DBMS based on relational models.

Output device or unit : It is an item of hardware design to produce or present output. There are many types of output units such as printer, VDU etc.

Package : It is a computer software supplied for ready use along with manuals and other instructions.

Palmtop : It is a small computer that literary fits in anyone's palm.

Parallel processing : The simultaneous processing of data.

PASCAL : It is a high-level programme language widely used in teaching and training, and for general purpose use. It derived its name from the 17th century French mathematician Blaize Pascal. It facilitates the use of structured programming techniques.

PDA : A personal digital assistant (PDA), also known as a palmtop computer, or personal data assistant, is a mobile device that functions as a personal information manager.

Personal computer : It is a microcomputer, usually used by one person at a time.

Programme : A complete set of sequenced instructions used to direct a computer in the performance of a desired task.

Programmer : A person who is skilled in the writing of computer programmes.

PL/1 (Programme Language Number 1) : It is a high level programme language designed for both business and scientific applications, devised by IBM in the early 1960s, it is not widely used now.

PRECIS (Preserved Context Indexing System) : A type of index system.

PROM (Programmable Read Only Memory) : It is a ROM whose contents can be changed by the user. Information in PROMS does not disappear when power is turned off.

Punched Card : A card of 19.3 x 9.5 cm, usually divided into 80 vertical columns, numbered 1-8. It is again divided into 80 vertical columns, numbered 1-8. It is again divided into 12 rows from top to bottom. Each column of this card can represent one character. The position of holes punched determines the character.

Punched Paper Tape : It is a form widely used for telegraphy and computer data storage till the late 1970s. On the tape there are usually a track on which holes are punched representing bytes of data. With the help of a paper tape reader the tape is scanned and the data is transferred to a computer memory or printer.

RAM (Random Access Memory) : It is the main memory of a computer. It generally refers to the integrated circuit that makes up the memory itself. The computer stores data in distinct locations in RAM and then call it, after it, and restores it when needed.

Random Access : It is a storage device where access to information is random rather than sequential, it means the access is imperfect. It is a most common storage device.

RDBMS : RDBMS stands for Relational Database Management System. RDBMS data is structured in database tables, fields and records. Each RDBMS table consists of database table rows. Each database table row consists of one or more database table fields.

Real time : It is a term indicating the computer response to inputs (i.e., gives output at the same rate as the input).

Real-time processing : It is a computer processing which receives and processes data quickly enough to produce output almost immediately.

Registers : It is a temporary store for data to be processed. It is used by the CPU (Central Processing Unit) to interpret instructions and perform arithmetic and local operations.

Response time : It is the time the system takes to respond to a command with the appropriate action. In other words, it is the time taken by the computer since the input of instructions and getting the result.

Retrieval : It is the process of finding again and returning there from with a book or document or information.

RFID (Radio Frequency Identification Device) : It is an electromagnetic or electrostatic coupling in the radio frequency portion of the electromagnetic spectrum is used to transmit signals. An RFID system consists of an antenna and a transceiver, which read the radio frequency and transfer the information to a processing device, and a transponder, or tag, which is an integrated circuit containing the RF circuitry and information to be transmitted.

Ring network : It is one of the network styles. In this network the computers are connected to one another (like a ring). Whenever data are to be transmitted among any two computers it is always transmitted in a circle (like that of a ring).

ROM (Read Only Memory) : It is the memory in which data are stored permanently. These data are usually available when power is turned on. In ROMs the information is placed in the computer during the process of its manufacture. Information stored in ROMs does not disappear when the power is turned off.

Scanner : A scanner is an electronic device that captures images from photographic prints, posters, magazine pages, and similar sources for computer editing and display.

Scanning : The process of acquisition of an electronic image through its original that may be a text, photograph, manuscript, etc., into the computer using an electronic image scanner. An image is read or scanned at a predefined resolution and dynamic range.

Secondary storage : A storage that supplements the primary storage of computer. It generally has an operating speed slower than that of primary storage. It is often called auxiliary storage.

SDI (Selective Dissemination of Information) : It is a system of information retrieval, often with the help of a computer, for disseminating relevant information to users. It consists of mainly two profiles – interest profile and document profile.

Serials : The term includes periodicals, newspapers, annuals, and other monographs and proceedings and transactions of societies – that are issued in successive parts appearing at regular intervals. They are mostly meant to be continued indefinitely.

Sequential access : It is a storage device where access to information is in the order in which they appear. It means the order is of some value rather than being random.

SIRNET (Scientific and Industrial Research Network) : It is a computer communication network started by CSIR laboratories with main node at NISCAIR.

SLIM 21 : SLIM 21 is an integrated, multi-user, multi-tasking library information software for the Windows environment.

Software : It is the general term used for computer programmes. The set of programmes, procedures, etc. that makes the computer work.

SOUL : Software for University Libraries (SOUL) is a state-of-the-art integrated library management software designed and developed by the INFLIBNET Centre of UGC based on requirements of college and university libraries.

Source programme : It is the language of the text in a machine-aided translation system, to be translated to machine code (for example, COBOL, BASIC).

SPIN (Special Interest Network) : It is a network extending across a city or a region. They commonly consists of microcomputers and terminals connected by telephone lines (for example, DELNET, CALIBNET).

Spread-sheet : It is a number of processing programmes based on two or more dimensions arranged in rows and columns. Its main uses are for laying out neatly and processing the data in tables of accounts.

SQL (Structured Query Language) : A popular language for data retrieval.

Star Network : It is one of the network styles. In this network of computers each computer is linked with the server. Therefore, whenever data are to be transmitted among any two, it should always be routed through the server.

Storage or Memory Unit : It that part of a computer where data or programme instructions are stored in binary number form for later use. It is also called storage unit. It can accept data, hold (store) them and deliver the same when demanded. Computers generally have internal read only memory (ROM) and random access memory (RAM) chips, which can be accessed very quickly. Computers also have mass storage devices, such as cassette. Magnetic disks which are often referred to as secondary or audiliary memory devices.

Super computer : It is a very large, a very fast, a very powerful computer with a very large main store. They are generally used for complex scientific applications.

Synchronous Transmission : It is a mode of data communication in which each set of bits (making up a character) is transmitted in a strict time rhythm.

System : In computers it stands for combination of hardware, software, links, procedures and actions that helps people to carry out a task.

System analysis : Analyzing the system i.e., planning a computer data processing system.

System designed flow chart : A flow chart representing the designing of the system i.e., the program.

System software : It is a programme that controls all operations of a computer system. There are many kinds of operating systems, as each machine needs its own particular type of operating software. Sometimes many operating software programmes are used simultaneously for increasing efficiency.

Telecommunications : In computer technology it stands for the use of telephone cables and or broadcast radio waves for the transmission of information and data in the form of electro-magnetic signals.

Tele ordering : It is a form of mail order with the help of ISBN to the book-sellers for supply. This is done with the help of a central computer and to the terminals of the participating publishers.

Telnet : It allows one computer to communicate with another computer and internet users to log into other inter network computers to access online databases etc.

Time sharing : In a multi-processing system the processor divides the attention between the different tasks. The operating software is designed in a manner, it gives the processor a fixed time slot (e.g. $1/100^{th}$ of a second) for each task in turn. As a result each user feels that the system is working on his task alone.

Throughput : It is a term used for measuring the rate of data transfer through a processing system from input to output. It is used to measure the efficiency of a computer system.

Transistor : A controller of electronic signals that functions like a switch using a semi-conductor. It is generally used in the manufacture of various electronic equipment.

Transmission Control Protocol (TCP) : It is one of the core protocols of the Internet protocol suite (IP), and is so common that the entire suite is often called TCP/IP. TCP provides reliable, ordered and error-checked delivery of a stream of octets (in groups of eight) between programs running on computers connected to a local area network, intranet or the public Internet. It resides at the transport layer.

Turn-key system : It is an information technology system which is so simple to operate where the user need not acquire special knowledge at all to work with the system.

UNIMARC – The Universal MARC format was created by IFLA in 1977 with the primary purpose of facilitating the international exchange of bibliographic data in machine-readable form.

UNIX : It is a very popular operating system for 16-bit mini-and microcomputers designed by Bell Telephones.

Utility Programme : It is a small programme designed to carry out a single routine task (for example, error handling routines, transferring data files).

Vacuum tube : It is an electronic tube through which electrons move in a vacuum carrying current. Traditionally they were used to provide the functions of diodes and transistors.

Vector Processing : Processing of data by breaking down the problems into elements (vectors).

VIKRAM : It is packet-switched public data network to be established by the department of telecommunications.

Virtua : Virtua is a Library software package which is basically windows based client/server application.

WAN (Wide Area Network) : It is a network linking several organizations, may be at national level or at international level or at international level (e.g., NICNET, INFLIBNET).

Winchester disk : It is a metal disk of medium size permanently fixed in the microcomputers. Some modern Winchesters are removable in the same way as floppies.

Word Perfect : It is a word processing package frequently used in business.

Word-Processing : It is a system where the text can be input on a typewriter with computer-like functions. The same can be updated, amended in necessary, printed out, in a desired format and quantity.

Word Star : It is a word processing package frequently used in business.

Workstation : A workstation is a computer intended for individual use that is faster and more capable than a personal computer.

WORM : An optical disk where information can be written and the same can be read many times, but cannot be erased (Write Once and Read Many times).

Z39.50 : Z39.50 is an international standard client-server, application layer communications protocol for searching and retrieving information from a database over a TCP/IP computer network.

Index